DATE DUE

DEMCO 38-296

THE CONFESSION OF A FOOL

THE CONFESSION
OF A FOOL

BY AUGUST STRINDBERG

TRANSLATED BY

ELLIE SCHLEUSSNER

STEPHEN SWIFT
AND COMPANY LIMITED
16 KING STREET
COVENT GARDEN
MCMXII

HASKELL HOUSE PUBLISHERS LTD.
Publishers of Scarce Scholarly Books
NEW YORK, N. Y. 10012
1972

HASKELL HOUSE PUBLISHERS Ltd.

Publishers of Scarce Scholarly Books

280 LAFAYETTE STREET

NEW YORK. N. Y. 10012

Library of Congress Cataloging in Publication Data

Strindberg, August, 1849–1912.
    The confession of a fool.

    Translation of Le plaidoyer d'un fou.
    I. Schleussner, Ellie, tr. II. Title.
PT9814.P513 1972   843   79-39042
ISBN 0-8383-1397-3

Printed in the United States of America

Translated from the "Litterarisches Echo,"

August 15, 1911

STRINDBERG'S WORKS

(By I. E. Poritzky, Berlin)

THE republication of *The Confession of a Fool* represents the last link in the chain of Strindberg's autobiographical novels. A German version of the book was published as far back as 1893, but it was mutilated, abbreviated, corrupted, and falsified to such an extent that the attorney-general, misled by the revolting language, blamed the author for the misdeeds of the translator and prohibited the sale of the book. This was a splendid advertisement for this profound work, but there were many who would have rejoiced if the translation had been completely ignored. It distorted Strindberg's character and was the cause of many prejudices which exist to this day.

Schering's new translation is an attempt to make reparation for this crime. "It is impossible," he says, "that any attorney-general can now doubt the high morality of this book." Strindberg himself has called it a *terrible book*, and has regretted that he ever wrote it. He has never published it in Swedish, his own language, because not only is it too personal in character, but it also revealed a still bleeding wound. It contains the relentless description of his first marriage, so superbly candid an account, that one is reminded of the last testament of a man for whom death has no longer any terror. We know from his fascinating novel *Separated*, how painful the burden was which he had to bear, and how

v

terribly he suffered during the period of his first marriage. So much so, indeed, that he had to write this book before he could face the thought of death with composure. Doubtless, a man for whom life holds no longer any charm would give us a genuinely truthful account of his inner life, and there is no denying that a book which takes its entire matter from the inner life is of vastly greater importance and on an immeasurably higher level than a million novels, be they written ever so well. The great importance of *The Confession of a Fool* lies in the fact that it depicts the struggle of a highly intellectual man to free himself from the slavery of sexuality, and from a woman who is a typical representative of her sex.

Apart from this, it is an intense joy from an artistic point of view to follow the " confessor " through the book, as he looks at himself from all sides in order to gain self-knowledge; that he conceals nothing from us, not even those deep secrets which he would fain keep even in the face of death. One *sees* Strindberg brooding over his own soul to fathom its depths. He plumbs its hidden profoundnesses, he takes to pieces the inner wheels of his mechanism, so as to know for himself and to show us how he is made and what is the cause of the instinct which drives him to confess and to create. He opens wide his heart and lets us see that he carries in his breast his heaven and also his horrible hell. We see angels and devils fighting in his soul for supremacy, and the divine in him stepping between them with its creative Let there be !

THE CONFESSION OF A FOOL

PART I

I

IT was on the thirteenth of May, 1875, at Stockholm.

I well remember the large room of the Royal Library which extended through a whole wing of the Castle, with its beechen wainscoting, brown with age like the meerschaum of a much-used cigar-holder. The enormous room, with its rococo beadings, garlands, chains and armorial bearings, round which, at the height of the first floor, ran a gallery supported by Tuscan columns, was yawning like a great chasm underneath my feet; with its hundred thousand volumes it resembled a gigantic brain, with the thoughts of long-forgotten generations neatly arranged on shelves.

A passage running from one end of the room to the other divided the two principal parts, the walls of which were completely hidden by shelves fourteen feet high. The golden rays of the spring sun were falling through the twelve windows, illuminating the volumes of the Renaissance, bound in white and gold parchment, the black morocco bindings mounted with silver of the seventeenth century, the red-edged volumes bound in calf of a hundred years later, the green leather bindings which were the fashion under the Empire, and the cheap covers of our own time. Here theologians were on neighbourly terms with apostles of magic, philosophers hobnobbed

B

with naturalists, poets and historians dwelt in peace side by side. It reminded one of a geological stratum of unfathomable depth where, as in a puddingstone, layer was piled upon layer, marking the successive stages arrived at by human folly or human genius.

I can see myself now. I had climbed on to the encircling gallery, and was engaged in arranging a collection of old books which a well-known collector had just presented to the library. He had been clever enough to ensure his own immortality by endowing each volume with his ex-libris bearing the motto "Speravit infestis."

Since I was as superstitious as an atheist, this motto, meeting my gaze day after day whenever I happened to open a volume, had made an undeniable impression on me. He was a lucky fellow, this brave man, for even in misfortune he never abandoned hope. . . . But for me all hope was dead. There seemed to be no chance whatever that my drama in five acts, or six tableaux, with three transformation scenes on the open stage, would ever see the footlights. Seven men stood between me and promotion to the post of a librarian—seven men, all in perfect health, and four with a private income. A man of twenty-six, in receipt of a monthly salary of twenty crowns, with a drama in five acts stowed away in a drawer in his attic, is only too much inclined to embrace pessimism, this apotheosis of scepticism, so comforting to all failures. It compensates them for unobtainable dinners, enables them to draw admirable conclusions, which often have to make up for the loss of an overcoat, pledged before the end of the winter.

Notwithstanding the fact that I was a member of a learned Bohemia, which had succeeded an older, artistic Bohemia, a contributor to important newspapers and excellent, but badly paying magazines, a partner in a society founded for the purpose of translating Hartmann's

Philosophy of the Unconscious, a member of a secret federation for the promotion of free love, the bearer of the empty title of a "royal secretary," and the author of two one-act plays which had been performed at the Royal Theatre, I had the greatest difficulty to make ends meet. I hated life, although the thought of relinquishing it had never crossed my mind; on the contrary, I had always done my best to continue not only my own existence but also that of the race. It cannot be denied that pessimism, misinterpreted by the multitude and generally confused with hypochondria, is really a quite serene and even comforting philosophy of life. Since everything is relatively nothing, why make so much fuss, particularly as truth itself is mutable and short-lived? Are we not constantly discovering that the truth of yesterday is the folly of to-morrow? Why, then, waste strength and youth in discovering fresh fallacies? The only proven fact is that we have to die. Let us live then! But for whom? For what purpose? Alas! . . .

When Bernadotte, that converted Jacobite, ascended the throne and all the rubbish which had been discarded at the end of the last century was re-introduced, the hopes of the generation of 1860, to which I belonged, were dashed to the ground with the clamorously advertised parliamentary reform. The *two houses,* which had taken the place of the *four estates,* consisted for the greater part of peasants. They turned Parliament into a sort of town council, where everybody, on the best of terms with everybody else, looked after his own little affairs, without paying the least regard to the great problems of life and progress. Politics were nothing more nor less than a compromise between public and private interests. The last remnants of faith in what was then "the ideal" were vanishing in a ferment of bitterness. To this must be added the religious reaction which marked the period after the death of Charles XV, and the beginning of the reign of Queen Sophia of Nassau. There were plenty of reasons, therefore, to account for an enlightened pessimism, reasons other than personal ones. . . .

The dust caused by the rearrangement of the books was choking me. I opened the window for a breath of fresh air and a look at the view beyond. A delicious breeze fanned my face, a breeze laden with the scent of lilac and the rising sap of the poplars. The lattice-work was completely hidden beneath the green leaves of the honeysuckle and wild vine; acacias and plane trees, well acquainted with the fatal whims of a northern May, were still holding back. It was spring, though the skeleton of shrub and tree was still plainly visible underneath the tender young green. Beyond the parapet with its Delft vases bearing the mark of Charles XII, the masts of the anchored steamers were rising, gaily decorated with flags in honour of the May-day festival. Behind them glittered the bottle-green line of the bay, and from its wooded shores on either side the trees were mounting higher and higher, gradually, like steps, pines and Scotch firs on one side and soft green foliage on the other. All the boats lying at anchor were flying their national colours, more or less symbolic of the different nations. England with the dripping scarlet of the blood of her famous cattle; Spain striped red and yellow, like the Venetian blinds of a Moorish balcony; the United States with their striped bed-tick; the gay tricolour of France by the side of the gloomy German flag with its sinister iron cross close to the flagstaff, ever reminiscent of mourning; the jerkinet of Denmark; the veiled tricolour of Russia. They were all there, side by side, with outspread wings, under the blue cover of the northern sky. The noise of carriages, whistles, bells and cranes lent animation to the picture; the combined odours of oil, leather, salt herrings and

groceries mingled with the scent of the lilac. An easterly
wind blowing from the open sea, cooled by the drift ice
of the Baltic, freshened the atmosphere.

I forgot my books as soon as I turned my back to
them and was leaning out of the window, all my senses
taking a delicious bath; below, the guards were marching
past to the strains of the march from *Faust*. I was so
intoxicated with the music, the flags, the blue sky, the
flowers, that I had not noticed the porter entering my
office in the meantime with the mail. He touched my
shoulder, handed me a letter and disappeared.

Hm! . . . a letter from a lady.

I hastily opened the envelope, anticipating some delightful adventure . . . surely it must be something of
that sort . . . it was!

"Meet me punctually at five o'clock this afternoon
before No. 65 Parliament Street. You will know me by
the roll of music in my hand."

A short time ago a little vixen had made a fool of me,
and I had sworn to take advantage of the first favourable
opportunity to revenge myself. Therefore I was willing
enough. There was only one thing which jarred on me;
the commanding, dictatorial tone of the note offended my
manly dignity. How could this unknown correspondent
dare to attack me unawares in this manner? What were
they thinking of, these women, who have such a poor
opinion of us men? They do not ask, they command
their conquests!

As it happened I had planned an excursion with some
of my friends for this very afternoon. And, moreover,
the thought of a flirtation in the middle of the day in one
of the principal streets of the town was not very alluring.

At two o'clock, however, I went into the chemical
laboratory where the excursionists had arranged to

assemble. They were already crowding the ante-room :
doctors and candidates of philosophy and medicine, all
of them anxious to learn the programme of the entertain-
ment in store. I had made up my mind in the meantime,
and with many apologies refused to be one of the party.
They clamoured for my reasons. I produced my letter
and handed it to a zoologist who was looked upon as an
expert in all matters pertaining to love; he shook his head
while perusing it.

"No good, that . . ." he muttered disconnectedly;
"wants to be married . . . would never sell herself . . .
family, my dear old chap . . . straight path . . . but
do what you like. You'll find us in the Park, later on,
if the spirit moves you to join us, and I have been wrong
about the lady. . . ."

At the hour indicated I took up my position near the
house mentioned, and awaited the appearance of the
unknown letter-writer.

The roll of music in her hand, what was it but a proposal of marriage? It differed in no way from the an-
nouncements on the fourth page of certain newspapers.
I suddenly felt uneasy; too late—the lady had arrived
and we stood looking at each other.

My first impression—I believe in first impressions—
was quite vague. She was of uncertain age, between
twenty-nine and forty, fantastically dressed. What was
she? Artist or blue-stocking? A sheltered woman or
one living a free and independent life? Emancipated or
cocotte? I wondered. . . .

She introduced herself as the fiancée of an old friend
of mine, an opera singer, and said that he wished me to
look after her while she was staying in town. This was
untrue, as I found out later on.

She was like a little bird, twittering incessantly. After
she had talked for half-an-hour I knew all about her; I

knew all her emotions, all her thoughts. But I was only half interested, and asked her if I could do anything for her.

"I take care of a young woman!" I exclaimed, after she had explained what she wanted. "Don't you know that I am the devil incarnate?"

"You only think you are," she replied; "but I know you thoroughly. You're unhappy, that's all. You ought to be roused from your gloomy fancies."

"You know me thoroughly? You really think so? I'm afraid all you know is the now antiquated opinion your fiancé has of me."

It was no use talking, my "charming friend" was well informed and knew how to read a man's heart, even from a distance. She was one of those obstinate creatures who strive to sway the spirits of men by insinuating themselves into the hidden depths of their souls. She kept up a large correspondence, bombarded all her acquaintances with letters, gave advice and warning to young people, and knew no greater happiness than to direct and guide the destinies of men. Greedy of power, head of a league for the salvation of souls, patroness of all the world, she had conceived it her mission to save me!

She was a schemer of the purest water, with little intelligence but a great deal of female impudence.

I began to tease her by making fun of everything, the world, men, religion. She told me my ideas were morbid.

"Morbid! My dear lady, my ideas morbid? They are, on the contrary, most healthy and of the latest date. But what about yours now? They are relics of a past age, commonplaces of my boyhood, the rubbish of rubbish, and you think them new? Candidly speaking, what you offer me as fresh fruit is nothing but preserved stuff in badly soldered tins. Away with it! It's rotten! You know what I mean."

She left me without a word of good-bye, furious, unable to control herself.

When she had gone I went to join my friends in the Park, and spent the evening with them.

I had not quite got over my excitement on the following morning when I received a communication from her. It was a vainglorious letter in which she overwhelmed me with reproaches, largely tempered by forbearance and compassion; she expressed ardent wishes for my mental health, and concluded by arranging a second meeting, and stating that we ought to pay a visit to her fiancé's aged mother.

As I rather pride myself on my manners, I resigned myself to my fate; but, determined to get off as cheaply as possible, I made up my mind to appear perfectly indifferent to all questions relating to religion, the world and everything else.

But how wonderful! The lady, dressed in a tightly fitting cloth dress, trimmed with fur, and wearing a large picture hat, greeted me most cordially; she was full of the tender solicitude of an elder sister, avoided all dangerous ground, and was altogether so charming that our souls, thanks to a mutual desire to please, met in friendly talk, and before we parted a feeling of genuine sympathy had sprung up between us.

After having paid our call we took advantage of the lovely spring day and went for a stroll.

I am not sure whether it was from an imperative desire to pay her out, or whether I felt annoyed at having been made to play the part of a confidant; whatever it was, the iniquitous idea occurred to me to tell her, in strict confidence, that I was practically engaged to be married; this was only half a lie, for I was really paying at that time a good deal of attention to a certain lady of my acquaintance.

On hearing this, her manner changed. She talked to me like a grandmother, began to pity the girl, questioned me about her character, her looks, her social status, her circumstances. I painted a portrait well calculated to excite her jealousy. Our eager conversation languished. My guardian angel's interest in me waned when she suspected a rival who might possibly be equally anxious to save my soul.

We parted, still under the influence of the chill which had gradually arisen between us.

When we met on the following day we talked exclusively of love and my supposed fiancée.

But after we had visited theatres and concerts for a week and taken numerous walks together, she had gained her object. The daily intercourse with her had become a habit of which I felt unable to break myself. Conversation with a woman who is above the commonplace has an almost sensual charm. The souls touch, the spirits embrace each other.

One morning, on meeting her as usual, I found her almost beside herself. She was full of a letter which she had just received. Her fiancé was furiously jealous. She accused herself of having been indiscreet; he was recommending her the utmost reserve in her intercourse with me: he seemed to have a presentiment that the matter would end badly.

"I can't understand such detestable jealousy," she said, deeply distressed.

"Because you don't understand the meaning of the word 'love,'" I answered.

"Love! Ugh!"

"Love, my dear lady, is consciousness of possession in its greatest intensity. Jealousy is but the fear of losing what one possesses."

"Possesses! Disgusting!"

"Mutually possesses, since each possesses the other."

But she refused to understand love in that sense. In her opinion love was something disinterested, exalted, chaste, inexplicable.

She did not love her fiancé, but he was head over ears in love with her.

When I said so she lost her temper, and then confessed that she had never loved him.

"And yet you contemplate marrying him?"

"Because he would be lost if I didn't."

"Always that mania for saving souls!"

She grew more and more angry; she maintained that she was not, and never had been, really engaged to him.

We had caught each other lying; what prospects!

There remained nothing for me to do now but to make a clean breast of it, and contradict my previous statement that I was "as good as engaged." This done, we were at liberty to make use of our freedom.

As she had now no longer any cause for jealousy, the game began afresh, and this time we played it in deadly earnest. I confessed my love to her—in writing. She forwarded the letter to her fiancé. He heaped insults on my head—by post.

I told her that she must choose between him and me. But she carefully refrained from doing so, for her object was to have me, him, and as many more as she could get, kneeling at her feet and adoring her. She was a flirt, a *mangeuse d'hommes*, a chaste polyandrist.

But, perhaps for want of some one better, I had fallen in love with her, for I loathed casual love-affairs, and the solitude of my attic bored me.

Towards the end of her stay in town I invited her to pay me a visit at the library. I wanted to dazzle her, show myself to her in impressive surroundings, so as to overawe this arrogant little brain.

I dragged her from gallery to gallery, exhibiting all
my bibliographical knowledge. I compelled her to admire
the miniatures of the Middle Ages, the autographs of
famous men. I evoked the great historical memories held
captive in old manuscripts and prints. In the end her
insignificance came home to her and she became embarrassed.

"But you are a very learned man!" she exclaimed.

"Of course I am," I laughed.

"Oh, my poor old mummer!" she murmured, alluding
to her friend, the opera singer, her so-called fiancé.

But if I had flattered myself that the mummer was now
finally disposed of, I was mistaken. He was threatening
to shoot me—by post; he accused me of having robbed
him of his future bride. I proved to him that he could
not have been robbed, for the simple reason that he had
not possessed anything. After that our correspondence
ceased and gave way to a menacing silence.

Her visit was drawing to an end. On the eve of her
departure I received a jubilant letter from her, telling
me of an unexpected piece of good luck. She had read
my play to some people of note who had influence with
stage managers. The play had made such an impression
on them that they were anxious to make my acquaintance. She would tell me all the details in the afternoon.

At the appointed hour I met her and accompanied her
on a shopping expedition to make a few last purchases.
She was talking of nothing but the sensation my play had
created, and when I explained to her that I hated patronage of any sort, she did her utmost to convert me to her
point of view. I paid little attention to her and went on
grumbling. The idea of ringing at unknown front doors,
meeting strangers and talking to them of everything
except that which was nearest to my heart, was hateful
to me; I could not whine like a beggar for favours.

I was fighting her as hard as I could when suddenly she
stopped before a young, aristocratic-looking lady, very
well, even elegantly dressed, with movements full of
softness and grace.

The lady, whom she introduced as Baroness X, said
a few words to me which the noise of the crowd rendered
all but inaudible. I stammered a reply, annoyed at
having been caught in a trap set for me by a wily little
schemer. For I felt certain the meeting had been pre-
meditated.

A few seconds more and the Baroness had gone, but
not without having personally repeated the invitation
which my companion had already brought me a little
earlier in the afternoon.

The girlish appearance and baby face of the Baroness,
who must have been at least twenty-five years of age,
surprised me. She looked like a schoolgirl; her little face
was framed by roguish curls, golden as a cornfield on
which the sun is shining; she had the shoulders of a
princess and a supple, willowy figure; the way in which
she bowed her head expressed at the same time candour,
respect and superiority.

And this delicious, girlish mother had read my play
without hurt or injury? Was it possible?

She had married a captain of the Guards, was the
mother of a little girl of three, and took a passionate
interest in the theatre, without, however, having the
slightest prospect of ever being able to enter the profession herself; a sacrifice demanded from her by the rank
and position not only of her husband, but also of her
father-in-law, who had recently received the appointment
of a gentleman-in-waiting.

This was the position of affairs when my love-dream
melted away. A steamer was bearing my lady-love into
the presence of her mummer. He would vindicate his

rights now and take a delight in making fun of my letters to her : just retribution for having laughed at his letters in the company of his inamorata while she was staying here. On the landing-stage, at the very moment of our affectionate farewell, she made me promise to call on the Baroness without delay. These were the last words we exchanged.

The innocent daydreams, so different from the coarse orgies of learned Bohemia, left a void in my heart which craved to be filled. The friendly, seemingly harmless intercourse with a gentlewoman, this intercourse between two people of opposite sexes, had been sweet to me after my long solitude, for I had quarrelled with my family and was, therefore, very lonely. The love of home life, which my Bohemian existence had deadened for a while, was reawakened by my relations with a very ordinary but respectable member of the other sex. And, therefore, one evening at six o'clock, I found myself at the entrance gate of a house in North Avenue.

How ominous! It was the old house which had belonged to my father, the house in which I had spent the most miserable years of my childhood, where I had fought through the troubles and storms of adolescence, where I had been confirmed, where my mother had died, and where a stepmother had taken her place. I suddenly felt ill at ease, and my first impulse was one of flight. I was afraid to stir up the memories of the misery of my youth and early manhood. There was the courtyard with its tall ash trees ; how impatiently I used to wait for the tender young green on the return of spring ; there was the gloomy house, built against a sand-quarry, the unavoidable collapse of which had lowered the rents.

But in spite of the feeling of depression caused by so many melancholy memories, I pulled myself together, entered, walked upstairs and rang the bell.

As I stood listening to the sound echoing through the house, I had a feeling that my father would presently come and open the door to me. But a servant appeared and disappeared again to announce me. A few seconds afterwards I stood face to face with the Baron, who gave me a hearty welcome. He was a man of about thirty years of age, tall and strong, with a noble carriage and the perfect manners of a gentleman. His full, slightly swollen face was animated by a pair of intensely sad blue eyes. The smile on his lips was for ever giving way to an expression of extraordinary bitterness, which spoke of disappointments, plans miscarried, illusions fled.

The drawing-room, once upon a time our dining-room, was not furnished in any particular style. The Baron, who bore the name of a famous general, a Turenne or Condé of our country, had filled it with the portraits of his ancestors, dating back to the Thirty Years' War; heroes in white cuirasses with wigs of the time of Louis XIV. Amongst them hung landscapes of the Düsseldorf school of painting. Pieces of old furniture, restored and gilded, stood side by side with chairs and easy-chairs of a more modern date. The whole room seemed to breathe an atmosphere of peace and domestic love.

Presently the Baroness joined us; she was charming, almost cordial, simple and kind. But there was a certain stiffness in her manner, a suspicion of embarrassment which chilled me until I discovered a reason for it in the sound of voices which came from an adjacent room. I concluded that she had other visitors, and apologised for having called at an inconvenient time. They were playing whist in the next room, and I was forthwith introduced to four members of the family : the gentleman-in-waiting, a retired captain, and the Baroness's mother and aunt.

As soon as the old people had sat down again to play, we younger ones began to talk. The Baron mentioned his great love of painting. A scholarship, granted him by the late King Charles XV, had enabled him to pursue his studies at Düsseldorf. This fact constituted a point of contact between us, for I had had a scholarship from the same king, only in my case it had been granted for literary purposes.

We discussed painting, the theatre, the personality of our patron. But gradually the flow of conversation ceased, largely checked by the whist players, who joined in every now and then, laying rude fingers on sensitive spots, tearing open scarcely healed wounds. I began to feel ill at ease in this heterogeneous society and rose to go. The Baron and his wife, who accompanied me to the door, dropped their constrained manner as soon as they were out of earshot of the old people. They asked me to a friendly dinner on the following Saturday, and after a little chat in the passage we parted as old friends.

II

PUNCTUALLY at three o'clock on the following Saturday
I started for the house in North Avenue. I was received
like an old friend and unhesitatingly admitted to the
intimacies of the home. Mutual confidences added a
delightful flavour to the meal. The Baron, who was dissatisfied with his position, belonged to a group of mal-
contents which had arisen under the new rule of King
Oscar. Jealous of the great popularity which his late
brother had enjoyed, the new ruler took pains to neglect
all plans fostered by his predecessor. The friends of the
old order, its frank joviality, its toleration and progressive
endeavour, stood aside, therefore, and formed an intellectual opposition without, however, taking any part in
party politics. While we sat, evoking the ghosts of the
past, our hearts were drawn together. All prejudices
nursed in the heart of the commoner against the aristocracy, which since the parliamentary reform of 1865 had
gradually receded more and more into the background,
vanished and gave place to a feeling of sympathy for the
fallen stars.

The Baroness, a native of Finland, was a new-comer in
Sweden, and not sufficiently informed to take part in our
conversation. But as soon as dinner was over she went
to the piano and began to sing, and both the Baron and
I discovered that we possessed an hitherto unsuspected
talent for the duets of Wennerberg.

The hours passed rapidly.

We amused ourselves by casting the parts and reading

16

a short play which had just been played at the Royal
Theatre.

But suddenly our spirits flagged and the inevitable
pause ensued ; that awkward pause which is sure to occur
after exhaustive efforts to shine and make conquests.
Again the memories of the past oppressed me and I grew
silent.

"What's the matter? " asked the Baroness.

"There are ghosts in this house," I replied, trying to
account for my silence. "Ages ago I lived here—yes,
yes, ages ago, for I am very old."

"Can't we drive away those ghosts? " she asked, looking at me with a bewitching expression, full of motherly
tenderness.

"I'm afraid we can't ; that's the privilege of some one
else," laughed the Baron ; "she alone can banish the
gloomy thoughts. Come now, you are engaged to Miss
Selma ? "

"No, you are mistaken, Baron ; it was love's labour
lost."

"What! is she bound to some one else? " asked the
Baron, scrutinising my face.

"I think so."

"Oh, I'm sorry! That girl's a treasure. And I'm
certain that she is fond of you."

And forthwith the three of us began to rail against the
unfortunate singer, accusing him of attempting to compel
a woman to marry him against her will. The Baroness
tried to comfort me by insisting that things were bound
to come right in the end, and promised to intercede for
me on her next trip to Finland, which was to take place
very shortly.

"No one shall succeed," she assured me, with an angry
flash in her eyes, "in forcing that dear girl into a
marriage of which her heart doesn't approve."

c

It was seven o'clock as I rose to go.   But they pressed me so eagerly to spend the evening with them that I almost suspected them of being bored in each other's company, although they had only been married for three years, and Heaven had blessed their union with a dear little girl.   They told me that they expected a cousin, and were anxious that I should meet her and tell them what I thought of her.

While we were still talking, a letter was handed to the Baron.   He tore it open, read it hastily, and, with a muttered exclamation, handed it to his wife.

"Incredible!" she exclaimed, glancing at the contents, and, after a questioning look at her husband, she continued: "She's my own cousin, you know, and her parents won't permit her to stay at our house because people have been gossiping."

"It's preposterous!" exclaimed the Baron.   "A mere child, pretty, innocent, unhappy at home, who likes being with us, her near relatives . . . and people gossiping!   Bah!"

Did a sceptic smile betray me?   His remark was followed by a dead silence, a certain confusion, badly concealed under an invitation to take a turn round the garden.

I left after supper, about ten o'clock, and no sooner had I crossed the threshold than I began to ponder on the happenings of that eventful day.

In spite of every appearance of happiness, and notwithstanding their evident affection, I felt convinced that my friends harboured a very formidable skeleton in their cupboard.   Their wistful eyes, their fits of absent-mindedness, something unspoken, but felt, pointed to a hidden grief, to secrets, the discovery of which I dreaded.

Why in the world, I asked myself, do they live so quietly, voluntary exiles in a wretched suburb?   They were like two shipwrecked people in their eagerness to pour out their hearts to the first comer.

The Baroness in particular perplexed me. I tried to call up her picture, but was confused by the wealth of contradictory characteristics which I had discovered in her, and from which I had to choose. Kindhearted, amiable, brusque, enthusiastic, communicative and reserved, cold and excitable, she seemed to be full of whims, brooding over ambitious dreams. She was neither commonplace nor clever, but she impressed people. Of Byzantine slenderness, which allowed her dress to fall in simple, noble folds, like the dress of a St. Cecilia, her body was of bewitching proportions, her wrists and ankles exquisitely beautiful. Every now and then the pale, somewhat rigid features of her little face warmed into life and sparkled with infectious gaiety.

It was difficult to say who was master in the house. He, the soldier, accustomed to command, but burdened with a weak constitution, seemed submissive, more, I thought, from indifference than want of will-power. They were certainly on friendly terms, but there was none of the ecstasy of young love. When I made their acquaintance they were delighted to rejuvenate themselves by calling up the memories of the past before a third person. In studying them more closely, I became convinced that they lived on relics, bored each other, and the frequent invitations which I received after my first call proved that my conclusions were correct.

On the eve of the Baroness's departure for Finland I called on her to say good-bye. It was a lovely evening in June. The moment I entered the courtyard I caught sight of her behind the garden railings; she was standing in a shrubbery of aristolochias, and the transcendent beauty of her appearance came upon me almost with a

C 2

shock.   She was dressed in a white *piqué* dress, richly embroidered, the masterpiece of a Russian serf; her chain, brooches and bangles of alabaster seemed to throw a soft light over her, like lamplight falling through an opalescent globe.   The broad green leaves threw death-like hues on her pale face, with its shining coal-black eyes.

I was shaken, utterly confused, as if I were gazing at a vision.   The instinct of worship, latent in my heart, awoke, and with it the desire to proclaim my adoration. The void which had once been filled by religion ached no longer; the yearning to adore had reappeared under a new form.   God was deposed, but His place was taken by woman, woman who was both virgin and mother; when I looked at the little girl by her side, I could not understand how that birth had been possible, for the relationship between her and her husband seemed to put all sexual intercourse out of the question; their union appeared essentially spiritual.   Henceforth this woman represented to me a soul incarnate, a soul pure and unapproachable, clothed with one of those radiant bodies which, according to the Scriptures, clothe the souls of the dead.   I worshipped her—I could not help worshipping her.   I worshipped her just as she was, as she appeared to me at that moment, as mother and wife; wife of a particular husband, mother of a particular child.   Without her husband my longing to worship could not have been satisfied, for, I said to myself, she would then be a widow, and should I still worship her as such?   Perhaps if she were mine— my wife? . . . No! the thought was unthinkable.   And, moreover, married to me, she would no longer be the wife of this particular man, the mother of this particular child, the mistress of this particular house.   Such as she was I adored her, I would not have her otherwise.

Was it because of the melancholy recollections which the house always awakened in me, or was it because of the instincts of the commoner who never fails to admire the upper classes, the purer blood?—a feeling which would die on the day on which she stood less high—the adoration which I had conceived for her resembled in every point the religion from which I had just emancipated myself. I wanted to adore, I was longing to sacrifice myself, to suffer without hope of any other reward but the ecstasies of worship, self-sacrifice and suffering.

I constituted myself her guardian angel. I wanted to watch over her, lest the power of my love should sweep her off her feet and engulf her. I carefully avoided being alone with her, so that no familiarity which her husband might resent should creep in between us.

But to-day, on the eve of her departure, I found her alone in the shrubbery. We exchanged a few commonplaces. But presently my excitement rose to such a pitch that it communicated itself to her. Gazing at her with burning eyes, I saw the desire to confide in me forming itself in her heart. She told me that the thought of a separation from husband and child, however short, made her miserable. She implored me to spend as much of my leisure with them as I could, and not to forget her while she was looking after my interests in Finland.

"You love her very much—with all your heart, don't you?" she asked, looking at me steadfastly.

"Can you ask?" I replied, depressed by the painful lie.

For I had no longer any doubt that my May dream had been nothing more than a fancy, a whim, a mere pastime.

Afraid of polluting her with my passion, fearful of entangling her against my will in the net of my emotions, intending to protect her against myself, I dropped the perilous subject and asked after her husband. She pulled a face, evidently interpreting my somewhat strange behaviour quite correctly. Perhaps, also—the suspicion rose in my mind much later—she found pleasure in the thought that her beauty confused me. Or, maybe, she was conscious at that moment of the terrible power she had acquired over me, a Joseph whose coldness was only assumed, whose chastity was enforced.

"I'm boring you," she said smilingly; "I'd better call for reinforcements."

And with a clear voice she called to her husband, who was in his room upstairs.

The window was thrown open and the Baron appeared, a friendly smile on his open countenance. A few minutes later he joined us in the garden. He was wearing the handsome uniform of the Guards and looked very distinguished. With his dark-blue tunic, embroidered in yellow and silver, his tall, well-knit figure, he formed an exquisite contrast to the slender woman in white who stood at his side. They were really a strikingly handsome couple; the charms of the one served but to heighten those of the other. The sight of them was an artistic treat, a brilliant spectacle.

After dinner the Baron proposed that we should accompany his wife on the steamer as far as the last customs station. This proposal, to which I gladly agreed, seemed to give the Baroness a great deal of pleasure; she was delighted with the prospect of admiring the Stockholm Archipelago from the deck of a steamer on a beautiful summer night.

At ten o'clock on the following evening we met on board the steamer a short time before the hour of starting. It was a clear night; the sky was a blaze of brilliant orange, the sea lay before us, calm and blue.

We slowly steamed past the wooded shores, in a light which was neither day nor night, but had the qualities of both, and impressed the beholder as being sunrise and sunset at the same time.

After midnight our enthusiasm, which had been kept alive by the constantly changing panorama and the memories which it called up, cooled a little. We were fighting against an overwhelming desire to sleep. The early dawn found us with pallid faces, shivering in the morning breeze. We suddenly became sentimental; we swore eternal friendship; it was fate that had thrown us together—we dimly discerned the fatal bond which was to connect our lives in the future. I was beginning to look haggard, for I had not yet regained my strength after an attack of intermittent fever; they treated me like an ailing child; the Baroness wrapped her rug round me and made me drink some wine, all the while talking to me with a mother's tenderness. I let them have their way. I was almost delirious with want of sleep; my pent-up feelings overflowed; this womanly tenderness, the secret of which none but a motherly woman knows, was a new experience to me. I poured out on her a deluge of respectful homage; over-excited by sleeplessness, I became lightheaded, and gave the reins to my poetical imagination.

The wild hallucinations of the sleepless night took shape, vague, mystic, unsubstantial; the power of my suppressed talent revealed itself in light visions. I spoke for hours, without interruption, drawing inspiration from two pairs of eyes, which gazed at me fascinated. I felt as if my frail body was being consumed by the burning fire of my imagination. I lost all sense of my corporeal presence.

Suddenly the sun rose, the myriads of islets which seem to be swimming in the bay appeared enveloped in flames; the branches of the pines glowed like copper, the slender needles yellow as sulphur; the window-panes of the cottages, dotted along the shore, sparkled like golden mirrors; the columns of smoke rising from the chimneys indicated that breakfasts were being cooked; the fishing-boats were setting sail to bring in the outspread nets; the sea-gulls, scenting the small herring underneath the dark green waves, were screaming themselves hoarse. But on the steamer absolute silence reigned. The travellers were still fast asleep in their cabins, we alone were on deck. The captain, heavy with sleep, was watching us from the bridge, wondering, no doubt, what we could be talking about.

At three o'clock in the morning the pilot cutter appeared from behind a neck of land, and parting was imminent.

Only a few of the larger islands now separated us from the open sea; the swell of the ocean was already distinctly discernible; we could hear the roar of the huge breakers on the steep cliffs at the extreme end of the land.

The time to say good-bye had arrived. They kissed one another, he and she, full of painful agitation. She took my hand in hers and pressed it passionately, her eyes full of tears; she begged her husband to take care of me, and implored me to comfort him during her absence.

I bowed, I kissed her hand without a thought of the proprieties, oblivious of the fact that I was betraying my secret.

The engines stopped, the steamer slowed down, the pilot took up his position between decks. Two steps towards the accommodation ladder—I descended, and found myself at the side of the Baron in the pilot cutter.

The steamer towered above our heads. Leaning against the rail, the Baroness looked down upon us with a sad smile, her innocent eyes brimming over with tears. The propeller slowly began to move, the giant got under way again, her Russian flag fluttering in the breeze. We were tossing on the rolling waves, waving our handkerchiefs. The little face grew smaller and smaller, the delicate features were blotted out, two great eyes only remained gazing at us fixedly, and presently they too were swallowed up like the rest. Another moment and only a fluttering bluish veil, attached to a Japanese hat, was visible, and a waving white handkerchief; then only a white spot, a tiny white dot; now nothing but the unwieldy giant, wrapped in grey smoke. . . .

We went ashore at the Pilots and Customs Station, a popular summer resort. The village was still asleep; not a soul was on the landing-stage, and we turned and watched the steamer altering her course to starboard, and disappearing behind the rocky island which formed the last bulwark against the sea.

As the steamer disappeared the Baron leaned against my shoulder, and I fancied I could hear a sob; thus we stood for a while without speaking a word.

Was this excessive grief caused by sleeplessness—by the exhaustion following a long vigil? Had he a presentiment of misfortune, or was it merely the pain of parting with his wife? I couldn't say.

We went to the village, depressed and taciturn, in the hope of getting some breakfast. But the inn was not yet astir. We walked through the street and looked at the closed doors, the drawn blinds. Beyond the village we came upon an isolated spot with a quiet pool. The water was clear and transparent, and tempted us to bathe our eyes. I produced a little case and took from it a clean handkerchief, a toothbrush, a piece of soap and a bottle of eau de Cologne. The Baron laughed at my fastidiousness, but, nevertheless, availed himself gratefully of the chance of a hasty toilet, borrowing from me the necessary implements.

On returning to the village I noticed the smell of coal-smoke coming from the direction of the alder trees on the shore. I implied by a gesture that this was a last farewell greeting brought by the wind from the steamer. But the Baron pretended not to understand my meaning.

He was a distressing sight at breakfast, with his big, sleepy head sunk on his breast, and his swollen features. Both of us suffered from self-consciousness; he was in a gloomy mood and kept up an obstinate silence. Once he seized my hand and apologised for his absent-mindedness, but almost directly afterwards he relapsed into gloom. I made every effort to rouse him, but in vain; we were out of harmony, the tie between us was broken. An expression of coarseness and vulgarity had stolen into his face, usually so frank and pleasant. The reflection of the charm, the living beauty of his beloved wife had vanished; the uncouth man had appeared.

I was unable to guess at his thoughts. Did he suspect my feelings? To judge from his behaviour he must have been a prey to very conflicting emotions, for at one minute he pressed my hand, calling me his best, his only friend, at the next he seemed oblivious of my presence.

I discovered with a feeling of dismay that we only lived in her and for her. Since our sun had set we seemed to have lost all individuality.

I determined to shake him off as soon as we got back to town, but he held on to me, entreating me to accompany him to his house.

When we entered the deserted home, we felt as if we had entered a chamber of death. A moisture came into our eyes.

Full of confusion and embarrassment, I did not know what to do.

"It's too absurd," I said at last, laughing at myself; "here are a captain of the Guards and a royal secretary whimpering like——"

"It's a relief," he interrupted me.

He sent for his little girl, but her presence only aggravated the bitter feeling of regret at our loss.

It was now nine o'clock in the morning. He had come to the end of his powers of endurance, and invited me to take a nap on the sofa while he went to lie down on his bed. He put a cushion under my head, covered me with his military cloak and wished me a sound sleep, thanking me cordially for having taken compassion on his loneliness. His brotherly kindness was like an echo of his wife's tenderness; she seemed to fill his thoughts completely.

I sank into a deep sleep, dimly aware, at the moment before losing consciousness, of his huge form stealing to my improvised couch with a murmured question as to whether I was quite comfortable.

It was noon when I awoke. He was already up. He hated the idea of being alone, and proposed that we should breakfast together in the Park. I readily fell in with his suggestion.

We spent the day together, talking about all sorts of things, but every subject led us back to her on whose life our own lives seemed to have been grafted.

III

I SPENT the two following days alone, yearning for the solitude of my library, the cellars of which, once the sculpture rooms of the museum, suited my mood. The large room, built in the rococo style and looking on to the "Lions' Court," contained the manuscripts. I spent a great deal of time there, reading at haphazard anything which seemed old enough to draw my attention from recent events. But the more I read, the more the present melted into the past, and Queen Christine's letters, yellow with age, whispered into my ears words of love from the Baroness.

To avoid the company of inquisitive friends, I shunned my usual restaurant. I could not bear the thought of degrading my tongue by confessing my new faith before those scoffers; they should never know. I was jealous of my own personality, which was henceforth consecrated to her only. As I went through the streets, I had a vision of acolytes walking before me, their tinkling bells announcing to the passers-by the approach of the Holy of Holies enshrined in the monstrance of my heart. I imagined myself in mourning, deep mourning for a queen, and longed to bid the crowd bare their heads at the passing of my stillborn love, which had no chance of ever quickening into life.

On the third day I was roused from my lethargy by the rolling of drums and the mournful strains of Chopin's Funeral March. I rushed to the window and noticed the

28

captain marching by at the head of his Guards. He looked up at my window and acknowledged my presence with a nod and a smile. The band was playing his wife's favourite piece, at his orders, and the unsuspicious musicians had no inkling that they played it in her honour for him and for me, and before an even less auspicious audience.

Half-an-hour later the Baron called for me at the library. I took him through the passages in the basement, overcrowded with cupboards and shelves, into the manuscript room. He looked cheerful, and at once communicated to me the contents of a letter he had received from his wife. All was going on well. She had enclosed a note for me. I devoured it with my eyes, trying hard to hide my excitement. She thanked me frankly and graciously for having looked after "her old man"; she said she had felt flattered by my evident grief at parting, and added that she was staying with my "guardian angel," to whom she was getting more and more attached. She expressed great admiration for her character, and, in conclusion, held out hopes of a happy ending. That was all.

So she was in love with me, this "guardian angel" of mine! This monster! The very thought of her now filled me with horror. I was compelled to act the part of a lover against my will; I was condemned to play an abominable farce, perhaps all my life long. The truth of the old adage that one cannot play with fire without burning one's fingers came home to me with terrible force. Caught in my own trap, I pictured to myself in my wrath the detestable creature who had forced herself upon me: she had the eyes of a Mongolian, a sallow face, red arms. With angry satisfaction I recalled her seductive ways, her suspicious behaviour, which more than once had set my friends wondering what species of woman it was with whom I was seen so constantly walking about the parks and suburbs.

The remembrance of her tricks, her attentions, her flattering tongue, gave me a kind of vicious pleasure. I remembered a way she had of pulling out her watch and showing a little bit of dainty underclothing. I remembered a certain Sunday in the Park. We were strolling along the broad avenues when she all at once proposed that we should walk through the shrubbery. Her proposal irritated me, for the shrubbery had an evil reputation, but she answered all my objections with a short " Bother propriety ! "

She wanted to gather anemones under the hazel bushes. She left me standing in the avenue and disappeared behind the shrubs. I followed, confused. She sat down in a sheltered spot under an alder tree, spreading out her skirts and showing off her feet, which were small but disfigured by bunions. An uncomfortable silence fell between us. I thought of the old maids of Corinth. . . . She looked at me with an expression of childlike innocence . . . she was safe from me, her very plainness saved her, and, moreover, I took no pleasure in easy conquests.

Every one of these details, which I had always put away from me as odious, came into my mind and oppressed me, now that there seemed a prospect of winning her. I prayed fervently for the comedian's success.

But I had to be patient and hide my feelings.

While I was reading his wife's note, the Baron sat down at the table, which was littered with old books and documents. He was playing with his carved ivory baton, absent-mindedly, as if he were conscious of his inferiority in literary matters. He defeated all my attempts to interest him in my work with an indifferent, " Yes, yes, very interesting ! "

Abashed by the evidences of his rank, his neckpiece, the sash, the brilliant uniform, I endeavoured to readjust the balance by showing off my knowledge. But I only succeeded in making him feel uncomfortable.

The sword versus the pen! Down with the aristocrat, up with the commoner! Did the woman, when later on she chose the father of her children from the aristocracy of the brain, see the future, clairvoyantly, without being conscious of it?

In spite of his constant efforts to treat me as his equal, the Baron, without admitting it even to himself, was always constrained in my presence. At times he paid due deference to my superior knowledge, tacitly acknowledging his inferiority to me in certain respects; at other times he would ride the high horse; then a word from the Baroness was sufficient to bring him to his senses. In his wife's eyes the inherited coat of arms counted for very little, and the dusty coat of the man of letters completely eclipsed the full-dress uniform of the captain. Had he not been himself aware of this when he donned a painter's blouse and entered the studio at Düsseldorf as the least of all the pupils? In all probability he had, but still there always remained a certain refinement, an inherited tradition, and he was by no means free from the jealous hatred which exists between students and officers.

For the moment I was necessary to him, as I shared his sorrow, and therefore he invited me to dine with him.

After the coffee he suggested that we should both write to the Baroness. He brought me paper and pen, and compelled me to write to her, against my will; I racked my brain for platitudes under which to hide the thoughts of my heart.

When I had finished my letter I handed it to the Baron and asked him to read it.

"I never read other people's letters," he answered, with hypocritical pride.

"And I never write to another man's wife without that man's full knowledge of the correspondence."

He glanced at my letter, and, with an enigmatical smile, enclosed it in his own.

I saw nothing of him during the rest of the week, until I met him one evening at a street corner. He seemed very pleased to see me, and we went into a café to have a chat.

He had just returned from the country, where he had spent a few days with his wife's cousin. Without ever having met that charming person, I was easily able to draw a mental picture of her from the traces of her influence on the Baron's character. He had lost his haughtiness and his melancholy. There was a gay, somewhat dissipated look on his face, and he enriched his vocabulary by a few expressions of doubtful taste; even the tone of his voice was altered.

"A weak mind," I said to myself, "swayed by every emotion; a blank slate on which the lightest of women may write sense or folly, according to her sweet will."

He behaved like the hero in comic opera; he joked, told funny tales and was in boisterous spirits. His charm was gone with his uniform; and when, after supper, slightly intoxicated, he suggested that we should call on certain female friends of his, I thought him positively repulsive. With the exception of the neckpiece, the sash and the uniform, he really possessed no attractions whatever.

When his intoxication had reached its climax, he lost all sense of shame and began to discuss the secrets of his married life. I interrupted him indignantly and proposed that we should go home. He assured me that his wife allowed him full license during her absence. At first I thought this more than human, but later on it confirmed the opinion I had formed of the Baroness's naturally frigid temperament. We parted very early, and I returned to my room, my brain on fire with the indiscreet disclosures which I had been made to listen to.

This woman, although apparently in love with her husband, after a union of three years not only permitted him every freedom, but did so without claiming the same right for herself. It was strange, unnatural, like love without jealousy, light without shade. No! it was impossible; there must be another cause. He had told me the Baroness was naturally cold. That, too, seemed strange. Or was she really an embodiment of the virgin mother, such as I had already dimly divined? And was not chastity, purity of the soul, so closely linked to refinement of manners, a characteristic, an attribute of a superior race? I had not been deceived, then, in my youthful meditations when a young girl roused my admiration without in the least exciting my senses. Beautiful childish dreams! Charming ignorance of woman, that problem unspeakably more complex than a bachelor ever dreams of!

At last the Baroness returned, radiant with health; the memories awakened by meeting again the friends of her girlhood seemed to have rejuvenated her.

"Here is the dove with the olive branch," she said, handing me a letter from my so-called sweetheart.

With anything but genuine enjoyment I waded through the presumptuous twaddle, the effusions of a heartless blue-stocking, anxious to win independence by marriage—any marriage, and while I was reading I made up my mind to put an end to the matter.

"Do you know for certain," I asked the Baroness, "whether the lady is engaged to the singer or not?"

"Yes and no."

D

"Has she given him her word?"

"No."

"Does she want to marry him?"

"No."

"Do her parents wish it?"

"No."

"Why is she so determined to marry him, then?"

"Because . . . I don't know."

"Is she in love with me?"

"Perhaps she is."

"Then she is simply a husband-hunter. She has but one thought, to make a bargain with the highest bidder. She doesn't know what love is."

"What is love?"

"A passion stronger than all others, a force of nature absolutely irresistible, something akin to thunder, to rising floods, a waterfall, a storm——"

She gazed into my eyes, forgetting the reproaches which, in the interest of her friend, had risen to the tip of her tongue.

"And is your love for her a force like that?" she asked.

I had a strong impulse to tell her everything.

But, supposing I did? . . . The bond between us would be broken, and, without the lie which protected me from my criminal passion, I should be lost.

Afraid of committing myself, I asked her to drop the subject. I said that my cruel sweetheart was dead as far as I was concerned, and that all that remained for me to do was to forget her.

The Baroness did her utmost to comfort me, but she did not cloak the fact that I had a dangerous rival in the singer, who was on the spot and in personal contact with his lady-love.

The Baron, evidently bored by our conversation, interrupted us peevishly, telling us that we should end by burning our fingers.

"This meddling with other people's love affairs is utter folly!" he exclaimed, almost rudely; the Baroness's face flushed with indignation. I hastily changed the subject to avoid a scene.

The ball had been set rolling. The lie, originally a mere whim, grew. Full of apprehension and shame, I told myself fairy tales which I ended in believing. In them I played the part of the ill-starred lover, a part which came easy enough, for with the exception of the object of my tenderness, the fairy tales agreed in every detail with reality.

I was indeed caught in my own net. One day, on returning home, I found "her" father's card. I returned his call at once. He was a little old man, unpleasantly like his daughter, the caricature of a caricature. He treated me in every way as he would his prospective son-in-law. He inquired about my family, my income, my prospects. It was a regular cross-examination. The matter threatened to become serious.

What was I to do? Hoping to divert his attention from me, I made myself as insignificant as possible in his eyes. The reason of his visit to Stockholm was obvious. Either he wanted to shake off the singer, whom he disliked, or the lady had made up her mind to honour me with her hand if an expert should approve of her bargain.

I showed myself from my most unpleasant side, avoided every opportunity of meeting him, refused even an invitation to dinner from the Baroness; I tired my unlucky would-be father-in-law out by giving him the slip again and again, pleading urgent duty at the library, until I had gained my purpose, and he departed before the appointed time.

Did my rival ever guess to whom he was indebted for his matrimonial misery when he married his bride-elect? No doubt he never knew, and proudly imagined that he had ousted me.

D 2

An incident which to some extent affected our destiny
was the sudden departure of the Baroness and her little
daughter to the country. It was in the beginning of
August. For reasons of health she had chosen Mariafred,
a small village on the Lake of Mälar, where at the moment
the little cousin happened to be staying with her parents.

This hurried departure on the day after her home-
coming struck me as very extraordinary; but, as it was
none of my business, I made no comment. Three days
passed, then the Baron wrote asking me to call. He appeared to be restless, very nervous and strange. He told
me that the Baroness would be back almost immediately.

"Indeed!" I exclaimed, more astonished than I cared
to show.

"Yes! . . . her nerves are upset, the climate doesn't
suit her. She has written me an unintelligible letter
which frightens me. I have never been able to understand her whims . . . she gets all sorts of fantastic ideas
into her head. Just at present she imagines that you
are angry with her!"

"I!"

"It's too absurd!" he continued, "but don't take
any notice of it when she returns; she's ashamed of her
moods; she's proud, and if she thought you disapproved
of her, she would only commit fresh follies."

"It has come at last," I said to myself; "the catastrophe is imminent!" And from that moment my
thoughts were bent on flight, for I had no desire to figure
as the hero of a romance of passion.

I refused the next invitation, making excuses which
were badly invented and wrongly understood. The result
was a call from the Baron; he asked me what I meant by
my unfriendly conduct? I did not know what explanation
to give, and he took advantage of my embarrassment and
exacted a promise from me to join them in an excursion.

I found the Baroness looking ill and worn out; only

the black eyes in the livid face seemed alive and shone with unnatural brilliancy. I was very reserved, spoke in indifferent tones and said as little as possible.

On leaving the steamer, we went to a famous hotel where the Baron had arranged to meet his uncle. The supper, which was served in the open, was anything but gay. Before us spread the sinister lake, shut in by gloomy mountains; above our heads waved the branches of the lime trees, the blackened trunks of which were over a hundred years old.

We talked commonplaces, but our conversation was dull and soon languished. I fancied that I could feel the after-effects of a quarrel between my hosts, which had not yet been patched up and was on the verge of a fresh outbreak. I ardently desired to avoid the storm, but, unfortunately, uncle and nephew left the table to discuss business matters. Now the mine would explode!

As soon as we were alone the Baroness leaned towards me and said excitedly—

"Do you know that Gustav is angry with me for coming back unexpectedly?"

"I know nothing about it."

"Then you don't know that he'd been building on meeting my charming cousin on his free Sundays?"

"My dear Baroness," I exclaimed, interrupting her, "if you want to bring charges against your husband, hadn't you better do it in his presence?"

. . . What had I done? It was brutal, this harsh, uncompromising rebuke, flung into the face of a disloyal wife in defence of a member of my own sex.

"How dare you!" she cried, amazed, changing colour. "You're insulting me!"

"Yes, Baroness, I am insulting you."

All was over between us, for ever.

As soon as her husband returned she hastened towards him, as if she were seeking protection from an enemy.

The Baron noticed that something was wrong, but he could not understand her excitement.

I left them at the landing-stage, pretending that I had to pay a visit at one of the neighbouring villas.

I don't know how I got back to town. My legs seemed to carry a lifeless body; the vital node was cut, I was a corpse walking along the streets.

Alone! I was alone again, without friends, without a family, without anything to worship. It was impossible for me to recreate God. The statue of the Madonna had fallen down; woman had shown herself behind the beautiful image, woman, treacherous, faithless, with sharp claws! When she attempted to make me her confidant, she was taking the first step towards breaking her marriage vows; at that moment the hatred of her sex was born in me. She had insulted the man and the sex in me, and I took the part of her husband against her. Not that I flattered myself with being a virtuous man, but in love man is never a thief, he only takes what is given to him. It is woman who steals and sells herself. The only time when she gives unselfishly is when she betrays her husband. The prostitute sells herself, the young wife sells herself; the faithless wife only gives to her lover that which she has stolen from her husband.

But I had not desired this woman in any other way than as a friend. Protected from me by her child, I had always seen her invested with the insignia of motherhood. Always seeing her at the side of her husband, I had never felt the slightest temptation to indulge in pleasures which are gross in themselves, and ennobled only by entire and exclusive possession.

I returned to my room annihilated, completely crushed, more lonely than ever, for I had dropped my Bohemian friends from the very outset of my relations with the Baroness.

IV

I OCCUPIED in those days a fairly large attic with two windows which looked on the new harbour, the bay and the rocky heights of the southern suburbs. Before the windows, on the roof, I had managed to create a garden of tiny dimensions. Bengal roses, azaleas and geraniums provided me in their turn with flowers for the secret cult of my Madonna with the child. It had become a daily habit with me to pull down the blinds towards the evening, arrange my flower-pots in a semicircle, and place the picture of the Baroness, with the lamplight full on it, amongst them. She was represented on this portrait as a young mother, with somewhat severe, but deliciously pure features, her delicate head crowned with a wealth of golden hair. She wore a light dress which reached up to her chin and was finished off with a pleated frill; her little daughter, dressed in white, was standing on a table by the side of her, gazing at the beholder with pensive eyes. How many letters "to my friends" had I not written before this portrait and sent off on the following morning addressed to the Baron! These letters were at that time the only channel into which I could pour my literary aspirations, and my inmost soul was laid bare in them.

To open a career for the erratic, artistic soul of the Baroness, I had tried to encourage her to seek an outlet for her poetic imagination in literary work. I had provided her with the masterpieces of all literatures, had taught her the first principles of literary composition by furnishing endless summaries, commentaries and analyses, to which I added advice and practical illustrations. She had been only moderately interested, for she doubted her literary talent from the outset. I told her that every educated person possessed the ability to write at least a letter, and was therefore a poet or author *in posse*. But it was all in vain; the passion for the stage had taken firm hold of her obstinate brain. She insisted that she was a born elocutionist, and, because her rank prevented her from following her inclination and going on the stage (an ardently desired contingency), she posed as a martyr, heedless of the disastrous consequences which threatened to overtake her home life. Her husband sympathised with my benevolent efforts, undertaken in the hope of saving the domestic peace of the family from shipwreck. He was grateful, although he had not the courage to take an active and personal interest in the matter. The Baroness's opposition notwithstanding, I had continued my efforts and urged her in every letter to break the fateful spell which held her, and make an effort to write a poem, a drama, or a novel.

"Your life has been an eventful one," I said to her in one of my letters; "why not make use of your own experience?" And, quoting from Börne, I added, "Take paper and pen and be candid, and you are bound to become an authoress."

"It's too painful to live an unhappy life all over again," she had replied. "I want to find forgetfulness in art; I want to merge my identity into characters different from my own."

I had never asked myself what it was that she wanted to forget. I knew nothing of her past life. Did she shrink from allowing me to solve the riddle? Was she afraid of handing me the key to her character? Was she anxious to hide her true self behind the personalities of stage heroines, or did she hope to increase her own magnitude by assuming the identities of her superiors?

When I had come to the end of my arguments, I suggested that she should make a start by translating the works of foreign authors; I told her this would help to form her style and make her known to publishers.

"Is a translator well paid?" she asked.

"Fairly well," I replied, "if she knows her business."

"Perhaps you will think me mercenary," she continued, "but work for its own sake doesn't attract me."

Like so many women of our time, she was seized with the mania of earning her own living. The Baron made a grimace plainly indicative of the fact that he would far rather see her taking an active interest in the management of her house and servants, than contributing a few shillings towards the expenses of a neglected home.

Since that day she had given me no peace, begging me to find her a good book and a publisher.

I had done my utmost, and had succeeded in procuring for her two quite short articles, destined for "Miscellaneous Items" in one of the illustrated magazines, which did not, however, remunerate its contributors. For a whole week I heard nothing of the work, which could easily have been accomplished in a couple of hours. She lost her temper when the Baron teasingly called her a sluggard; in fact, she was so angry that I saw he had touched a very sore spot, and stopped all further allusions, afraid of making serious mischief between the couple.

This was how matters stood at the time of my rupture with her.

. . . I sat in my attic with her letters before me on the table. As I re-read them, one after the other, my heart ached for her. She was a soul in torment, a power wasted, a voice unable to make itself heard, just like myself. This was the secret of our mutual sympathy.

I suffered through her as if she were a diseased organ grafted on my sick soul, which had itself become too blunted and dull to sense the pleasure of exquisite pain.

And what had she done that I should deprive her of my sympathy? In a moment of jealousy she had complained to me of her unhappy marriage. And I had repulsed her, I had spoken harshly to her, when I ought to have reasoned with her; it would not have been an impossible task, for hadn't her husband told me that she allowed him every licence?

I was seized with an immense compassion for her; no doubt, in her soul lay, shrouded in profound mystery, fateful secrets, physical and psychical aberrations. It seemed to me that I should be guilty of a terrible wrong if I let her come to ruin. When my depression had reached its climax I began a letter to her, asking her to forgive me. I begged her to forget what had happened, and tried to explain the painful incident by a misunderstanding on my part. But the words would not come, my pen refused to obey me. Worn out with fatigue, I threw myself on my bed.

The following morning was warm and cloudy, a typical August morning. At eight o'clock I went to the library, melancholy and depressed. As I had a key, I was able to let myself in and spend three hours in perfect solitude before the general public began to arrive. I wandered through the passages, between rows of books on either side, in that exquisite solitude which is not loneliness, in close communion with the great thinkers of all times. Taking out a volume here and there, I tried to fix my mind on some definite subject in order to forget the painful scene of yesterday. But I could not banish the desecrated image of the fallen Madonna from my mind. When I raised my eyes from the pages, which I had read without understanding a word, I seemed to see her, as in a vision, coming down the spiral staircase, which wound in endless perspective at the back of the galleries. She lifted the straight folds of her blue dress, showing her perfect feet and slender ankles, looking at me furtively, with a sidelong glance, tempting me to the betrayal of her husband, soliciting me with that treacherous and voluptuous smile which I had yesterday seen for the first time. The apparition awakened all the sensuality which had lain dormant in my heart for the last three months, for the pure atmosphere which surrounded her had kept away from me all lascivious thoughts. Now all the passion which burnt in me concentrated itself on a single object. I desired her. My imagination painted for me the exquisite beauty of her white limbs. I selected a work on art which contained illustrations of all the famous sculptures in the Italian museums, hoping to discover this woman's formula by systematic scientific research. I wanted to find out species and genus to which she belonged. I had plenty to choose from.

Was she Venus, full-bosomed and broad-hipped, the normal woman, who awaits her lover, sure of her triumphant beauty?

No!

Juno, then, the fertile mother, who keeps her regal charms for the marriage-bed?

By no means!

Minerva, the blue-stocking, the old maid, who hides her flat bosom under a coat of mail?

On no account!

Diana then, the pale goddess of night, fearful of the sun, cruel in her enforced chastity, more boy than girl, modest because she needs must be so—Diana, who could not forgive Actæon for having watched her while bathing? Was she Diana? The species, perhaps, but not the genus!

The future will speak the last word! With that

delicate body, those exquisite limbs, that sweet face, that proud smile, that modestly veiled bosom, could she be yearning for blood and forbidden fruit? Diana? Yes, unmistakably Diana!

I continued my research; I looked through a number of publications on art stored up in this incomparable treasure-house of the State, so as to study the various representations of the chaste goddess.

I compared; like a scientist, I proved my point, again and again rushing from one end of the huge building to the other to find the volumes to which I was being referred.

The striking of a clock recalled me from the world of my dreams; my colleagues were beginning to arrive, and I had to enter on my daily duties.

I decided to spend the evening at the club with my friends. On entering the laboratory, I was greeted with deafening acclamations, which raised my spirits. The centre of the room was occupied by a table dressed like an altar, in the middle of which stood a skull and a large bottle of cyanide of potassium. An open Bible, stained with punch spots, lay beside the skull. Surgical instruments served as bookmarkers. A number of punch-glasses were arranged in a circle all round. Instead of a ladle a retort was used for filling the glasses. My friends were on the verge of intoxication. One of them offered me a glass bowl containing half-a-pint of the fiery drink, and I emptied it at one gulp. All the members shouted the customary "Curse it!" I responded by singing the song of the ne'er-do-wells—

> Deep potations
> And flirtations
> Are life's only end and aim . . .

After this prelude an infernal row arose, and, amid shouts of applause, I delivered myself of a stream of vulgar platitudes, abusing and insulting women in high-flown verses, mixed with anatomical terms.   Intoxicated with the coarse suggestions, the vulgar profanation, I surpassed myself in heaping insults on the head of my Madonna.   It was the morbid result of my unsatisfied longing.   My hatred for the treacherous idol broke out with such virulence that it afforded me a sort of bitter comfort.   My messmates, poor devils, acquainted with love in its lowest aspect only, listened eagerly to my vile denunciations of a lady of rank, who was utterly beyond their reach.

The drunkenness increased.   The sound of men's voices delighted my ears after I had passed three months amid sentimental whining, mock modesty and hypocritical inno-cence.   I felt as if I had torn off the mask, thrown back the veil under which Tartuffe concealed his cupidity.   In imagination I saw the adored woman indulging every whim and caprice, merely to escape the boredom of a dull existence.   All my insults, my infamous invectives and abuse I addressed to her, furious with the power in me which successfully strove against my committing a crime.

At this moment the laboratory appeared to me to be a hallucination of my over-excited brain, the temple of monstrous orgies in which all the senses participated. The bottles on the shelves gleamed in all the colours of the rainbow : the deep purple of red lead; the orange of potash, the yellow of sulphur, the green of verdigris, the blue of vitriol.   The atmosphere was thick with tobacco smoke ; the smell of the lemons, used in brewing the punch, called up visions of happier countries.   The piano, intentionally out of tune and badly treated, groaned Beethoven's march in a manner which made it unrecognis-able.   The pallid faces of the revellers see-sawed in the blue-black smoke which rose from the pipes.   The lieu-tenant's sash, the black beard of the doctor of philosophy, the physician's embroidered shirt front, the skull with its empty sockets; the noise, the disorder, the abominable discords, the lewd images evoked, bewildered and confused my maddened brain, when suddenly, with one accord, there arose a cry uttered by many voices—

"To the women, you men!"

The whole assembly broke into the song—

> Deep potations
> And flirtations
> Are life's only end and aim . . .

Hats and overcoats were donned, and the whole horde trooped out. Half-an-hour later we had arrived at our destination. The fires in the huge stoves spluttered and crackled, stout was ordered, and the saturnalias, which rendered the remainder of the night hideous, began.

V

WHEN I awoke on the following morning in my own bed in broad daylight, I was surprised to find that I had regained complete mastery over myself. Every trace of unhealthy sentimentality had disappeared; the cult of the Madonna had been forgotten in the excesses of the night. I looked upon my fantastic love as a weakness of the spirit or the flesh, which at the moment appeared to me to be one and the same thing.

After I had had a cold bath and eaten some breakfast, I returned to my daily duties, content that the whole matter was at an end. I plunged into my work, and the hours passed rapidly.

It was half-past twelve when the porter announced the Baron.

"Is it possible?" I said to myself, "and I had been under the impression that the incident was closed!"

I prepared myself for a scene.

The Baron, radiant with mirth and happiness, squeezed my hand affectionately. He had come to ask me to join in another excursion by steamer, and see the amateur theatricals at Södertelje, a small watering-place.

I declined politely, pleading urgent business.

"My wife," he recommenced, "would be very pleased if you could manage to come. . . . Moreover, Baby will be one of the party. . . ." Baby, the much-discussed cousin. . . .

He went on urging me in a manner at once irresistible and pathetic, looking at me with eyes so full of melancholy that I felt myself weakening. But instead of frankly accepting his invitation, I replied with a question—

"The Baroness is quite well?"

"She wasn't very well yesterday; in fact, she was really ill, but she is better since this morning. My dear fellow," he added after a slight pause, "what passed between you the night before last at Nacka? My wife says that you had a misunderstanding, and that you are angry with her without any reason."

"Really," I answered, a little taken aback, "I don't know myself. Perhaps I had a little too much to drink. I forgot myself."

"Let's forget all about it then, will you?" he replied briskly, "and let us be friends as before. Women are often strangely touchy, as you know. It's all right, then; you'll come, won't you? To-day at four. Remember, we are counting on you. . . ."

I had consented! . . .

Unfathomable enigma! A misunderstanding! . . . But she had been ill! . . . Ill with fear . . . with anger . . . with . . .

The fact that the little unknown cousin was about to appear upon the scene added a new interest, and with a beating heart I went on board the steamer at four o'clock, as had been arranged.

The Baroness greeted me with sisterly kindness.

"You're not angry with me because of my unkind words?" she began. "I'm very excitable. . . ."

"Don't let us speak about it," I replied, trying to find her a seat behind the bridge.

"Mr. Axel . . . Miss Baby! . . ."

The Baron was introducing us. I was looking at a girl of about eighteen, of the soubrette type, exactly what I had imagined. She was small, very ordinary-looking, dressed simply, but with a certain striving after elegance.

But the Baroness! Pale as death, with hollow cheeks, she looked more fragile than ever. Her bangles jingled at her wrists; her slender neck rose from her collar, plainly showing the blue arteries winding towards the ears which, owing to the careless way in which she had arranged her hair, stood out from her head more than usual. She was badly dressed, too. The colours of her frock were crude, and did not blend. I could not help thinking that she was downright plain, and, as I looked at her, my heart was filled with compassion, and I cursed my recent conduct towards her. This woman a coquette? She was a saint, a martyr, bearing undeserved sorrow.

The steamer started. The lovely August evening on the Lake of Mälar tempted one to peaceful dreams.

Was it accidental or intended? The little cousin and the Baron were sitting side by side at a distance sufficiently great to prevent our overhearing each other. Leaning towards her, he talked and laughed incessantly, with the gay, rejuvenated face of an accepted lover.

From time to time he looked at us, slyly, and we nodded and smiled back.

"A jolly girl, the little one, isn't she?" remarked the Baroness.

"It seems so," I answered, uncertain how to take her remark.

"She knows how to cheer up my melancholy husband. I don't possess that gift," she added, with a frank and kindly smile at the group.

And as she spoke the lines of her face betrayed suppressed sorrow, tears held back, superhuman resignation; across her features glided, cloud-like, those incomprehensible reflections of kindness, resignation and self-denial, common to pregnant women and young mothers.

Ashamed of my misinterpretation of her character, tor-

E

tured by remorse, nervous, I suppressed with difficulty the
tears which I felt rising to my eyes.

"But aren't you jealous?" I asked, merely for the sake
of saying something.

"Not at all," she answered, quite sincerely and without
a trace of malice. "Perhaps you'll think it strange, but
it's true. I love my husband; he is very kind-hearted;
and I appreciate the little one, for she's a nice girl. And
there is really nothing wrong between them. Shame on
jealousy, which makes a woman look plain; at my age one
has to be careful."

And, indeed, she looked so plain at that moment that it
wrung my heart. Acting thoughtlessly, on impulse, I
advised her, with fatherly solicitude, to put a shawl round
her shoulders, pretending that I was afraid of her catching
cold. She let me arrange the fleecy fabric round her face,
framing it, and transforming her into a dainty beauty.

How pretty she was when she thanked me smilingly!
A look of perfect happiness had come into her face; she
was grateful like a child begging for caresses.

"My poor husband! How glad I am to see him a little
more cheerful! He is full of trouble! . . . If you only
knew!"

"If I'm not indiscreet," I ventured, "then, for
Heaven's sake, tell me what it is that makes you so unhappy. I feel that there is a great sorrow in your life.
I have nothing to offer you but advice; but, if I can in
any way serve you, I entreat you to make use of my
friendship."

My poor friends were in financial difficulties: the
phantom of ruin—that ghastly nightmare!—was threatening them. Up to now the Baron's inadequate income had
been supplemented by his wife's dowry. But they had
recently discovered that the dowry existed on paper only,
it being invested in worthless shares. The Baron was on

the point of sending in his papers, and looking out for a cashier's billet in a bank.

"That's the reason," she concluded, "why I want to make use of the talent I possess, for then I could contribute my share to the necessary expenses of the household. It's all my fault, don't you see? I'm to blame for the difficulties in which he finds himself; I've ruined his career. . . ."

What could I say or do in such a sad case which went far beyond my power of assistance? I attempted to smooth away her difficulties, to deceive myself about them.

I assured her that things would come all right, and, in order to allay her fears, I painted for her the picture of a future without cares, full of bright prospects. I quoted the statistics of national economy to prove that better times were coming in which her shares would improve; I invented the most extraordinary remedies; I conjured up a new army organisation which would bring in its train unexpected promotion for her husband.

It was all pure invention, but, thanks to my power of imagination, courage and hope returned to her, and her spirits rose.

After landing, and while we were waiting for the commencement of the play, we went for a walk in the Park. I had not, as yet, exchanged one word with the cousin. The Baron never left her side. He carried her cloak, devoured her with his eyes, bathed her in a flood of words, warmed her with his breath, while she remained callous and self-possessed, with vacant eyes and hard features. From time to time, without apparently moving a muscle of her face, she seemed to say things to which the Baron replied with shrieks of laughter, and, judging from his animated face, she must have been indulging pretty freely in repartee, innuendoes and double-entendres.

E 2

At last the doors opened, and we went in to take our seats, which had not been reserved.

The curtain rose. The Baroness was blissfully happy to see the stage, smell the mingled odours of painted canvas, raw wood, rouge and perspiration.

They played *A Whim*. A sudden indisposition seized me, the result of the distressing memories of my vain efforts to conquer the stage, and also, perhaps, the consequence of the excesses of the previous night. When the curtain fell, I left my seat and made my way to the restaurant, where I refreshed myself with a double-absinthe, and remained until the performance was over.

My friends met me after the play, and we went to have supper together. They seemed tired, and unable to hide their annoyance at my flight. Nobody spoke a word while the table was being laid. A desultory conversation was started with the greatest difficulty. The cousin remained mute, haughty, reserved.

We discussed the menu. After consulting with me, the Baroness ordered *hors d'œuvres*. Roughly—too roughly for my unstrung nerves, the Baron countermanded the order. Lost in gloomy thoughts, I pretended not to hear him, and called out "*Hors d'œuvres* for two!" for her and for me, as she had originally ordered.

The Baron grew pale with anger. There was thunder in the air, but not another word was spoken.

I inwardly admired my courage in thus answering a rudeness with an insult, bound to have serious consequences in any civilised country. The Baroness, encouraged by the way in which I had stood up for her, began teasing me in order to make me laugh. But in vain. Conversation was impossible; nobody had anything to say, and the Baron and I exchanged angry glances. In the end my opponent whispered a remark in his neighbour's ear; in reply she made a grimace, nodded, pronounced a few syllables without moving her lips, and regarded me scornfully.

I felt the blood rising to my head, and the storm would have burst there and then if an unexpected incident had not served as a lightning conductor.

In an adjacent room a boisterous party had been strumming the piano for the last half-hour; now they began singing a vulgar song, with the doors standing wide open.

The Baron turned to the waiter: "Shut that door," he said curtly.

The door had hardly been closed when it was again burst open. The singers repeated the chorus, and challenged us with impertinent remarks.

The moment for an explosion had arrived.

I jumped up from my chair; with two strides I was at the door and banged it in the faces of the noisy crew. Fire in a powder-barrel could not have had a more rousing effect than my determined stand against the enemy.

A short struggle ensued, during which I kept hold of the door-handle. But the door yielded to the vigorous pull from the other side, and I was dragged towards the howling mob, who threw themselves upon me, eager for a hand-to-hand tussle.

At that moment I felt a touch on my shoulder, and heard an indignant voice asking "these gentlemen whether they had no sense of honour, that they attacked in a body one single opponent?" . . .

It was the Baroness who, under the stress of a strong emotion, forgetting the dictates of convention and good manners, betrayed warmer feelings than she probably was aware of.

The fight was over. The Baroness regarded me with searching eyes.

"You're a brave little hero," she said. "I was trembling for you."

The Baron called for the bill, asked to see the landlord and requested him to send for the police.

After this incident perfect harmony reigned amongst us. We vied in expressions of indignation about the rudeness of the natives. All the suppressed wrath of jealousy and wounded vanity was poured on the heads of those uncouth louts.

And later on, as we sat drinking punch in one of our own rooms, our old friendship burst into fresh flames; we forgot all about the police, who, moreover, had failed to put in an appearance.

On the following morning we met in the coffee-room, full of high spirits, and in our inmost hearts glad to have done with a disagreeable business, the consequences of which it would have been difficult to foretell.

After the first breakfast we went for a walk on the banks of the canal, in couples, and with a fair distance between us. When we had arrived at a lock where the canal made a strong curve, the Baron waited and turned to his wife with an affectionate, almost amorous smile.

" D'you remember this place, Marie ? " he asked.

" Yes, yes, my dear, I remember," she answered, with a mingled expression of passion and sadness.

Later on she explained his question to me.

" It was here where he first told me of his love . . . one evening, under this very birch-tree, while a brilliant shooting-star flashed across the sky."

" That was three years ago," I completed her explanation, " and you are reviving old memories already. You live in the past because the present doesn't satisfy you."

" Oh, stop ! " she exclaimed; " you've taken leave of your senses. . . . I loathe the past, and I am grateful to my husband for having delivered me from a vain mother whose doting tyranny was ruining me. No, I adore my husband, he's a loyal friend to me. . . ."

"As you like, Baroness; I'll agree with anything, to please you."

At the stated hour we went on board to return to town, and after a delightful passage across the blue sea, with its thousands of green islands, we arrived in Stockholm, where we parted.

I had made up my mind to return to work, determined to tear this love out of my heart, but I soon found that I had reckoned without forces much stronger than myself. On the day after our excursion I received an invitation to dinner from the Baroness; it was the anniversary of her wedding-day. I could not think of a plausible excuse, and, although I was afraid of straining our friendship, I accepted the invitation. To my great disappointment, I found the house turned upside down, undergoing the process of a general cleaning; the Baron was in a bad temper, and the Baroness sent her apologies for the delayed dinner. I walked up and down the garden with her irritable, hungry husband, who seemed unable to control his impatience. After half-an-hour's strenuous effort my powers of entertaining him were exhausted, and conversation ceased. He took me into the dining-room.

Dinner was laid, and the appetisers [1] had been put on the table, but the mistress of the house was still invisible.

"If we took a snack standing," said the Baron, "we should be able to wait."

Afraid of offending the Baroness, I did my utmost to dissuade him, but he remained obstinate, and being, as it were, between two fires, I was compelled to acquiesce in his proposal.

At last the Baroness entered: radiant, young, pretty;

[1] Note of the translator: It is customary in Sweden to begin dinner with savoury sandwiches, which are usually placed on a side-table. These sandwiches are intended to excite the appetite of the diners, and are called "appetisers"

she was dressed in a diaphanous silk frock, yellow, like ripe corn, with a mauve stripe, reminiscent of pansies; this was her favourite combination of colours. The well-cut dress suited her girlish figure to perfection, and emphasised the beautiful contour of the shoulders and the curve of the exquisitely modelled arms.

I handed her my bunch of roses, wishing her many happy returns of the day; I also took good care to put all the blame for our rude impatience on the Baron.

When her eyes fell on the disordered table, she pursed up her lips and addressed a remark to her husband which was more stinging than humorous; he was not slow to reply to the undeserved rebuke. I threw myself into the breach by recalling the incidents of the previous day which I had already discussed with the Baron.

"And what d'you think of my charming cousin?" asked the Baroness.

"She's very amiable," I replied.

"Don't you agree with me, my dear fellow, that the child is a perfect treasure?" exclaimed the Baron, in a voice which expressed parental solicitude, sincere devotion and pity for this imp of Satan, supposed to be martyred by imaginary tyrants.

But in spite of the stress laid by her husband on the word "child," the Baroness continued mercilessly—

"Just look how that dear Baby has changed the style in which my husband does his hair!"

The parting which the Baron had been accustomed to wear had indeed disappeared. Instead of it, his hair was dressed in the manner of the young students, his moustache waxed—a style which did not suit him. Through an association of ideas, my attention was drawn to the fact —which, however, I kept to myself—that the Baroness, too, had adopted from the charming cousin certain details of dressing her hair, of wearing her clothes, of manner

even. It made me think of the elective affinities of the
chemists, in this case acting on living beings.

The dinner dragged on, slowly and heavily, like a cart
which has lost its fourth wheel, and wearily lumbers along
on the three remaining ones. But the cousin, henceforth
the indispensable complement of our quartet, which, without her, was beginning to be out of harmony, was expected
to come later on and take coffee with us.

At dessert I proposed a toast to the married couple, in
conventional terms, without spirit or wit, like champagne
which has grown flat.

Husband and wife, animated by the memories of the
past, kissed tenderly, and, in mimicking their former fond
ways, became affectionate, amorous even, just as an actor
will feel genuinely depressed when he has been feigning
tears.

Or was it that the fire was still smouldering underneath
the ashes, ready to burst into fresh flames if fanned by a
skilful hand? It was impossible to guess how matters
stood.

After dinner we went into the garden and sat in the
summer-house, the window of which looked on to the
street. Digestive processes did not favour conversation.
The Baron stood at the window, absent-mindedly watching
the street, in the hope of catching a glimpse of the cousin.
Suddenly he darted off like an arrow, evidently with the
intention of going to meet the expected guest.

Left alone with the Baroness, I at once became embarrassed; I was not naturally self-conscious, but she had
a queer way of looking at me and paying me compliments
on certain details of my appearance. After a long, almost
painful silence, she burst out laughing, and pointing in
the direction in which the Baron had disappeared, she
exclaimed—

"Dear old Gustav, he is head-over-ears in love!"

"It looks like it," I replied. "And you are really not jealous?"

"Not at all," she assured me. "I'm in love myself with the pretty little cat. And you?"

"Oh, I'm all right. I don't want to be rude, but I shall never feel in the least in sympathy with your cousin."

And this was true. From the first moment I had taken a dislike to this young woman, who, like myself, was of middle-class origin. She saw in me the odious witness, or rather the dangerous rival, hunting in the preserves which she had reserved for herself, and from which she hoped to force her way into society. Her keen grey eyes had at once recognised in me an acquaintance of whom she could make no use; her plebeian instinct scented an adventurer in me. And up to a certain point she was right, for I had entered the Baron's house in the hope of finding a patron for my unfortunate drama; unluckily, the relations between my friends and the stage were non-existent, a mere fabrication of my friend from Finland, and, with the exception of a few compliments, my play had never been mentioned.

It was also undeniable that there was a marked difference in the Baron's manner whenever his charmer was present. He was fickle and easily impressed, and evidently beginning to regard me with the eyes of the sorceress.

We had not long to wait; the pair appeared at the garden gate, merrily talking and laughing.

The girl was brimming over with fun and merriment; she used bad language, a little too freely perhaps, but with excellent taste; she uttered double-entendres with such an appearance of perfect innocence that it was impossible to credit her with the knowledge of the meaning of her ambiguous words. She smoked and drank without forgetting for one single moment that she was a woman, and, what is more, a young woman. There was nothing masculine about her, nothing emancipated, nor was she in the least prudish. She was certainly amusing, and time passed quickly.

But what surprised me most and ought to have been a warning to me, was the excessive mirth with which the Baroness greeted any doubtful remark which fell from the girl's lips. Then a wild laugh, a cynical expression would flit over her countenance, giving evidence that she was deeply versed in the secrets of excess.

While we were thus amusing ourselves, the Baron's uncle joined our little party. A retired captain, a widower of many years' standing, very chivalrous, of pleasing manners, a little daring in his old-fashioned courteousness, he was, thanks to his connection with the family, the declared favourite of these ladies, whose affections he had succeeded in winning.

He looked upon it as his right to fondle them, kiss their hands, pat their cheeks. As he came in, both of them fell on his neck with little exclamations of pleasure.

"Take care, my little ones! Two at a time is too much for an old fellow like me. Take care! You are burning yourselves. Quick, down with your hands, or I won't be responsible for anything."

The Baroness held her cigarette, poised between her lips, towards him.

"A little fire, please, uncle!"

"Fire! Fire! I'm sorry I can't oblige you, my child, my fire has gone out," he answered slyly.

"Has it?"

She boxed his ears with her finger-tips. The old man seized her arm, held it between his hands and felt it up to her shoulder.

"You're not as thin as you look, my darling," he said, stroking her soft flesh through her sleeve.

The Baroness did not object. The compliment seemed

to please her. Playfully, smilingly, she pushed up her sleeve, exposing a beautifully-modelled arm, daintily rounded and white as milk. Almost immediately, however, remembering my presence, she hastily pulled it down again; but I had seen a spark of the consuming fire which burned in her eyes, an expression which comes into the face of a woman in the transports of love.

The burning match which I held between my fingers, with the intention of lighting a cigarette, accidentally dropped between my coat and waistcoat.

With a terrified scream, the Baroness rushed at me and tried to extinguish the flame between her fingers.

"Fire! Fire!" she shrieked, her cheeks scarlet with excitement.

Losing my self-control, I started back and pressed her hand against my breast, as if to smother the smouldering fire; then, shamefacedly releasing myself and pretending that I had escaped a very real danger, I thanked the Baroness, who was still unable to control her agitation.

We talked till supper-time. The sun had set, and the moon rose behind the cupola of the Observatory, illuminating the apple trees in the orchard. We amused ourselves by trying to differentiate between the apples suspended from the branches and half-hidden by the leaves, which looked sedge-green in the pale moonlight. The ordinary blood-red Calville seemed but a yellow spot; the greyish Astrachan apple had turned green, the Rennet a dark, brownish red, and the others had changed colour in proportion. The same thing had happened with the flowers.

The dahlias presented to our eyes unknown tints, the stocks shone in the colours of another planet, the hues of the Chinese asters were indefinable.

"There, you see, Baroness," I said, commenting on the

phenomenon, "how everything in the world is imaginary. Colour does not exist in the abstract; everything depends on the nature of the light. Everything is illusion."

"Everything?" she said softly, remaining standing before me and gazing at me with eyes magnified by the darkness.

"Everything, Baroness!" I lied, confused by this living apparition of flesh and blood, which at the moment terrified me by its unearthly loveliness.

The dishevelled golden hair formed a luminous aureole round her pale, moonlit face; her exquisitely proportionate figure rose by my side, tall and straight and more slender than ever in the striped dress, the colours of which had changed to black and white.

The stocks breathed their voluptuous perfumes, the crickets chirped in the grass, wet with the falling dew, a gentle breeze rustled in the trees, twilight wrapped us round with its soft mantle; everything invited to love; nothing but the cowardice of respectability kept back the avowal which trembled on my lips.

Suddenly an apple dropped from a wind-shaken bough and fell at our feet. The Baroness stooped, picked it up and gave it to me, with a significant gesture.

"Forbidden fruit!" I murmured. "No, thank you." And to efface the impression of this blunder, which I had committed against my will, I hastened to improvise a satisfactory, explanation of my words, hinting at the parsimony of the owner. "What would the owner say if he saw me?"

"That you are at least a knight without reproach," she replied disapprovingly, glancing at the shrubbery which effectively screened the Baron and her cousin from indiscreet observers.

When we rose from the supper-table the Baron proposed that we should accompany "the dear child" home. At the front door he offered her his arm, and then turned to me.

"Look after my wife, old man," he said, "and prove to her that you really are the perfect cavalier I know you to be." His voice was full of tender solicitude.

I felt ill at ease. As the evening was warm the Baroness, leaning lightly on me, was carrying her scarf in her hand, and from her arm, the graceful outline of which was plainly perceptible through the thin silk, emanated a magnetic current which excited in me an extraordinary sensitiveness. I imagined that I could detect, at the height of my deltoid muscle, the exact spot where the sleeve of her under-garment ended. My sensitiveness was intensified to such a degree that I could have traced the whole anatomy of that adorable arm. Her biceps, the great elevator which plays the principal part when two people embrace each other, pressed mine, flesh against flesh, in supple rhythms. In walking along, side by side, I could distinguish the curve of her hips through the skirts which brushed against my legs.

"You walk splendidly, you must be a perfect dancer," she said, as if to encourage me to break an embarrassing silence.

And after a few moments, during which she must have felt the quivering of my overstrung nerves, she asked, a little sarcastically, with the superiority of a woman of the world—

"Are you shivering?"

"Yes, I'm cold."

"Then why not put on your overcoat?"

Her voice was soft and velvety, like a caress.

I put on my coat, a veritable straight jacket, and so was better protected against the warmth which flowed from her body into mine.

The sound of her little feet, keeping time with my footsteps, drew our nervous systems so closely together that I felt almost as if I were walking on four feet, like a quadruped.

In the course of that fateful walk a pruning occurred of the kind which gardeners call "ablactation," and which is brought about by bringing two boughs into the closest proximity.

From that day I no longer belonged to myself. She had inoculated me with her blood; our nerves were in a state of high tension; the unborn lives within her yearned for the quickening fiat which would call them into existence; her soul craved for union with my spirit, and my spirit longed to pour itself into this delicate vessel. Had all this happened to us without our knowledge? Impossible to say.

Once more back in my room, I determinately faced the question of the future. Should I flee from danger and forget, should I try to make my fortune abroad? The idea flashed through my mind to go to Paris, the centre of civilisation. Once there, I would bury myself in the libraries, be lost in the museums. In Paris I should produce a great work.

No sooner had I conceived this plan, than I took the necessary steps to carry it out. After a month had elapsed I was in a position to pay my farewell visits.

An unexpected incident which happened very opportunely served as a convenient pretext with which to cloak my flight. Selma, my whilom Finnish friend, was having her banns published. I was, therefore, so to speak, compelled to seek forgetfulness and healing for my wounded heart in distant countries. Anyhow, it was as good an excuse as any I could think of.

My departure was delayed for a few weeks in deference to the entreaties of my friends, who were dreading the equinoctial gales; I had decided to go by steamer to Havre.

Furthermore, my sister's wedding was to take place early in October, and this necessitated a further postponement of my project.

During this time I received frequent invitations from the Baroness. The cousin had returned to her parents, and the three of us generally spent the evenings together. The Baron, unconsciously influenced by the strong will of his wife, seemed more favourably disposed towards me; moreover, my impending departure had reassured him completely, and he treated me with his former friendliness.

One evening the Baroness's mother was entertaining a small circle of intimate friends, when the Baroness, stretched out listlessly on the sofa, suddenly put her head on her mother's lap and loudly confessed her intense admiration for a well-known actor. Did she want to torture me, to see the effect which such a confession would have on me? I don't know. But the old lady, tenderly stroking her daughter's hair, looked at me.

"If ever you write a novel," she said, "let me draw your attention to this particular type of passionate womanhood. It's an extraordinary type! She's never happy unless she is in love with some one else beside her husband."

"It's quite true what mamma says," agreed the Baroness, "and just at present I'm in love with that man! He's irresistible!"

"She's mad," laughed the Baron, wincing, yet anxiously trying to appear unconcerned.

Passionate womanhood! The words sank into my heart, for, jesting apart, those words spoken by an old woman, and that old woman her own mother, must have contained more than a grain of truth.

VI

My departure was imminent. On the eve of my
leaving I invited the Baron and his wife to a bachelor's
dinner in my attic. To hide the meanness of the furniture, my little home was wearing its Sunday clothes, and
had the appearance of a sacred temple. My damaged
wicker sofa was pushed against the wall between the two
window recesses, one of which was filled by my writing-
table and the improvised garden, the other by my book-
shelves; an imitation tiger-skin was thrown over it, and
held in its place by invisible tacks.

The left was taken up by my large bed-sofa, with its
gaudy tick cover. Above it, on the side wall, hung a
vividly-coloured map of the world. On the right-hand
side stood my chest of drawers with its swing glass, both
in the Empire style and decorated with brass ornaments;
a wardrobe with a bust of plaster of Paris and a wash-
stand, for the moment banished behind the window cur-
tains, completed the furniture. The walls, with their
decorations of framed sketches, made a gay and varied
show.

A china chandelier, of the shape which is occasionally
met with in churches and which I had discovered at an
antiquary's, was suspended from the ceiling. The cracks
were skilfully concealed by a wreath of artificial ivy which
I had found some little time ago at my sister's. Beneath
the three-armed chandelier stood the dining-table. A
basket filled with Bengal roses, which glowed red among
the dark foliage, was placed on the white damask table-
cloth, and the roses, reaching up to and mingling with

the drooping ivy shoots, gave the whole the effect of a flower show. Round the basket which held the roses stood an array of wine glasses, red, green and opal, which I had bought cheaply, at a sale, for each of them had a flaw. The same thing applied to the dinner service : plates, salt-cellars and sugar-bowl of Chinese, Japanese and Swedish porcelain.

I had but a dozen cold dishes to offer to my friends, most of them chosen more with an eye to their decorative value than because they were good to eat, for the meal was to consist principally of oysters. My landlady had good-naturedly lent me the indispensable articles for the banquet, an unprecedented event in my attic. . . . At last everything was satisfactorily arranged, and I could not help admiring the setting : these mingled touches betrayed on a small scale the inspiration of a poet, the research of a scientist, the good taste of an artist. The fondness for dainty food, the love of flowers, suggested the love of women. If the table had not been laid for three, one might have guessed at an intimate feast for two, the first delights of a love-adventure, instead of a feast of reconciliation which it actually was. My room had not seen a female visitor since that horrible woman whose boots had left ineradicable traces on the woodwork of my sofa. The looking-glass on the chest of drawers had reflected no female figure since then. And now a woman of blameless life, a mother, a lady of education and refinement, was coming to consecrate this place which had seen so much work, misery and pain. And, I thought in a transport of poetic inspiration, it is indeed a sacred festival, since I am prepared to sacrifice my heart, my peace, perhaps my life, to ensure the happiness of my friends.

Everything was ready when I heard footsteps on the fourth floor landing. I hastily lit the candles, for the

last time straightened the basket containing the roses,
and a moment later my guests, exhausted with having
climbed four flights of stairs, stood panting before my
door.

I opened. The Baroness, dazzled by the lights, clapped
her hands as if she were admiring a successful stage setting.

"Bravo ! " she exclaimed, "you are a first-class stage
manager."

"Yes," I replied, "I occasionally amuse myself with
play-acting, for the sake of discipline and patience."

I took off her cloak, bade her be welcome, and made her
sit down on the sofa. But she could not keep still.
With the curiosity of a woman who has never been in a
bachelor's chambers, but has gone straight from her
father's house to that of her husband, she began to
examine the room. She seized my penholder, handled
my blotter, searched about as if she were determined to
discover a secret. Strolling to my book-shelves, she
glanced curiously at the back of the volumes. In passing
the looking-glass she stopped for a few seconds to arrange
her hair and push the end of a piece of lace into the opening of her blouse. She examined the furniture, piece by
piece, and smelt the flowers, all the time uttering little
cries of delight.

When she had finished her voyage of discovery round
my room, she asked me, naïvely, without any *arrière-
pensée*, seeking with her eyes a piece of furniture which
appeared to be missing—

"But where do you sleep ? "

"On the sofa."

"Oh, how jolly a bachelor's life must be ! "

And the forgotten dreams of her girlhood awoke in
her brain.

"It's often very dull," I replied.

"Dull to be one's own master, have one's own home,
F 2

be free from all supervision! Oh, what would I not give
to be independent! Matrimony is abominable! Isn't it
so, darling?" She turned towards the Baron, who had
been listening to her good-naturedly.

"Yes, it *is* dull," he agreed, smilingly.

Dinner was ready and the banquet began. The first
glass of wine made us feel merry, but all of a sudden,
remembering the occasion for our unceremonious meeting,
a feeling of sadness mingled with our enjoyment. We
began to talk of the pleasant days we had spent together.
In imagination we again passed through all the little adven-
tures of our excursions. And our eyes shone, our hearts
beat more quickly, we shook hands and clinked glasses
with one another.

The hours passed rapidly, and we realised with growing
distress that the moment of parting was approaching. At
a sign from his wife the Baron produced an opal ring from
his pocket and held it out to me.

"Here, my dear old fellow," he said, "take this little
keepsake as a token of our gratitude for the friendship
which you have shown us. May fate give you your heart's
desire! This is my sincerest wish, for I love you as a
brother and respect you as a man of honour! A pleasant
journey! We will not say 'farewell,' but 'to the day of
our next meeting.'"

As a man of honour? Had he guessed my motive?
Read my conscience? Not at all! . . . For in well-chosen
words, anxious to explain his little speech, he burst out
into a string of abuse of poor Selma; he accused her of
having broken her word, of having sold herself to a man
who . . . well, to a man whom she did not love, a man
who owed his happiness merely to my extraordinary
decency.

My extraordinary decency! I felt ashamed, but,
carried away by the sincerity of this simple heart, which

judged a little too hastily, perhaps, I suddenly felt very
unhappy, inconsolably unhappy, and I kept up the lie
dressed in the outer semblance of truth.

The Baroness, deceived by my clever acting, misled by
my assumed indifference, believed me to be in earnest, and
with motherly tenderness tried to comfort me.

"Have done with her!" she urged; "forget all about
her. There are plenty of girls, far better than she is.
Don't fret, she's not worth crying for, since she couldn't
even wait for you. Besides, I may tell you now—I've
heard things about her. . . ."

And with a pleasure which she was quite unable to
conceal, she proceeded to disgust me still further with my
supposed idol.

"Just think," she exclaimed, "she practically proposed to an officer of good family, and she made herself
out to be ever so much younger than she is . . . she's
nothing but a common flirt, take my word for it."

A disapproving gesture from the Baron made her realise
her mistake; she pressed my hand and apologised, looking
at me with eyes so wistful and tender that I felt as if I
should die of grief. The Baron, slightly intoxicated,
made sentimental speeches, took me into his confidence,
overwhelmed me with brotherly love, attacked me with
endless toasts, which seemed to lose themselves in infinity.
His swollen face beamed benevolently. He looked at me
with his caressing, melancholy eyes; their glance dissipated
every shadow of doubt of the sincerity of his friendship
which I might have entertained. Surely he was nothing
but a big, good-natured child, of unquestionable integrity;
and I made a vow to behave honourably towards him,
even if it should kill me.

We rose from the table to say good-bye, perhaps for
ever. The Baroness burst out sobbing, and hid her face
on her husband's shoulder.

" I must be mad," she exclaimed, " to be so fond of this dear boy that his going away almost breaks my heart ! "

And with an outburst of affection, at once pure and impure, interested and disinterested, passionate and full of angelic tenderness, she put her arms round my neck and kissed me in her husband's presence ; then she made the sign of the cross over me and turned to go.

My old charwoman, who was waiting on the threshold, wiped her eyes, and we all shed tears. It was a solemn moment, never to be forgotten. The sacrifice had been made.

I went to bed at one o'clock in the morning, but I was unable to sleep ; fear of missing the steamer kept me awake. Worn out by the farewell parties which had been following one on the top of the other for a week, my nerves unhinged from too much drinking, stupid from idleness, overwrought by the excitement of the evening, I tossed between the sheets until the day broke. Knowing that my will-power was temporarily enfeebled, and loathing railway journeys, because the shaking and jolting is injurious to the spine, I had elected to travel by steamer ; moreover, this would prevent any attempt on my part to draw back. The boat was to start at six o'clock in the morning, and the cab called for me at five. I started on my way alone.

It was a windy October morning, foggy and cold. The branches of the trees were covered with hoar frost. When I arrived on the North Bridge, I imagined for a second that I was the victim of an hallucination : there was the Baron, walking in the same direction as my cab. Contrary to our agreement, he had risen early, and had come to see me off. Deeply touched by this unexpected proof of friendship, I felt altogether unworthy of his affection, and full of remorse for ever having thought evil of him.

We arrived at the landing-stage. He accompanied me

on board, examined my cabin, introduced himself to the captain, and recommended me to his special attention. He behaved like an elder brother, a devoted friend, and we said good-bye to each other, deeply moved.

"Take care of yourself, old man," he said. "You are not looking well."

I really felt quite ill, but I pulled myself together until the mooring ropes were cast adrift.

Then a sudden terror of this long and senseless journey seized me, a frantic desire to throw myself into the water and swim to the shore. But I had not the strength to yield to my impulse, and remained standing on deck, undecided what to do, waving my handkerchief in response to my friend's greeting until he disappeared, blotted out by the vessels which rode at anchor in the roads.

The boat was a heavily loaded cargo steamer, with but one cabin on the main deck. I went to my berth, stretched myself on the mattress and pulled the blankets over me, determined to sleep through the first twenty-four hours, so as to prevent any attempt at escape on my part. I must have been unconscious for half-an-hour, when I suddenly started from my sleep as if I had received an electric shock, a very ordinary result of dissipation and sleeplessness.

In a second the whole dreary reality had flashed into my mind. I went on deck to exercise my stiff limbs. I watched the barren brown shores receding before my eyes, the trees stripped of their leaves, the yellowish-grey meadows; in the hollows of the rocks snow was already lying. The water looked grey with sepia-coloured spots; the sky was leaden and full of gloom; the dirty deck, the uncouth sailors—everything contributed to deepen my depression. I felt an unspeakable longing for human companionship, but there did not appear to be a single passenger—not one! I climbed on to the bridge to look

for the captain. I found him a bear of the worst description, absolutely unapproachable. I was a prisoner for
ten days, solitary, cast away among people without understanding, without feeling. It was torture.

I resumed my walk on deck, up and down, in all direc-
tions, as if my restless movements could increase the speed
of the boat. My burning brain worked under high pressure; a thousand ideas flashed into my mind in a second;
the suppressed memories rose, pushing and chasing each
other. A pain like toothache began to torment me, but
in my confusion I could neither describe nor locate it.
The further the steamer advanced into the open sea, the
greater became the strain. I felt as if the bond which
bound me to my native country, to my family, to her, was
tearing asunder. Deserted by everybody, tossing on the
high seas between heaven and earth, I seemed to be losing
all foothold, and in my loneliness I felt afraid of everything and everybody. It was, doubtless, a sign of consti-
tutional weakness, for I remembered that as a boy I had
cried bitter tears on a pleasure trip, at the sudden thought
of my mother; I was twelve years old then, but, bodily,
I was developed far in advance of my years. The reason,
in my opinion, was that I had been born prematurely, or
perhaps even attempts had been made to suppress life
before it could properly be said to have come into existence. Such things happen only too frequently in large
families. At any rate, I felt sure that this was the cause
of the despondency which invariably overcame me when
I was about to make a change in my surroundings. Now,
in tearing myself away from my familiar environment, I
was tormented with dread of the future, the unknown
country, the ship's crew. Impressionable, like every prematurely born child, whose exposed nerves are waiting for
the still bleeding skin; defenceless like a crab which,
having cast its shell, seeks protection underneath the

stones, and feels every change of the sinking barometer, I wandered about, trying to find a soul stronger than mine, take hold of a firm hand, feel the warmth of a human presence, look into a friendly eye. Like a squirrel in its cage, I ran round the upper deck, picturing to myself the ten days of suffering which awaited me. I remembered that I had only been on board for an hour! A long hour, more like a day of agony . . . and not a glimmer of hope at the end of this accursed journey! I tried to reason with myself, and all the time rebelled against reason.

Who compelled me to go? Who had a right to blame me if I returned? . . . Nobody! And yet! . . . Shame, the fear of making myself a laughing-stock, honour! No! No! I must abandon all hope. Moreover, the boat would not call anywhere on her way to Havre. Forward then, and courage!

But courage depends on strength of body and mind, and at the moment I lacked both. Haunted by my dreary thoughts, I turned towards the lower deck, for by now I knew the upper deck down to its smallest details, and the sight of its rails, rigging and tackling bored me like a book read until one knows it by heart. On my way I almost tumbled over a person seeking shelter from the wind behind the cabin. It was an old lady, dressed in black, with grey hair and a careworn face.

She gazed at me attentively, with sympathetic eyes. I walked up to her and spoke to her. She answered me in French, and we soon became acquainted.

After the exchange of a few commonplaces, we confided to each other the purpose of our journey. She was not travelling for pleasure. The widow of a timber-merchant, she had been staying with a relative in Stockholm, and was now on her way to visit her insane son, confined in a lunatic asylum at Havre.

Her account was so simple and yet so heartrending that it affected me strongly, and probably her story, impressing itself on the cells of my already overwrought brain, led up to what followed.

All of a sudden the lady ceased talking, and, gazing at me with a look of dismay, exclaimed sympathetically—

" Are you ill ? "

" I ? "

" Yes, you look ill. You should try and get some sleep."

" To tell you the truth, I never closed my eyes last night, and I am over-tired. I've been suffering from sleeplessness for some time, and nothing seems to be able to procure me the much-needed rest."

" Let me try. Go to bed at once. I will give you a draught that will send you to sleep standing."

She rose, pushed me gently before her, and forced me to go to bed. Then she disappeared for a moment and returned with a small flask, containing a sleeping draught. She gave me a dose in a spoon.

" Now you are sure to be able to sleep."

I thanked her, and she carefully covered me with the blankets. How well she understood what she was about ! She radiated warmth, that warmth which a baby seeks in the arms of its mother. Under the gentle touch of her hands I grew calm, and two minutes later unconsciousness began to steal over me. I seemed to have become an infant again. I saw my mother busying herself round my bed and caring for me. Gradually her fading features mingled and became one with the finely-chiselled face of the Baroness and the sympathetic expression of the compassionate nurse who had just left me. In the care of these women, who hovered round my bed, I faded away like a paling colour, went out like a candle, lost consciousness.

When I awoke I did not remember any dream, but a fixed idea haunted me, as if it had been suggested to me during my sleep : I must see the Baroness again, or I shall go out of my mind !

Shivering with cold, I sprang from my bed ; the salt-laden wind, penetrating through every chink and cranny, had made it damp. When I stepped out of my cabin the sky was pale grey, like iron. On deck the great waves washed the tackling, watered the planks and splashed my face with foam.

I looked at my watch and calculated the distance which the steamer must have travelled while I slept. In my opinion we were now in the archipelago of Norrköping ; all hope of return was therefore dead. Everything was strange to me, the scattered islands in the bay, the rugged coast, the shape of the cottages dotted along the shore, and the cut of the sails on the fishing-smacks. Amid these unfamiliar surroundings I felt the first pangs of homesickness. A sullen wrath choked me, I felt a wild despair in finding myself packed on this cargo-boat in spite of myself, in deference to a higher power, in the imperious name of Honour !

When my wrath had exhausted itself, my strength had come to an end. Leaning against the rail, I let the waves lash my burning face, while my eyes greedily devoured the coastline, eager to discover a ray of hope. And again and again my mind returned to the idea of swimming to the shore.

For a long time I stood gazing at the swiftly-receding outlines of the coast. The wind had dropped, and I grew calmer, rays of a tranquil happiness illuminated my soul ; the pressure on my surcharged brain grew less ; pictures of beautiful summer days, memories of my first youth came into my mind, although I was at a loss to understand why I should suddenly think of them. The boat was rounding a promontory : the roofs of red houses with white garlands rose above the Scotch firs ; a flagstaff became visible, the gay patchwork of the gardens, a bridge, a chapel, a church steeple, a graveyard. . . . Was it a dream ? A delusion ?

No, it was the quiet seaside place where I had spent many summers in my student days. Up there was the tiny house where I had passed a night, last spring, with her and him, after we had spent the day sailing on the sea and wandering through the woods. It was there—there—on the top of that hill, under the ash-trees, on the balcony, where I had seen her delicate face, illuminated by the sunshine of her golden hair, and crowned by the little Japanese hat with the blue veil, while her small, gloved hand had beckoned me to come to dinner. . . . She was there now, I could see her plainly, she was waving her handkerchief to me. . . . I could hear her melodious voice . . . but . . . what was happening ? The boat was slowing down, the engine stopped . . . the pilot cutter came to meet us . . . in an instant . . . a flash of thought—a single, obsessing thought, moved me with electric force—with the spring of a tiger I bounded up the stairs which led to the bridge—I stood before the captain —I shouted—

" Have me put ashore at once—or I shall go mad ! "

The captain looked at me sharply, scrutinisingly, and without vouchsafing a reply, dismayed as if he had looked into the face of an escaped lunatic, he called to the second officer and said, imperatively—

" Have this gentleman and his luggage put ashore. He is ill."

Before five minutes had elapsed, I was on board the pilot cutter ; they rowed with such vigour that we landed in a very short time.

I possess the remarkable gift of becoming blind and deaf

when it suits me.   I was walking along the road leading
to the hotel without having heard or seen anything hurtful
to my vanity ; neither a glance from the pilots, betraying
that they guessed my secret, nor a disparaging remark
from the man who was carrying my luggage.

Arrived at the hotel, I asked for a room, ordered an
absinthe, lighted a cigar and began to reflect.

"Had I gone mad?   Was I in such imminent peril of
insanity that an immediate landing had been necessary?"

In my present state of mind I was incapable of forming
an opinion, for a madman, according to the verdict of the
doctors, is not conscious of his mental disorder, and the
association of his ideas proves nothing against their irregu-
larity.   Like a scientist, I examined similar occurrences
which had happened to me before.

When I was still a boy at college, my nervous excitability, exaggerated by exasperating events, passion, the
suicide of a friend, distrust of the future, had been increased to such an extent that everything filled me with
apprehension, even in broad daylight.   I was afraid to
stay in a room by myself ; I was haunted by my own
spectre, and my friends took it in turns to spend the night
with me, while the candles burned and the fire crackled
in the stove.

Another time, in an attack of wild despair, following on
all sorts of misfortunes, I ran across country, wandered
through the woods, and at last climbed to the top of a
pine tree.   There I sat astride on a branch and made a
speech to the Scotch firs which spread out their branches
below me, endeavouring to drown their voices, imagining
that I was a speaker addressing an assembled crowd.   It
was not so very far from here, on an island where I had
spent many summers, and the headland of which was
plainly visible from where I stood.

Remembering that incident, with all its ridiculous

details, I could not help admitting to myself that, at any rate at times, I was subject to mental delusions.

What was I to do now? Should I communicate with my friends before the rumour of my attack had reached the town? But the disgrace and shame of having to acknowledge that henceforth I was on a level with the irresponsible! The thought was unbearable.

Lie, then! Double without being able to throw the pursuers off the scent. It went against the grain. Tormented by doubts, hesitating between different plans of escape from this maze, I longed to run away in order to be spared the terrible questions which awaited me. Like a wild beast which feels the approach of death, I thought of hiding myself in the wood to die.

With that idea in my mind, I went slowly through the narrow streets. I climbed over huge rocks, saturated and rendered slippery by the autumnal rains, crossed a stubble field, reached the little house where I once had lived. The shutters were tightly closed; the wild vine which covered the walls up to the roof was stripped of its leaves, and the green lattice-work was plainly visible. As I stood again upon that sacred spot, sacred to my heart because it had seen the first blossoming of our friendship, the sense of my loss, which for a time had been forced into the background, reasserted itself. Leaning against one of the supports of the wooden balcony, I wept like a forsaken child.

I remembered having read in the *Thousand and One Nights* that lovers fall ill with unsatisfied longing, and that their cure depends entirely on the possession of the beloved one. Snatches of Swedish folk-songs came into my mind, about young maidens who, in despair of ever being united to the object of their affections, waste away, and bid their mothers prepare their deathbeds for them. I thought of Heine, the old sceptic, who sings of the tribe of the Asra, "who die when they love." There could have been no doubt of the genuineness of my passion, for I had gone back to childhood, obsessed by one thought, one picture, one single, overpowering sensation, prostrating me and rendering me unable to do anything but sigh.

To distract my thoughts, I let my eyes travel over the glorious landscape spread out at my feet. The thousands of islands bristling with Scotch firs, with here and there a pine tree, which seemed to swim in the enormous bay, gradually decreased in size and transformed themselves into reefs, cliffs and sandbanks, until the huge archipelago terminated at the grey-green line of the Baltic, where the breakers dashed against the steep bulwarks of the remotest cliffs.

The shadows of the drifting clouds fell in coloured stripes on the surface of the water, passing from dark brown through all the shades of bottle-green and Prussian blue to the snowy white of the crested waves. Behind a fortress, situated on a steep cliff, rose a column of black smoke, ascending without a break from an invisible chimney, to be blown down again by the wind on to the foaming waves. All of a sudden the dark hull of the cargo-boat which I had just left came into view. The sight wrung my heart, for the steamer seemed like a witness of my disgrace. Like a shying horse, I bolted and fled into the wood.

Underneath the pointed arches of the Scotch firs, through the needles of which the wind whistled, my anguish increased. Here we had been walking together when the spring sunshine lay on the tender green, when the Scotch firs put forth their purple blossoms, which exhale a perfume like that of the wild strawberry; when the juniper scattered its yellow pollen into the wind; when the anemones pushed their white heads through the dead leaves under the hazel bushes. Her little feet had pressed the soft, brown moss, spread out like a rug, while with a silvery voice she had sung her Finnish songs. Guided by the clear light of remembrance, I found again the two gigantic trees, grown together in an unending embrace; the two trunks were bending to the violent gusts of the wind, and rubbed against each other with a grating noise. From here she had taken a little footpath to gather a water-lily which grew in a swamp.

With the zeal of a setter I tried to discover the trace of her pretty foot, the imprint of which, however light, I felt sure I could not miss. With bent shoulders and eyes glued to the ground, I searched the path without finding anything. The ground was covered with the footprints of the deer, and I might just as well have tried to follow the trail of a wood nymph, than discover the spot which the dainty shoe of the adored woman had trod. Nothing but mud-holes, refuse, fungi, toadstools, puff-balls, decaying and decayed, and the broken stalks of flowers. Arrived at the edge of the swamp, which was filled with black water, I found a certain fleeting comfort in the thought that it had once reflected the sweetest face in all the world. In vain I looked for the spot where the water lilies grew; it was covered up by dead leaves, blown down by the wind from the birch trees.

I retraced my footsteps and plunged into the heart of the forest; the soughing of the wind in the branches deepened with the growing size of the trees. In the very depth of despair I sobbed aloud, the tears raining down my cheeks; like a wild stag I trampled on the fungi and toadstools, tore up the young plants, dashed myself against the trees. What did I want? I didn't know myself. My pulses throbbed, an inexpressible longing to see her again came over me. She, whom I loved too deeply for desire, had taken possession of my soul. And now that everything was at an end, I longed to die, for life without her was impossible.

But, with the cunning of a madman, I decided to get some satisfaction out of my death by contracting pneumonia, or a similar fatal disease ; for in that case, I argued, I should have to be in bed for some time ; I could see her again and could kiss her hand in saying good-bye for ever.

Comforted by this sudden thought, I turned my steps towards the coast ; it was not difficult to find it, I had but to be guided by the roar of the breakers, which led me across the wood.

The coast was precipitous and the water deep, everything as it should be. With careful attention, which betrayed nothing of my sinister purpose, I undressed myself ; I hid my clothes in a plantation of alder trees and pushed my watch into a hole in the rock. The wind was cold ; at this time of the year, in October, the temperature of the water could be but a very few degrees above freezing-point. I took a run over the rocks and threw myself headlong into the water, aiming at a cleft between two gigantic waves. I felt as if I had fallen into red-hot lava. But I rose quickly to the surface, dragging up with me pieces of seaweed which I had glimpsed at the bottom, and the tiny vesicles of which were scratching my legs. I swam out into the open sea, breasting the huge waves, greeted by the laughter of the sea gulls and the cawing of the crows. When my strength began to fail, I turned and swam back to the cliff.

Now the moment of greatest importance had arrived. According to all instructions given to bathers, the real danger consists in remaining too long out of the water in a state of nudity. I sat down on the rock which was most fully exposed to the wind, and allowed the October gale to lash my bare back. My muscles, my chest immediately contracted, as if the instinct of self-preservation would protect the vital organs at any price. But I was unable to remain on the same spot, and, seizing the branch of an

G

alder tree, I climbed to its top. The tree swayed with the convulsive, uncontrollable movements of my muscles. In this way I succeeded in remaining in the same place for some time. The icy air scorched my skin like a red-hot iron.

At last I was convinced that I had attained my end, and hastily dressed myself.

In the meantime night had fallen. When I re-entered the wood it was quite dark. Terror seized me; I knocked my head against the lower branches of the trees, and was obliged to feel my way along. Suddenly, under the influence of my frantic fear, my senses became so acute that I could tell the variety of the trees which surrounded me by the rustling of their branches. What depth there was in the bass of the Scotch firs, with their firm and closely-set needles, forming, as it were, gigantic guitars; the tall and more pliable stems of the pines gave a higher note; their sibilant fife resembled the hissing of a thousand snakes; the dry rustling of the branches of the birch trees recalled to me memories of my childhood, with its mingled griefs and pleasures; the rustling of the dead leaves clinging to the branches of the oaks sounded like the rustling of paper; the muttering of the junipers was almost like the whispering voices of women, telling each other secrets. The gale tore off the branch of an alder tree, and it crashed to the ground with a hollow thud. I could have distinguished a pine cone from the cone of a Scotch fir by the sound it made in falling; my sense of smell detected the proximity of a mushroom, and the nerves of my large toe seemed to feel whether it trod on soil, clubmoss or maidenhair.

Guided by the acuteness of my sensations, I came to the enclosure of the graveyard, and walked up the wooden steps. I felt a momentary pleasure in the sound of the weeping willow lashing the tombstones which they over-

hung. At last, stiff with cold, shaking at every unexpected noise, I reached the village and walked past the
houses, which shone feebly in the dark, to the hotel.

As soon as I had arrived in my room I sent off a telegram
to the Baron, informing him of my sudden illness and
enforced landing. Then I drew up for him a full statement of my mental condition, mentioning my former
attacks, and asking him to keep the matter quiet. I gave
him to understand that my illness was caused by the
conduct of my unfaithful love, whose publicly announced
engagement had robbed me of all hope.

I went to bed exhausted, certain of having contracted
a fatal fever. Then I rang for the servant and asked her
to send for a doctor. On her reply that no doctor was
available, I begged her to send for a clergyman, so that
I could make my last wishes known to him.

And from that moment I was prepared to die or go out
of my mind.

The clergyman appeared almost immediately. He was
a man of about thirty, and looked like a farm labourer in
Sunday clothes. Red-haired and freckled, with a half-
vacant look in his eyes, he did not inspire me with sympathy; for a long time I could find no words, for I did not
know what to say to this man, who possessed neither
education, the wisdom of age, nor a knowledge of the
human heart.

He remained standing in the centre of the room, self-
conscious, like a provincial in the presence of the inhabitant
of a large city, until I motioned him to take a chair.

Then he began his cross-examination.

" You have sent for me, sir?   You are in trouble? "

" Yes."

" There is no happiness but in Jesus."

Although I was hankering after quite another sort of
happiness, I did not contradict him, and the evangelist

G 2

rambled on, uninterruptedly, monotonously, verbosely. The old tenets of the catechism lulled me gently to sleep, and the presence of a human being entering into spiritual relationship with my soul gave me new strength.

But the preacher, suddenly doubting my sincerity, interrupted his discourse with a question—

"Do you hold the true faith?"

"No," I replied, "but go on speaking, your words are doing me good. . . ." And he returned to his work.

The monotonous sound of his voice, the radiations from his eyes, the warmth which emanated from his body, affected me like a magnetic fluid. In half-an-hour's time I was fast asleep.

When I awoke, the mesmerist had gone; the servant brought me a sleeping-draught, with strict injunctions from the chemist to be careful, as the bottle contained sufficient poison to kill a man. Needless to say, as soon as she had turned her back, I drank the whole contents of the flask at a gulp. Then, firmly determined to die, I buried myself under the blankets, and sleep was not long in coming.

When I opened my eyes on the following morning I was not in the least surprised to find my room flooded by the rays of a brilliant sun, for my sleep had been visited by bright and rosy dreams.

"I dream, therefore I exist," I said to myself. I felt my body all over, so as to discern the height of the fever, or the presence of any signs of pneumonia. But, in spite of my firm resolution to bring about a crisis, my condition was fairly normal. My brain, although a little stupefied, functioned easily, no longer under the high pressure of the previous day, and twelve hours' sleep had fully restored the vigour which, thanks to bodily exercises of all descriptions, practised since my early youth, I usually enjoyed.

. . . A telegram was handed to me. My friends were

informing me that they would arrive by the two o'clock boat.

I was overwhelmed with shame. What was I to say? What attitude was I to adopt? . . . I reflected. . . .

My reawakened manhood rebelled against humiliating resolutions; after a hasty review of the circumstances, I decided to remain at the hotel until I had completely recovered, and continue my journey by the next steamer. In this way honour would be saved, and the visit from my friends would be but one more leave-taking—the very last.

When I remembered what had occurred on the previous day, I hated myself. That I, the strong-minded, the sceptic, should have committed such absurdities! And that clergyman's visit! How was I to explain that? It was true, I had only sent for him in his official capacity, and, as far as I was concerned, he had but acted as a hypnotist! But to outsiders it was bound to look like a conversion. Monstrous confessions would very likely be hinted at, a criminal's last avowal of his crime on his death-bed. What a pretty topic for the villagers who stood in close communication with the town! What a treat for the porters!

A trip abroad, undertaken at once, was the only way out of this unbearable situation. Like a castaway, I spent the morning in walking up and down before the verandah, watching the barometer, studying the time-tables. Time passed fairly rapidly. The steamer appeared at the mouth of the estuary before I had made up my mind whether to walk to the landing-stage or remain at the hotel. As I had no desire to be stared at by an inquisitive crowd, I at last went to my room.

A few minutes later I heard the voice of the Baroness: she was making inquiries of the landlady about my health. I went out to meet her, and she almost kissed me before the eyes of all the by-standers. With a heart full to overflowing, she deplored my illness, which she regarded as the result of overwork, and advised me to return to town, and put off my journey until the spring.

She was beautiful to-day. In her closely-fitting fur coat, with its long and supple hairs, she looked like a llama. The sea-breezes had brought the blood to her cheeks, and in her eyes, magnified by the excitement of her visit, I could read an expression of infinite tenderness. In vain I begged her not to alarm herself on my account, and assured her that I had almost fully recovered. She found that I looked like a corpse, declared me unfit for work, and treated me like a child. And how sweetly she played the part of a mother! The tone of her voice was a caress; she playfully used terms of endearment; she wrapped her shawl round me; at table she spread my dinner-napkin over my knees, poured out some wine for me, looked after me in every way. I wondered why she did not thus devote herself to her child rather than to the man who was all the time striving to hide his passion, which threatened to defy all control.

In this disguise of the sick child, it seemed to me that I was like the wolf who, after having devoured the grandmother, lies down on her bed waiting for Little Red Riding-hood, that he may devour her also.

I blushed before this unsophisticated and sincere husband, who overwhelmed me with kindness, asked for no explanations. And yet I was not at fault. I obstinately hardened my heart, and received all the attentions which the Baroness showered on me with an almost insulting indifference.

At dessert, when the time for the return journey had come, the Baron proposed that I should return with them. He offered me a room in his house which, he said, was waiting to receive me. I am glad to say that my answer was a decided refusal. Terrified of this dangerous playing

with fire, I was firm in my decision. I would stay here for
a week to recover entirely, and then return to town to my
old attic.

In spite of all their objections, I persisted. Strange;
as soon as I pulled myself together and made a determined
stand, the Baroness became almost hostile to me. The
more I vacillated and humoured her whims, the fonder she
seemed of me, the more she praised my wisdom, my
amiability. She swayed and bewildered me, but as soon
as I opposed her seriously, she turned her back on me and
treated me with dislike, almost with rudeness.

While we were discussing the Baron's proposal to live
under one roof, she drew a glowing picture of such an
arrangement, dwelling on the pleasantness of being able
to see one another at any time without a previous
invitation.

"But, my dear Baroness," I objected, "what would
people say if you were to receive a bachelor into your
young *ménage*?"

"What does it matter what people say?"

"But your mother, your aunt? Moreover, my man's
pride rebels against a measure which is only permissible
in the case of a minor."

"Bother your man's pride! Do you think it manly to
perish without opening your lips?"

"Yes, it behoves a man to be strong."

She grew angry, and refused to admit that a man's case
differed from that of a woman. Her woman's logic
confused my brain. I turned to the Baron, whose answering smile showed plainly what a small opinion he had of
female brain-power.

About six o'clock the steamer weighed anchor and bore
my friends away. I returned to the hotel alone.

It was a splendid evening. The sun had set in an
orange-coloured sky, white stripes were lying on the deep

blue water, a coppery moon was rising behind the Scotch firs.

I was sitting at a table in the dining-room, lost in thought, now mournful, now serene, and did not notice the landlady until she stood close by me.

"The lady who's just left is your sister, isn't she?" she asked.

"Not at all."

"Isn't she? How strangely you resemble one another! I should have sworn that you are brother and sister."

I was not in the mood to continue such a conversation, but it left me in a ferment of thoughts.

Had my constant intercourse with the Baroness affected the expression of her features? Or had the expression of her face influenced mine during this six months' union of our souls? Had the instinctive desire to please one another at any price been the cause of an unconscious selection of gestures and expressions, suppressing the less pleasing in favour of the more seductive? It was not at all unthinkable that a blending of our souls had taken place, and that we no longer belonged to ourselves. Destiny, or rather instinct, had played its fateful, inevitable part; the ball had been set rolling, overthrowing and destroying everything that barred its way: honour, reason, happiness, loyalty, wisdom, virtue!

. . . And this guilelessness to propose to receive under her roof an ardent young man, a man of the age when the passions are so strong that control is often almost impossible! Was she vicious, or had love obscured her reason? Vicious! No, a thousand times no! I appreciated her candid ways, her gaiety, her sincerity, her motherly tenderness. That she was eccentric, that her mind was badly balanced, she had herself acknowledged in speaking of her faults—but vicious? No! Even the little tricks which she occasionally resorted to in order to cheer me up were much more the tricks of a mature woman who amuses herself by teasing and bewildering a timid youth, and then laughs at his confusion, than those of a coquette whose object it is to excite a man's passions.

But I must exorcise the demon, and continue to mislead my friends. I sat down at the writing-table and wrote a letter on the hackneyed subject of my unhappy love affair. I added two impassioned poems entitled " To Her "— poems which could be understood in two ways. It was open to the Baroness to be annoyed.

Letter and poems remained unanswered; perhaps the trick had grown threadbare, perhaps the subject was no longer found interesting.

The calm and tranquil days which followed hastened my recovery. The surrounding landscape seemed to have adopted the favourite colours of the adored woman. The wood, in which I had spent hours of purgatory, now smiled on me. Never in my morning rambles did I find as much as the shadow even of a painful memory lurking in its deep recesses, where I had fought with all the demons of the human heart. Her visit, and the certainty that I should see her again, had given me back life and reason.

VII

KNOWING from experience that nobody who returns unexpectedly is quite welcome, it was not without a feeling of constraint, not without misgivings, that I called on the Baroness as soon as I was back in town.

In the front garden everything proclaimed the winter; the trees were bare, the garden seats had been removed; there were gaps in the fence where the gates had been; the wind was playing with the withered leaves on the paths; the cellar holes were stuffed with straw.

I found it difficult to breathe in the close atmosphere of the drawing-room, heated by a tiled stove. Fixed to the walls, the stoves had the appearance of sheets suspended from the ceiling, large and white. The double-windows hung in their hinges, every chink was pasted over with paper; the space between the inner and outer windows was filled with snow-white cotton wool, giving the large room the appearance of a death-chamber. In imagination I endeavoured to strip it of its semi-fashionable furniture, and recall its former aspect of rough homeliness. In those days the walls had been bare, the floor plain deal; the memory of the black dining-table, which could boast of no cover and with its eight legs resembled a huge spider, called up the severe faces of my father and stepmother.

The Baroness received me cordially, but her melancholy face betrayed grief. Both uncle and father-in-law were there, playing cards with the Baron in an adjoining room. I shook hands with the players, and then returned with the Baroness into the drawing-room. She sat down

in an arm-chair underneath the lamp and took up
some crochet work. Taciturn, morose, not at all
pretty, she left the conversation entirely to me, and
since she made no replies, it soon degenerated into
a monologue.

I watched her from my chimney corner as she sat with
drooping head, bending over her work. Profoundly
mysterious, lost in thought, she seemed at times oblivious
of my presence. I wondered whether I had called at an
inconvenient time, or whether my return to town had
really created the unfavourable impression which I had
half anticipated. All at once my eyes, travelling round
the room, were arrested by a display of her ankles underneath the tablecloth. I beheld her finely-shaped calf,
clothed in a white stocking; a gaily embroidered garter
belted that charming muscle which turns a man's brain
because it stimulates his imagination and tempts him to
the construction of the whole of the remaining form.
Her arched foot with its high instep was dressed in a
Cinderella's slipper.

At the time I took it for an accident, but later on I
learned that a woman is always conscious of being looked
at when she exhibits more than her ankles. Fascinated
by the sight I changed the conversation, and aptly turned
it on the subject of my supposed love affair.

She drew herself up, turned towards me, and glanced
at me sharply.

"You can at least pride yourself on being a faithful
lover!"

My eyes remained riveted on the spot underneath the
tablecloth, where the snowy stocking shone below the
cherry-coloured ribbon. With an effort I pulled myself
together; we looked at each other; her pupils shone large
in the lamplight.

"Unfortunately I can!" I replied dryly.

The sound of the falling cards and the exclamations of the players accompanied this brief passage of arms.

A painful silence ensued. She resumed her crochet work, and with a quick movement allowed the skirts to drop over her ankles. The spell was broken. My eyes were gazing at a listless woman, badly dressed. Before another quarter of an hour had gone by I took my leave, pretending that I did not feel well.

As soon as I arrived in my attic I brought out my play, which I had resolved to re-write. Hard work would help me to get over this hopeless love, otherwise bound to end in a crime from which inclination, instinct, cowardice and education made me shrink. And once more I decided to break off these fatal relations.

An unexpected incident came to my assistance: two days later the cataloguing of a library, belonging to a collector who lived at some distance from the town, was offered to me.

And thus I came to pitch my tent in a spacious room, lined with books up to the ceiling, of an old manor house dating from the seventeenth century. Sitting there, I could let my imagination travel through all the epochs of my country's history. The whole Swedish literature was represented, from the old prints of the fifteenth century to the latest publications. I gave myself up to my work, eager to find forgetfulness—and I succeeded. A week had elapsed and I had never once missed my friends. On Saturday, the day on which the Baroness generally was "at home," an orderly brought me an invitation from the Baron, full of friendly rebuke for having kept away from them for so long. I was half-pleased, half-sorry to find myself able to send an amiable refusal in reply, regretting that my time was no longer my own.

When a second week had gone by another orderly, in full dress, brought me another communication; this time

it came from the Baroness. It was a rather curt request
to call and see her husband, who, she said, was laid up
with a cold. She begged me to let them have news of
me. It was impossible to make further excuses, and so
I went.

The Baroness did not look well, and the slightly indis-
posed Baron seemed bored. He was in bed, and I was
asked to go and see him. The sight of this Holy of
Holies, which I had been spared up to now, excited my
instinctive repugnance; this sharing of a common room by
a married couple, this perpetual presence of a witness on
the thousand occasions which demand privacy, revolted
me. The large bed which the Baron occupied, brazenly
proclaimed the intimacies of their union; the heap of
pillows, piled up by the side of the sick man, boldly
marked the wife's place. The dressing-table, the wash-
stands, the towels, everything struck me as being unclean
and I had to make myself blind to overcome my disgust.

After a few words at the foot end of the bed, the
Baroness invited me to take a glass of liqueur in the
drawing-room, and, as if she had divined them, she gave
expression to my thoughts as soon as we were alone. In
short, disjointed sentences she poured out her heart to me.

"Isn't it wretched?"

"What?"

"You know what I mean. . . . A woman's existence:
without an object in life, without a future, without
occupation. It's killing me!"

"But your child, Baroness! It will soon be time to
begin her education. . . . And she may have brothers
and sisters. . . ."

"I will have no more children! Am I in the world
for the sole purpose of being a nurse?"

"Not a nurse, but a mother in the highest meaning
of the word, equal to her task."

"Mother or housekeeper! Thank you! One can hire a housekeeper! It's easier. And then? How am I to occupy myself? I have two maids, excellent substitutes. No! I want to live. . . ."

"Go on the stage?"

"Yes!"

"But that's out of the question!"

"I know that only too well! And it irritates me, makes me stupid . . . kills me!"

"What about a literary career? It's not in such bad repute as the stage!"

"The dramatic art is, in my opinion, the highest of all arts. Come what may, I shall never cease to regret the fact that I have missed my vocation. And what have I got in exchange? . . . A disappointment!"

The Baron called to us, and we returned to his bedside.

"What was she talking about?" he asked me.

"We were talking about the theatre," I replied.

"She's crazy!"

"Not as crazy as you think," retorted the Baroness, and left the room, slamming the door.

"She doesn't sleep at night," began the husband, growing confidential.

"No?"

"She plays the piano, she lies on the sofa, or, rather, she chooses the hours of the night to do her accounts. For heaven's sake, my dear young sage, tell me what I'm to do to put an end to this madness!"

"Perhaps if she had a large family?" I ventured.

He pulled a face, then he tried to look unconcerned.

"She was very ill after her first baby was born . . . and the doctor has warned her . . . and moreover, children cost so much. . . . You understand?"

I understood, and I took care not to refer again to the subject. I was too young at the time to know that it is the patient who orders the doctor what to prescribe for her.

Presently the Baroness returned with her little girl, and began to put her to bed in her small iron cot. But the little one refused to be undressed, and began to scream. After a few futile attempts to calm her, her mother threatened her with the rod.

I cannot bear to see a child being punished without losing my temper. I remember on one such occasion raising my hand against my own father. I allowed my anger to get the better of me, and interfered.

" Allow me," I said . . . " but do you think that a child cries without a reason ? "

" She's naughty."

" Then there's some cause for it. Perhaps she's sleepy, and our presence and the lamplight irritate her."

She agreed, taken aback, and, perhaps, conscious that her shrewish conduct had produced an unfavourable impression on me.

This glimpse of her home life cured me for some weeks of my love, and I must confess that the scene with the rod had contributed more than anything else to my disillusion.

The autumn dragged on monotonously and Christmas drew near. The arrival of a newly-married couple from Finland, friends of the Baroness, brought a little more life in our relationship, which had lost much of its charm. Thanks to the Baroness, I received numerous invitations, and presented myself in evening dress at suppers, dinners and occasionally even at a dance.

While moving in this, her world, which in my opinion lacked dignity, I could not help noticing that the Baroness, under cover of an exaggerated candour, paid a great deal of attention to the young men, watching me furtively all the while, however, to see the effect of her conduct on me.

Irritated and disgusted by her brazen flirtations, which I considered bad form, I responded by a callous indifference. It hurt me that the woman whom I adored should behave like a vulgar coquette.

She always seemed to be enjoying herself immensely, and prolonged the parties till the small hours of the morning; I became more and more convinced that she was discontented and bored with her home life; that her longing for an artistic career was dictated by a petty vanity, a desire to be seen and enjoy herself. Vivacious, full of exuberant spirits, of a restless disposition, she possessed the art to shine; she was always the centre of a crowd, more in consequence of a certain gift to attract people than because of her natural charms. Her great vitality, her nervous excitability, compelled the most refractory to listen to her, to pay homage to her. And I also noticed that as soon as her nervous force was exhausted, the spell was broken, and she was left sitting alone and unnoticed in a quiet corner. Ambitious, yearning for power, perhaps heartless, she took care that the men paid her every attention; the society of women had no attraction for her.

Doubtless, she had made up her mind to see me at her feet, doting, vanquished, sighing. One day, after an evening of triumph, she told one of her friends that I was head over ears in love with her. When I called at her friend's house a short time afterwards, I stupidly remarked that I had hoped to meet the Baroness.

"Oh, indeed!" laughed the lady of the house, "you haven't come to see me then! How unkind of you!"

"Well, I haven't. To tell you the truth, I'm here by appointment."

"A tryst, then!"

"You may call it so, if you like! Anyhow, you'll give me credit for having put in a prompt appearance!"

The meeting had indeed been arranged by the Baroness. I had but carried out her instructions in calling. She had given me away to save her own skin.

I paid her out by spoiling a number of parties for her, for my absence robbed her of the enjoyment which she drew from the contemplation of my sufferings. But I had to pay a heavy penalty! Watching the houses to which I knew her to be invited, I plunged the dagger into my heart, trembling with jealous rage whenever I saw her, in the arms of a partner, gliding past the windows in her blue silk dress, with her sunny curls rising and falling in the quick movements of the dance, with her charming figure, on the tiniest feet in the world.

VIII

WE had navigated the cape of the New Year and spring was approaching. We had spent the winter in gay festivities, in intimate companionship, the three of us. But it had all been very dreary: we had quarrelled and become reconciled, fought battles and made armistices, teased one another and become the best of friends again. I had stayed away and had come back.

Now March was near, a fateful month in the countries of the north, because passion becomes all-powerful and the destinies of lovers are fulfilled: vows are broken, the ties of honour, of family, of friendship are set aside.

The Baron was on duty early in the month, and invited me to spend a day with him at the guard-house. I accepted his invitation. A son of the people, a descendant of the middle-classes, cannot but be impressed by the insignia of the highest power in the land. At the side of my friend I walked along the passage, continually saluted by passing officers; I listened to the rattling of the swords; the "Who goes there?" of the sentinels, the beating of the drums. We arrived at the guard-room. The military decorations of the room stirred my imagination; the portraits of the great generals filled me with reverence; the colours taken at Lützen and Leipzic, the new flags, the bust of the reigning king, the helmets, the resplendent breast-pieces, the plans of battles, all these roused in me that feeling of uneasiness which the lower classes feel in contemplating the symbols of the ruling powers. And in his impressive surroundings the personality of the captain became more imposing; I kept close to his side in case any unpleasantness should arise.

98

As we entered a lieutenant rose and saluted, standing, and I, too, felt myself the superior of these lieutenants, the sworn foes of the sons of the people, and the authors' rivals in the favour of the ladies.

A soldier brought us a bowl of punch, and we lighted our cigars. The Baron, anxious to amuse me, showed me the Golden Book of the regiment, an artistic collection of sketches, water paintings and drawings, all of them representing distinguished officers, who had during the last twenty years belonged to the Royal Guards; portraits of the men who had been the envy and admiration of my school friends, whom they had aped in their boyish games. It tickled my middle-class instincts to see all those favourites of fortune caricatured in this book, and counting on the applause of the democratic Baron, I indulged in little sallies at the expense of those disarmed rivals. But the boundary-line of the Baron's democratic sympathies differed from mine, and he resented my sallies; the spirit of caste prevailed : he turned the leaves more quickly, and did not stop until he came to a large drawing representing the insurrection of 1868.

"Look at this! " he said, with a sarcastic smile, "how we charged into that mob! "

"Did you take part in it ? "

"Didn't I! I was on duty that day, and my orders were to protect the stand opposite the monument which the mob was attacking. A stone hit my helmet. I was serving out the cartridges, when a royal messenger on horseback arrived and stopped my little band from firing. But I remained proof-butt and target for the stones thrown by the crowd. That's all I ever got for my democratic sympathies."

And after a pause he continued, still laughing and trying to catch my eye—

"You remember the occasion ? "

H 2

"Perfectly," I said; "I was walking in the procession of the students." But I did not mention the fact that I was one of that special mob on which he had been so anxious to fire. My sense of justice had been outraged because that particular stand had been reserved for a favoured few and denied to the people on a public festival. I had been on the side of the attacking party, and had not forgotten the stones which I had flung at the soldiers.

The moment I heard him pronounce the word "mob" with aristocratic disdain, I remembered and understood my feeling of discomfort in entering the enemy's fortress, and the sudden change which had come over my friend's features at my sarcasms depressed me. The hatred of race, the hatred of caste, tradition, rose between us like an insurmountable barrier, and as I regarded him sitting there, the sword between his knees—a sword of honour, the hilt of which was ornamented with the name and crown of the royal giver—I felt strongly that our friendship was but an artificial one, the work of a woman, who constituted the only link between us. The haughty tone of his voice, the expression of his face, seemed more and more in harmony with his surroundings and took him further and further away from me. To bridge over the gulf which separated us, I changed the conversation and inquired after his wife and little daughter. Instantly his brow cleared, his features relaxed and resumed their normal expression of good-nature. Seeing him look at me with the benevolent eyes of the ogre caressing Tom Thumb, I made bold to pull three hairs out of the ogre's beard.

"Cousin Matilda is expected at Easter, isn't she?" I asked.

"She is."

"I shall make love to her."

He emptied his glass. "You can try," he sneered, with a murderous scowl.

"Try? Is it possible that her affections are otherwise engaged?"

"Not . . . that I know of! But . . . I think I may say that. . . . Well, you can try!"

And with a tone of deepest conviction—

"You may be sure to get your money's worth!"

This sneering remark was an insult, and roused my desire to defy him. If I made love to that other woman, it might not only save me from my criminal passion, but it would also give satisfaction to the Baroness, whose legitimate feelings had been outraged.

It had grown dark. I rose to go home. The captain accompanied me past the sentinels. We shook hands at the barrier gate, which he slammed after me as if he wanted to challenge me.

Spring had come. The snow had melted, the streets were free from ice. Half-starved children were selling little bunches of liverwort in the streets. The windows of the flower-shops glowed with azaleas, rhododendron and other early blossoms; golden oranges gleamed in the greengrocers' shops; lobsters, radishes and cauliflower appeared on the costers' barrows. Under the North Bridge the waves reflected the rays of the sun. On the quays the steamers were being newly rigged and painted in sea-green and scarlet. The men who had grown weak in the winter darkness, recovered in the sunlight. Woe to the weakling when love gives free play to the long-restrained passions!

The pretty little she-devil had arrived, and was staying with the Baroness.

I paid her a great deal of attention. She had apparently been informed of my designs, and consequently she amused herself with me. We had been playing a duet, and she was leaning against my left arm with her right shoulder.

The Baroness noticed it and winced. The Baron glared at me with jealous rage. At one moment he was jealous of his wife, at the next he accused me of flirting with the cousin. Whenever he left his wife, to whisper in a corner to Matilda, and I started a conversation with the Baroness, he lost his temper and interrupted our conversation with an irrelevant question. I answered him with a sarcastic smile, and sometimes I took no notice whatever of him.

One evening we were all having supper in the strictest family circle. The mother of the Baroness was present. She had grown fond of me, and with the prevision frequently met with in old women, suspected that something was going on behind the scenes.

Following an impulse of motherly love, dreading some unknown danger, she seized my hands, and holding me with her eyes said gravely—

"I'm sure that you're a man of honour. I don't know what's going on in this house. But promise me that you will watch over my daughter, my only child, and if ever anything should happen . . . which must not happen, promise that you will come to me and tell me everything."

"I promise," I answered, and kissed her hand in the Russian fashion, for she had been married to a Russian for many years and had been left a widow not very long ago.

And I shall keep my promise!

We were dancing on the edge of a crater. The Baroness had grown pale, emaciated, plain. The Baron was jealous, rude and insolent. If I stayed away for a day or two, he sent for me, received me with open arms and tried to explain everything by a misunderstanding, while in reality we understood each other only too well.

The Lord knows what was going on in this house!

One evening the charming Matilda had retired into her

bedroom to try on a ball dress. The Baron quietly disappeared soon after, leaving me alone with his wife. After half-an-hour had gone by, I asked what had become of her husband?

"He's playing lady's maid to Matilda," she replied.

I understood. Presently, evidently regretting her words, she added—

"There's no harm in it; they're relations. One shouldn't be too ready to think evil!"

Then she changed her tone.

"Are you jealous?"

"Are you?"

"Perhaps I shall be by and by."

"God grant that you will be soon! It's the wish of a true friend."

The Baron returned, and with him the girl, dressed in a pale green evening dress, cut very low.

I pretended to be dazzled by her appearance, and screening my eyes with both my hands, exclaimed—

"Don't you know that it's dangerous to look at you?"

"Isn't she lovely?" asked the Baroness in a strange voice.

After a short time the couple withdrew, and for the second time we were left by ourselves.

"Why are you so unkind to me these days?" she asked, with tears in her voice, gazing at me wistfully, with the eyes of an ill-treated dog.

"I? . . . I had no idea that . . ."

"You've changed towards me; I wonder why. . . . If I'm to blame in any way. . . ."

She pushed her chair closer to mine, looked at me with luminous eyes, trembled and . . . I jumped up.

"The Baron's absence is really extraordinary, don't you think so? This confidence on his part is insulting!"

"What d'you mean?"

"It's not right of him to leave his wife alone with a young man and shut himself up with a girl. . . ."

"You're right, it's an insult to me. . . . But your manners ! . . ."

"Never mind my manners ! It's hateful ! I shall despise you if you won't be more jealous of your dignity. . . . What are those two doing ? "

"He's interested in Matilda's ball dress ! " she answered, with an innocent face and a fleeting smile. "What do you want me to do ? "

"A man doesn't assist a woman at her toilet unless there are certain relations between them."

"She is a child, he says, and looks upon him as a father."

"I should never allow any children to play 'papa and mamma,' much less grown-up people."

The Baroness rose, went out of the room and returned with her husband.

We spent the rest of the evening in making experiments with animal magnetism. I made a few passes over her forehead, and she acknowledged that it calmed her nerves. But all of a sudden, just as she was going into a trance, she shook herself, started to her feet, and looked at me with troubled eyes.

"Let me go ! " she exclaimed; "I won't ! You are bewitching me ! "

"It's your turn now to try your magnetic powers," I said, and I submitted to the same treatment to which I had subjected her.

I sat with half-closed eyes; there was deep silence on the other side of the piano ; my glances strayed to the legs and the lyre-shaped pedal of the instrument and . . . I thought I must be dreaming, and sprang up from my chair. At the same moment the Baron appeared from behind the piano and offered me a glass of punch.

The four of us raised our glasses. The Baron looked at his wife—

"Drink to your reconciliation with Matilda," he pleaded.

"Your health, little witch!" exclaimed the Baroness with a smile, and turning to me she added—

"I must tell you we quarrelled about you!"

For a moment I did not know how to reply. Then I asked her to explain her words.

"No, no! no explanation!" answered a chorus of voices.

"That's a pity," I replied; "in my opinion we've been playing ' hide-and-seek ' far too long."

The rest of the evening passed amid general constraint.

"Well, I don't care!" I muttered on my way home, searching my conscience.

What was the meaning of all this? Was it nothing but the innocent whim of a fantastic mind? Two women quarrelling over a man! They must be jealous, then. Was the Baroness mad that she gave herself away in such a manner? I did not think so. I felt sure there was something else at the bottom of it.

"What *is* going on in this house?" I asked myself, brooding over the strange scene which had startled me in the evening, the very improbability of which made me hesitate to believe that I had seen anything really wrong.

This senseless jealousy, the apprehension of the old mother, the love of the Baroness, stimulated by the spring air, all this confused my mind, seethed and fermented in my brain, and after spending a sleepless night, I decided for a second time not to see her again, and so prevent the threatening calamity.

With this intention I arose in the morning and wrote her a sensible, candid and humble letter; in carefully chosen language I protested against an excessive abuse of friendship; firmly, without any explanation, I asked for forgiveness of my sins, blamed myself for having caused ill-feeling between relatives, and goodness knows what else I said!

The result was that I met the Baroness, as if by accident, on leaving the library at my usual time. She stopped me on the North Bridge, and we walked together through one of the avenues leading to Charles XII Square. Almost with tears in her eyes she entreated me to come back, not to ask for explanations, but just to be one of them again as in the old days.

She was charming this morning. But I loved her too dearly to compromise her.

"Leave me! You are ruining your reputation," I said, watching the passers-by, whose curious glances embarrassed us. "Go home at once, or I shall leave you standing here!"

She looked at me with eyes so full of misery that I longed to kneel down before her, kiss her feet and ask her forgiveness.

But instead I turned my back on her and hastily disappeared down a side street.

After dinner I went home to my attic, glowing with the satisfaction of a duty done, but with a broken heart. Her eyes haunted me.

A short rest gave me back my determination. I rose and looked at the almanac which hung on the wall. It was the thirteenth of March. "Beware the Ides of March!" These famous words, which Shakespeare quotes in his *Julius Cæsar*, sounded in my ears as the servant entered, bringing me a note from the Baron.

In it he begged me to spend a lonely evening with him, saying that his wife was not well and that Matilda was going out.

I had not the nerve to refuse, and so I went.

The Baroness, more dead than alive, met me in the drawing-room, pressed my hand against her heart and thanked me warmly for having resolved not to rob her of a friend, a brother, for the sake of a mere nothing, a misunderstanding.

"I really think she's going out of her mind," laughed the Baron, releasing me from her hands.

"I *am* mad, I know, mad with joy that our friend has come back to us after he had decided to leave us for ever."

And she burst into tears.

"She's been suffering a great deal," explained her husband, disconcerted by this scene.

And, indeed, she looked as if she were in a high fever. A sombre fire burned in her eyes, which seemed to take up half of the little face; her cheeks were of a greenish pallor. The sight of her hurt me. Her frail body was shaken by fits of coughing.

Her uncle and father-in-law arrived unexpectedly. The fuel in the great stove was replenished, and we sat down before the fire, without lighting the lamps, to enjoy the cosy hour of the gathering twilight.

She took a seat by my side, while the three men began to talk politics.

I saw her eyes shine through the dusk, I felt the warmth which radiated from her body.

Her skirts brushed against me, she leaned over to say something meant for me alone, and attacked me with a whispered question—

"Do you believe in love?"

"No!"

My "no" struck her like a blow, for I had at the same time jumped up and changed my seat.

She must be mad, I thought; and afraid of a scene I suggested that we should have the lamps lighted.

During supper uncle and father-in-law discussed cousin

Matilda to their heart's content, praising her domesticity, her skill in needlework.   The Baron, who had drunk several glasses of punch, burst out into extravagant eulogies and deplored, with alcoholic tears, the unkind treatment to which the " dear child " was subjected at home.   But when apparently in the very depth of sympathetic sorrow, he suddenly pulled out his watch and prepared to leave us, as if called away by the stern voice of duty.

" You must excuse me, gentlemen," he said, " but I have promised Baby to meet her and see her home.   Don't let me disturb you, I shall be back in an hour."

The old Baron, his father, vainly tried to detain him ; his artful son insisted on keeping his word and slipped away, after having extracted a promise from me to await his return.

We remained at table for another quarter of an hour and then went into the drawing-room ; the two old gentlemen soon left us and retired to the uncle's room, which the nephew had fitted up for him a little while ago.

I cursed fate for having caught me in a trap which I had done my utmost to avoid.   I steeled my throbbing heart ; proudly, as a cock raises his comb, I raised my head ; my hair bristled like the hair of a sheep dog, and I determined to crush at the outset any attempt to create a tearful or amorous scene.

Leaning against the stove I smoked my cigar, silent, cold and stiff, awaiting events.

The Baroness was the first to speak.

" Why do you hate me ? "

" I don't hate you."

" Remember how you treated me only this morning ! "

" Please, don't speak of it ! "

The unaccustomed rudeness of my replies, for which

there was no adequate reason, was a strategical error. She saw through me and changed her tactics.

" You wanted to run away from me," she continued. "Shall I tell you why I suddenly went to Mariafred? "

" Probably for the same reason for which I decided to go to Paris."

" Then . . . it's clear," she said.

" And now? "

I expected a scene. But she remained calm and regarded me mournfully. I had to break the silence which was fraught with more danger than any words could possibly contain.

"Now that you know my secret," I said, " let me give you a word of warning. If you want me to come here occasionally, you mustn't ever lose your head. My love for you is of such an exalted nature, that I could live contentedly at your side, without any other wish but to see you. If you should ever forget your duty, if you should betray by as much as a look the secret which lies locked in our hearts, then I shall confess everything to your husband, come what will! "

Carried away by my words, full of enthusiasm, she raised her eyes to heaven.

"I swear it to you! . . . How strong and good you are! . . . How I admire you! Oh! but I'm ashamed! I should like to surpass your honesty . . . shall I tell Gustav everything? "

" If you like . . . but then we shall never meet again. After all, it's not his business. The feelings which animate my heart are not criminal; and even if he knew everything, would it be in his power to kill my love? No! Tha ̄ love the woman of my choice is my own affair as long as my passion does not infringe the rights of another. However, do as you please. I am prepared for anything! "

" No, no ! He must know nothing ; and since he permits himself every licence——"

" There I don't agree with you ! The cases are not
identical. If he chooses to degrade himself, so much the
worse for him. But that's no reason why——"

" No, no ! . . ."

The ecstasy was over. We had come back to earth.

" No ! No ! " I repeated. " And don't you agree
that it's beautiful, new, almost unique—to love, to tell
one another of it. . . . Nothing else ! "

" It's as beautiful as a romance," she cried, clapping
her hands like a child.

" But it doesn't generally happen like that in fiction ! "

" And how good it is to remain honest ! "

" The only thing to do ! "

" And we shall always meet as before, without
fear——"

" And without reproach——"

" And without misunderstandings ! And you are sure
that Matilda is nothing——"

" Oh ! hush ! "

The door opened. How commonplace ! The two old
gentlemen crossed the drawing-room carrying a dark
lantern.

" Notice how life is a medley of petty troubles and
divine moments ! " I said to her ; " notice how reality
differs from fiction. Could I dare to draw a scene like
this in a novel or a drama without being accused of being
humdrum ? Just think—a confession of love without
kisses, genuflexions or protestations, terminated by the
appearance of two old men throwing the light of a dark
lantern on the lovers ! And yet therein lies the secret of
Shakespeare's greatness, who shows us Julius Cæsar in
dressing-gown and slippers, starting from his sleep at
night, frightened by childish dreams."

The bell rang. The Baron and pretty Matilda were returning home. As he had a guilty conscience, he overwhelmed us with amiability. And I, eager to show myself in my new part, told him a barefaced lie.

"I've been quarrelling with the Baroness for the last hour!"

He gave us a scrutinising look, full of vindictiveness, and scenting the air like a hound, seemed to catch the wrong scent.

IX

WHAT unparalleled guilelessness it argues to believe that there could be love without passion! There was danger even in the secret which existed between us. It was like a child conceived in secrecy, it grew and strove to see the light.

Our longing to meet and compare notes increased; we yearned to live again through the last year in which we had been trying to deceive one another. We resorted to all kinds of trickery. I introduced the Baroness to my sister, who, having married the head-master of a school, a man with an old, aristocratic name, in a way belonged to her set.

We often met by appointment; our meetings were harmless to begin with, but after a while passion sprang up and desire awoke.

In the first days following our mutual confession, she gave me a packet of letters, written partly before, partly after the thirteenth of March. These letters, into which she had poured all her sorrow, all her love, had never been intended to reach me.

"*Monday.*

"MY DEAR FRIEND,

"I am longing to see you, to-day as always. I want to thank you for listening to me yesterday without that sarcastic smile with which it is now your rule to regard me! I turn to you trustfully, at a moment when I am in dire need of your friendship, and you cover your face with a mask. Why? Is it necessary that you should disguise your feelings? You have yourself admitted in one of your letters that it is a mask. I hope it is, I can see it is, and yet it hurts me, for it makes me think that I have committed a fault of some sort . . . and I wonder : What is he thinking of me?

" I am jealous of your friendship ; I am afraid that some day you might despise me. Tell me that it will never happen ! You must be good and loyal to me. You must forget that I am a woman—don't I only too often forget it myself !

" I was not angry with you for what you said yesterday, but it surprised and pained me. Do you really believe me capable of wanting to excite my husband's jealousy for the sake of taking a mean revenge? Think of the danger to which I should expose myself if I attempted to win him back through jealousy ! What should I gain? His anger would fall upon your head, and we should for ever be separated ! And what would become of me without you, who are dearer to me than life !

" I love you with a sister's tenderness, not with the whims of a coquette. . . . It is true that I have known moments when I longed, when it would have been heaven, to take your head into my hands, to look deep into your dear eyes, so full of wisdom ; and I am sure I should have kissed you on your forehead, but never in your life would you have received a purer kiss.

" I am not responsible for my affectionate temperament, and if you were a woman, I should love you just as much, provided that I could respect a woman as highly as I respect you. . . .

" Your opinion of Matilda makes me very happy. One has to be a woman to be pleased about such a thing. But what am I to do? Think of my position in case everybody sided with her ! And I am to blame for whatever happens. I encouraged this flirtation because I considered it no more serious than a child's game. Feel-

I

ing sure of his affection, I allowed my husband perfect liberty. The consequences have proved my error. . . ."

"*Wednesday.*

"He is in love with her and has told me so. The matter has surpassed all limits, and I have laughed at it. . . . Think: after seeing you to the door, he came back to me, took my hands, looked into my face—I trembled, for my conscience was not clear—and said entreatingly: 'Don't be angry with me, Marie! I love Matilda!' What was I to do? Should I cry or laugh? And he confessed this to me, to me who am tormented by remorse, forced to love you from afar, hopelessly! Oh, these stupid ideas of honour! How senseless they are! Let him indulge his passion! You are my dear love, and my woman's heart shall never get the better of me and make me forget my duties as a wife and mother. But . . . notice the conflicting double nature of my feelings . . . I love you both, and I could never live without him, the brave, honest friend of my heart . . . nor without you either."

"*Friday.*

"At last you have lifted the veil which for so long has hidden the secret of my heart. And you don't despise me! Merciful God! You even love me. You have spoken the words which you had determined to leave for ever unspoken. You love me! And I am a guilty woman, a criminal, because I love you in return. May God forgive me! For I love him too, and could not bear the thought of leaving him.

"How strange it is! . . . To be loved! Loved tenderly! By him and by you! I feel so happy, so calm, that my love cannot possibly be a crime! Surely I should feel remorse if it were—or am I so hardened?

" How ashamed I am of myself! It was I who had to speak the first word of love. My husband is here, he puts his arms round me, and I let him kiss me. Am I sincere? Yes! Why did he not take care of me while there was yet time?

" 'The whole is like a novel. What will be the end? Will the heroine die? Will the hero marry another? Will they be separated? And will the end be satisfactory from a moral point of view?

" If I were with you at this moment, I should kiss your brow with the same devotion with which the devotee kisses the crucifix, and I should put from me all baseness, all artificiality. . . .' "

Was this hypocrisy, or did I deceive myself? Were they nothing but passion, these semi-religious ecstasies? No, not passion only. The desire of propagation has become more complicated, and even with the lower animals moral characteristics are transmitted through sexual love. Therefore love affects both body and soul, and one is nothing without the other. If it were but passion, why should she prefer a delicate, nervous, sickly youth to a giant like him? If it were only the love of the soul, why this longing to kiss me, why this admiration for my small feet, my well-shaped hands and nails, my intellectual forehead, my abundant hair? Or were those hallucinations caused by the intoxication of her senses, excited by her husband's excesses? Or did she feel instinctively that an ardent youth like me would make her far more happy than the inert mass which she called her husband? She was no longer jealous of his body, therefore she had ceased looking upon him in the light of a lover. But she was jealous of my person, and therefore she was in love with me! . . .

One day, when visiting my sister, the Baroness was

seized with an attack of hysterics. She threw herself on the sofa and burst into tears, infuriated with the disgraceful conduct of her husband, who was spending the evening with Matilda at a regimental ball.

In a passionate outburst she threw her arms round me and kissed me on the forehead. I returned kiss for kiss. She called me by endearing names.

The bond between us was growing stronger and my passion was increasing.

In the course of the evening I recited Longfellow's "Excelsior" to her. Genuinely touched by this beautiful poem, I fixed my eyes on her, and as if she were hypnotised, her face reflected every shade of feeling expressed on my own. She had the appearance of an ecstatic, of a seer.

After supper her maid called for her with a cab to take her home. I meant to come no further with her than the street, but she insisted on my getting into the cab, and in spite of my protestations she ordered her maid to sit on the box, by the side of the driver. As soon as I was alone with her I took her in my arms, silently, without a word. I felt her delicate body thrill and yield under my kisses. But I shrank from crime—and left her at her door, unhurt, ashamed of herself and, perhaps, also a little angry.

I no longer had any doubts now; I saw clearly. She was trying to tempt me. It was she who had given the first kiss, she who had taken the initiative in everything. From this moment I was going to play the part of the tempter, for, although a man of firm principles on the point of honour, I was by no means a Joseph.

On the following day we met at the National Museum.

How I adored her as I saw her coming up the marble staircase, under the gilded ceiling, as I watched her little feet tripping over the flags of variegated stucco, her aristocratic figure clothed in a black velvet costume, trimmed with military braid. I hurried to meet her and, like a page, bent my knees before her. Her beauty, which had blossomed under my kisses, was striking. The rich blood in her veins shone through her transparent cheeks : this statue, almost the statue of an old maid, had quickened under my caresses, and grown warm at the fire of life. Pygmalion had breathed on the marble and held a goddess in his arms.

We sat down before a statue of Psyche, acquired in the Thirty Years' War. I kissed her cheeks, her eyes, her lips, and she received my kisses with a rapturous smile. I played the tempter, employing all the sophisms of the orator, all the arts of the poet.

"I entreat you," I said, "leave your polluted house; don't consent any longer to live this life of three—or you'll force me to despise you. Return to your mother, devote yourself to art; in a year you will be able to appear before the footlights. Then you will be free to live your own life."

She added fuel to the fire; I became more and more incensed and warmed to my subject. I deluged her with a flood of words, the object of which was to extract a promise from her to tell her husband everything, for then, I argued, we should no longer be responsible for the consequences.

"But supposing things end badly for us?" she interposed.

"Even if we should lose everything! I could no longer love you if I could no longer respect both of us. Are you a coward? Do you crave the reward and refuse to bring the sacrifice? Be as noble as you are beautiful, dare the fatal leap, even at the risk of perishing! Let everything be lost save our honour! If we go on like this, we shall both be guilty in a very short time, for my love is like lightning, which will strike you! I love you as the sun loves the dew—to drink it. Therefore, quick to the scaffold! Sacrifice your head so that you may keep your hands clean! Don't imagine that I could ever debase myself and be content to share you with a third, never, never!"

She feigned resistance, but in reality she threw a grain of powder into the open flames. She complained of her husband and hinted at things, the very thought of which made my blood boil.

He, the numskull, poor as myself, without prospects, indulged in the luxury of two mistresses, while I, the man of talent, the aristocrat of the future, sighed and writhed under the torture of my unsatisfied longings.

But all of a sudden she veered round and tried to calm my excited nerves by reminding me of our agreement to be brother and sister.

"No, not that dangerous game of brother and sister! Let us be man and woman, lover and beloved! This alone is worthy of ourselves! I adore you! I adore everything belonging to you, body and soul, your golden hair and your straightforwardness, the smallest feet that ever wore shoes in Sweden, your candour, your eyes which shine in the dusk, your bewitching smile, your white stocking and your cherry-coloured garter. . . ."

"What?"

"Yes, my lovely princess, I have seen everything! And now I want to kiss your throat and the dimples on your shoulders; I will smother you with my kisses, strangle you between my arms as with a necklet. My love for you fills me with the strength of a god. Did you think me delicate? I was an imaginary invalid, or, rather, I pretended to be ill! Beware of the sick lion! Don't come near his den or he will kill you with his caresses! Down with the dishonest mask! I want you and I will have you! I've wanted you from the first moment I set eyes on you! The story of Selma, the Finlander, is nothing but a fairy tale . . . the friendship of our dear Baron a lie . . . he loathes me, the man of the middle-classes, the provincial, the *déclassé*, as I loathe him, the aristocrat!"

This avalanche of revelations excited her very little, for it told her nothing new : she had been aware of it without my avowal.

And we separated with the firm resolution not to meet again until she had told her husband everything.

I spent the evening at home, anxious and uneasy, waiting for telegrams from the seat of war. To distract my thoughts, I emptied a sack containing old books and papers on the floor, and sat down among this litter to examine and classify it. But I found it impossible to concentrate my thoughts on my task ; I stretched myself out at full length, resting the back of my head on my hands and, my eyes fixed with a hypnotic stare on the candles burning in the old chandelier, I lost myself in a reverie. I was longing for her kisses, and thinking out plans of making her my own. As she was sensitive and strange, I felt that the utmost delicacy would be necessary, that I must allow matters to arrange themselves ; that a single clumsy movement would spoil everything.

I lighted a cigarette and imagined that I was lying in a meadow ; it amused me to view my little room from below. Everything seemed new to me. The sofa, the witness of many pleasant hours, brought me back to my dreams of love, which, however, were quickly paralysed by the fear that happiness would be wrecked on the rocks of my uncompromising principles.

Analysing the thought which had checked my ardour, I discovered in it a great deal of cowardice, fear of the

consequences, a little sympathy with the man who stood
in danger of being betrayed, a little disgust with the
unclean pell-mell; a little genuine respect for the woman
whom I could not bear to see degrading herself; a little
pity with the daughter, a mere nothing of compassion with
the mother of my beloved, in case of a scandal; and quite
in the background of my miserable heart a vague presentiment of the difficulty I should find later on, if ever I
should wish to sever our connection.

"No," I said to myself, "all or nothing! She must
be mine alone, and for ever!"

While I was thus musing, there came a gentle tapping
at my door, and almost simultaneously a lovely head
appeared in the opening, flooding my attic with sunshine,
and with its roguish smile drawing me away from my
papers into the arms of my beloved. After a hailstorm
of kisses on her lips, which were fresh with the cold
outside, I asked—

"Well, what has he decided to do?"

"Nothing! I haven't told him yet!"

"Then you are lost! Flee, unhappy woman!"

And keeping firm hold of her, I took off her close-
fitting fur coat, removed her beaded hat and drew her to
the fire. Then she found words.

"I hadn't the courage. . . . I wanted to see you once
again before the catastrophe, for God knows, he may
decide to divorce me. . . ."

I closed her lips with mine, pushed a little table to her
seat and brought from my cupboard a bottle of good wine
and two glasses. By the side of them I set a basket with
roses and two lighted candles, arranging everything in the
manner of an altar. For a footstool I gave her a priceless
old edition of Hans Sachs, bound in calf, furnished with
gold locks and ornamented with a portrait of Luther. I
had borrowed the book from the Royal Library.

I poured out some wine. I gathered a rose and fastened it in the golden thicket of her hair. My lips touched the glass raised to drink to her health, to our love. I knelt down before her and worshipped her.

"How beautiful you are! "

For the first time she saw me as a lover. She was delighted. She took my head between her hands, kissed it and smoothed with her fingers the tangled strains of my unruly hair.

Her beauty filled me with respect. I looked at her with veneration, as one looks at the statue of a saint. She was enchanted to see me without the hated mask ; my words intoxicated her, and she was filled with delirious joy when she found that my love for her was at once tender, respectful and full of ardour.

I kissed her shoes, blackening my lips ; I embraced her knees without touching the hem of her dress ; I loved her just as she was, fully dressed, chaste as an angel, as if she had been born clothed, with wings outside her dress.

Suddenly the tears came into my eyes, I could not have said why.

"Are you crying? " she asked. "What is the matter? "

"I don't know. I'm too happy, that's all."

"You, capable of tears! You, the man of iron! "

"Alas! I know tears only too well! "

Being a woman of experience, she imagined that she possessed the secret remedy for my secret sorrow.

She rose from the sofa and pretended to be interested in the papers scattered about on the floor.

"You seemed to be stretched out on the grass when I came in," she said, smiling archly. "What fun to make hay in the middle of the winter! "

She sat down on a pile of papers ; I threw myself down

beside her. Another hailstorm of kisses, the goddess stooped towards me, ready to surrender.

Gradually I drew her closer to me, holding her captive with my lips, so as not to give her time to break the spell my eyes had cast over her, and free herself. We sat on the "grass" like lovers, yielding to our passion like fully dressed angels, and rose up content, happy, without remorse, like angels who have not fallen.

Love is inventive! We had sinned without sinning, yielded without surrendering. How precious is the love of a woman of experience! She is merciful to the young apprentice; she finds her pleasure in giving, not in receiving. . . .

Suddenly she recovered her senses, remembered the claims of reality and prepared to go.

"Until to-morrow, then!"

"Until to-morrow!"

X

HE had been told everything, and she called herself guilty, for he had wept. He had wept scalding tears! Was it simplicity or artfulness on his part? Doubtless both. Love and delusion are inseparable, and it is difficult to know ourselves as we really are.

But he was not angry with us, and did not insist on separating us, on condition that we should respect his good name.

"He is more noble and generous than we are," she said in her letter, "and he still loves both of us."

What a milksop! He consented to receive in his house a man who had kissed his wife; he believed us to be sexless, able to live side by side, like brother and sister.

It was an insult to my manhood; henceforth he had ceased to exist for me.

I stayed at home, a prey to the bitterest disappointment. I had tasted the apple, and it had been snatched from me. My imperious love had repented; she was suffering from remorse; she overwhelmed me with reproaches—she, the temptress! A fiendish idea flashed through my mind. Had I been too reserved? Did she want to break with me because I had been too timid? Since the thought of the crime from which I shrank had not seemed to disturb her, her passion must be stronger than mine. . . . But come back to me once more, my love, and I will teach you better.

At ten o'clock I received a letter from the Baron, in which he said that his wife was seriously ill.

My reply was a request to be left in peace. "I have

been long enough the cause of unpleasantness between you ;
forget me, as I will forget you."

Towards noon a second letter arrived :

"Let us once more revive our old friendship. I have
always respected you, and, in spite of your error, I am
convinced that you have behaved like a man of honour.
Let us bury the past. Come back to me as a brother,
and the matter will be forgotten."

The pathetic simplicity, the perfect confidence of the
man touched me ; in my reply I mentioned my misgivings,
and begged him not to play with fire, but leave me in
future unmolested.

At three o'clock in the afternoon I received a last communication : the Baroness was dying ; the doctor had just
left her ; she had asked for me. The Baron entreated me
not to refuse her request, and I went. Poor me !

I entered. The room smelt of chloroform. The Baron
received me with great agitation and tears in his eyes.

"What's the matter ? " I asked, with the calmness of a
doctor.

"I don't know. But she has been at death's door."

"And the doctor, what did he say ? "

"He shook his head and said it was not a case for him."

"Has he given her a prescription ? "

"No."

He took me into the dining-room, which had been transformed into a sick-room. She was lying on a couch, stiff,
haggard ; her hair was falling over her shoulders, her eyes
glowed like red-hot coals. She moved her hand, and her
husband put it into mine. Then he returned into the
drawing-room and left us by ourselves. My heart remained unmoved ; I did not trust my eyes ; the unusual
spectacle roused my suspicions.

"Do you know that I nearly died ? "

"Yes."

" And you don't feel sorry ? "

" Oh yes ! "

" You are not moved, you have no look of sympathy, no look of commiseration."

" You have your husband ! "

" Hasn't he himself brought us together ? "

" What are you suffering from ? "

" I'm very ill.   I shall have to consult a specialist."

" Oh ! "

" I'm afraid !   It's terrible !   If you knew how I have suffered ! . . . Put your hand on my head . . . it does me good. . . . Now smile at me . . . your smile fills me with new life ! . . ."

" The Baron——"

" You are going ?   You are leaving me ? "

" What can I do for you ? "

She began to cry.

" You surely can't want me to play the lover here, close to your child, your husband ? "

" You are a monster !   A man without a heart !   A——"

" Good-bye, Baroness ! "

I went.   The Baron accompanied me through the drawing-room, but, quick though he was, he could not prevent me from catching sight of a woman's skirt disappearing through one of the other doors.

This awakened the suspicion in me that the whole had been a farce.

The Baron closed the door behind me with a bang which echoed through the staircase, and gave me the impression that I had been kicked out.

I felt sure that I had not been mistaken.   I had assisted at the *dénoûment* of a sentimental play with a double plot.

This mysterious illness, what was it ?   Hysteria ?   No. Science has given it the name of " nymphomania " ; freely translated it means, the desire of a woman for children, moderated and disguised by time and the conventions, but suddenly breaking out with irresistible force.

This woman, always living in a state of semi-celibacy, unwilling to take upon herself the burden of motherhood, and yet dissatisfied with the incompleteness of her married life, was driven into the arms of a lover, to the commission of a crime, and, at the very moment when she thought that her lover was incontestably hers, he slipped through her fingers, and he, too, left her unsatisfied.

How miserable a mistake was matrimony! How pitiful a passion was love!

When I had finished my analysis I had come to the conclusion that the unsatisfactory nature of their relationship had driven both husband and wife to seek happiness elsewhere. The disappointment at my flight had brought the Baroness back into the arms of her husband, whose love had received a fresh stimulus, and who would henceforth strive to make her more happy.

They were reconciled, and everything was at an end.

Exit the devil.

The curtain falls.

No, it was not at an end.

She visited me again in my room, and I drew from her a full confession, brutal in its candour.

In the first year of her marriage she knew nothing of the ecstasies of love. After her baby was born, her husband grew indifferent to her, and their relations became strained.

"Then you've never been happy with this man with the physique of a giant?"

"Never . . . sometimes perhaps . . . hardly ever."

"And now?"

She blushed.

"The doctor has advised him not to go on sinning against nature."

She sank back on the sofa and hid her face in her hands.

Excited by these intimate confessions, I made an attempt to put my arms round her. She offered no resistance, she trembled and breathed heavily, but suddenly she felt remorse and repulsed me.

Strange enigma which was beginning to provoke me!

What did she want from me? Everything! But she shrank from the real crime, the illegitimate child.

I took her in my arms and kissed her, I tried to rouse her passion. She freed herself and left me, but, I thought, a shade less disappointed than before.

And now, what?

Confess to the husband? It has been done.

Give him details? . . . There are no details to give.

She continued to visit me.

And whenever she came, she sat down on the sofa on the plea of fatigue.

I was ashamed of my timidity; furious at my humiliation; afraid that she might think me a fool; conflicting emotions wore away my self-control, and the day came when I watched her from my window, walking away slowly, until she was hidden by the turn of the street. I sighed heavily.

The son of the people had carried off the white skin, the plebeian had won the aristocrat, the swineherd had mated with the princess! But he had paid a heavy price.

A storm was brewing. All sorts of rumours circulated in the town. The fair fame of the Baroness had suffered.

Her mother asked me to call on her. I went.

"Is it true that you are in love with my daughter?"

"It is true."

"And are you not ashamed? "

"I glory in it."

"She has told me that she loves you."

"I was aware of that. . . . I am sorry for you. I regret the possible consequences, but what am I to do? No doubt it is a deplorable business, but we are not guilty, neither she nor I. When we discovered our danger, we warned the Baron. Wasn't that acting correctly? "

"I'm not complaining of your conduct now, but I must protect the honour of my daughter, of her child, of the family! Surely you don't want to ruin us? "

The poor old woman cried bitterly. She had put all her eggs in one basket: the aristocratic alliance of her daughter, which was to rehabilitate her own family. She roused my compassion, and I succumbed to her sorrow.

"Command me," I said; "I will do whatever you wish."

"Leave this place, go away from here, I implore you."

"I will do so, but on one condition."

"And that is? "

"That you will ask Miss Matilda to return to her family."

"Is that an accusation? "

"More than that, a denunciation. For I believe I'm right in saying that her presence at the Baron's house is not conducive to happiness."

"I agree with you. Oh, that girl! I shall tell her what I think of her! But you, you will leave to-morrow? "

"To-night, if you like."

At this stage the Baroness appeared, and unceremoniously interrupted our conversation.

"You must stay! You shall stay! " she said imperatively. "Matilda must go! "

"Why? " asked her mother, in amazement.

" Because I mean to have a divorce.   Gustav has treated me like an abandoned woman before Matilda's step-father. I shall prove to them that they're mistaken."

What a heartrending scene !   Is there a surgical operation so painful as the tearing asunder of family ties? All passions are let loose, all uncleanness hidden in the depth of the soul stands revealed.

The Baroness took me apart and repeated to me the contents of a letter from her husband to Matilda : abuse of us, and an assurance of his undying love for the girl, in terms which proved that he had deceived us from the very beginning.

The ball has now gained the volume of a rock ; it goes on rolling, and crushes alike the innocent and the guilty.

In spite of all the coming and going a settlement seemed as far off as ever.

Fresh misfortunes happened.   The bank did not pay the ordinary yearly dividend ; ruin was menacing.

The threatening poverty was made the pretext for the divorce, for the Baron could no longer maintain his family. For appearances' sake he asked his colonel whether his wife's proposed theatrical career would in any way interfere with his own.   The colonel gave him to understand that if his wife went on the stage, he would have to leave the service.   A splendid opportunity for abusing aristocratic prejudices !

During all this time the Baroness, under medical treatment for some internal trouble, continued to live at her husband's house, although they were now practically separated.   She was always in pain, irritable and despondent, and I found it impossible to rouse her from her deep depression ; my strenuous effort to inspire her with some of my youthful confidence was wasted.   In vain I drew for her glowing pictures of the career of an artist, the inde-

K

pendent life in a home of her own, a home like mine, where
she would enjoy freedom of body and soul. She listened
to me without replying; the stream of my words seemed
to galvanise her like a magnetic current, without penetrating to her consciousness.

An agreement between the two parties had been arrived
at at last. It was decided that after all legal formalities
had been complied with, the Baroness should proceed to
Copenhagen, where an uncle of hers was living. The
Swedish consul at Copenhagen would communicate with
her on her supposed flight from her husband's house, and
she would inform him of her wish to have her marriage
annulled. After that she would be free to make her own
plans for the future, and return to Stockholm. Her dowry
would remain in the possession of her husband, as well as
all the furniture, with the exception of a very few things;
the little girl would continue to live with her father, unless
the latter contracted a second marriage, but the Baroness
would have the right to see her child whenever she wished.

The financial question gave rise to a violent scene. To
save the remnants of a fortune which had almost disappeared, the father of the Baroness had made a will in which
he left everything to his daughter. Her scheming mother
had obtained possession of the inheritance, and was paying
her son-in-law a certain percentage. Since such a pro-
cedure was illegal, the Baron insisted that the will should
now come into force. The old mother-in-law, furious at
the reduction of her income, denounced her son-in-law to
her brother, Matilda's father, as the girl's lover. The
storm burst. The colonel threatened to cashier the
Baron; a law-suit was impending.

Now, the Baroness left no stone unturned to save the
father of her child. And to clear him I was made the
scapegoat.

I was prevailed upon to write a letter to Matilda's father, in which I took the sins of everybody and the responsibility for all the mischief on my own shoulders, called God to witness that the Baron and the girl were innocent, and asked the offended father to forgive me for all the crimes I had committed—I, the only penitent one!

It was a beautiful action and a good one, and the Baroness loved me for it as a woman loves a man who has allowed her to trample on his honour, his self-respect, his good name.

In spite of my resolution not to be mixed up in these unsavoury family matters, I had been unable to steer clear of them.

The mother-in-law paid me many visits, and, always appealing to my love for her daughter, tried to incite me against the Baron, but in vain; I took my orders from no one but the Baroness.   Moreover, on this point I sided with the father.   As he was taking charge of the child, the dowry, imaginary or otherwise, belonged undoubtedly to him.

Oh, this month of April!   What a springtime of love! The beloved woman on the sick-bed, intolerable meetings at which the two families washed their dirty linen, which I certainly never had the least desire to come into contact with; tears; rudeness; a chaos which brought to light everything base that had hitherto been hidden under the veneer of education.

That comes of raising a nest of hornets about one's ears! . . .

No wonder that love suffered under such conditions. Where is the charm of a woman who is always worn out with contention, whose conversation bristles with legal terms?

Again and again I attempted to instil into her my thoughts of consolation and hope, even though they were

K 2

often anything but spontaneous, for I had come to the end of my nerve-power; and she accepted everything, sucked my brain dry, consumed my heart. In exchange she looked upon me as a dustbin, into which she threw all her rubbish, all her grief, all her troubles, all her cares.

In this hell I lived my life, dragged on my misery, worked for a bare sufficiency. When she came to see me of an evening and found me working, she sulked; and it was not until I had wasted a couple of hours with tears and kisses that I succeeded in convincing her of my love.

She conceived love as never-ending admiration, a servile readiness to please, unceasing sacrifice.

I was crushed down by my heavy responsibility. I could see the moment not very far off when misery, or the birth of a child, would force me into a premature marriage. She had claimed but three thousand francs for one year, with which she intended to defray the costs of her artistic training. I had no faith in her dramatic career. Her pronunciation still betrayed her Finnish descent, and her features were too irregular for the stage. To keep her from brooding I made her repeat poetry. I constituted myself her teacher. But she was too much occupied with her disappointments, and when, after a rehearsal, she had to admit that her progress was very small, she was inconsolable.

How dreary our love was! Instead of being the source from which flowed strength to cope with our difficulties, it was a prolonged torture.

Joy was no sooner born than it was slain, and we parted, dissatisfied, robbed of the greatest happiness life has to give. A poor phantom was our love!

But my monogamic nature recoiled from change. Our love, sad as it was, was yet the source from which sprang exquisite spiritual joys, and my inextinguishable longing was the guarantee for its endurance.

XI

It was on the first of May. All the necessary documents had been signed. Her departure was fixed for the day after to-morrow. She came to me and threw her arms round me.

"Now I belong to you alone; take me!"

As we had never discussed marriage, I did not quite understand what she meant, and we sat in my little attic, sad and thoughtful. Everything was permitted to us now, but temptation had diminished. She accused me of indifference, and I proved the contrary to her. Thereupon she accused me of sensuality.

Adoration, incense it was what she wanted!

She had hysterics, and complained that I no longer loved her. Already! . . .

After half-an-hour of flattery and blandishments she grew calmer, but she was not really herself until she had reduced me to tears of despair. Then she made a fuss of me.

The more humble I was, the more I knelt before her, small and miserable, the more she loved me. She hated strength and manliness in me; to win her love I had to pretend to be wretched, so that she could pose as the stronger, play "little mother" and console me.

We had supper in my room; she laid the table and prepared the meal. After supper I claimed the rights of a lover, and she made no resistance.

How wonderful is the rejuvenating power of love! A young girl lay in my arms, trembling, and brutality was transformed into tenderness. Surely the animal had no part in this union of souls! Alas! is it ever possible to say where the spiritual ends and the animal begins?

Reassured on the question of her health, she gave herself to me whole-heartedly; she was radiant with joy, content and happy; her beauty shone out; her eyes sparkled. My poor attic had become a temple, a sumptuous palace; I lighted the broken chandelier, my reading lamp, all the candles, to illuminate our happiness, the joy of living, the only thing which makes our miserable lives endurable.

For these moments of rapture accompany us on our thorny pilgrimage through life; the memory of these fleeting hours helps us to live, and outlive our former selves.

"Don't speak ill of love," I said to her. "Worship nature in all her forces; honour God, who compels us to be happy in spite of ourselves!"

She made no reply, for she was happy. Her yearning was stilled; my kisses had driven the warm blood through her beating heart into her cheeks; the flame of the candle was mirrored in her eyes moist with tears; the rainbow tints of her veins appeared more vivid, like the plumage of the birds in the springtime. She looked like a girl of sixteen, so delicate, so pure were her contours; the dainty head with its masses of golden hair, half-buried in the cushions, might have been a child's.

Thus she reclined on my sofa, like a goddess, allowing me to worship her, while she regarded me with furtive glances, half shamefaced, half provoking.

How chaste in her abandonment is the beloved woman when she surrenders herself to the caresses of her lover! And man, though her superior mentally, in only happy when he has won the woman who is his true mate. My former flirtations, my love affairs with women of a lower class, appeared to me like crimes, like a sin against the race. The white skin, the perfect feet, the delicate hands, were they signs of degeneration? Were they not rather on a par with the glossy skin of the wild beast, its slim, sinewy legs, which show hardly any muscle? The beauty of a woman is the sum total of characteristics which are worthy of transmission through the agency of the man who can appreciate them. This woman had been pushed aside by her husband; therefore she no longer belonged to him, for she had ceased to please him. He could see no beauty in her, and it was left to me to achieve the blossoming of a flower, the rare loveliness of which the seer, the elect only, could perceive.

Midnight was striking. From the barracks close by came the "Who goes there?" of the relieving guards. It was time to part.

I accompanied my beloved on her way home, and, as we were walking along side by side, I tried to kindle in her the fire of my enthusiasm, my new hopes; I startled her with the plans which her kisses had ripened in me. She came closer, as if to find strength in contact with me, and I gave her back tenfold what I had received from her.

When we had arrived at the high railings she noticed that she had forgotten her key. How annoying! But, bent on showing her my mettle by penetrating into the lion's den, I climbed the railings, dashed across the courtyard and knocked at the front door, prepared for a stormy reception from the Baron. My throbbing heart was thrilled by the thought of fighting my rival before her eyes. The favoured lover was transformed into a hero! But, luckily, it was only a servant who came to open the door, and we said good-night to each other formally, calmly, with the maid, who had not taken the trouble to respond to our "Good-evening," looking on in contemptuous silence.

Henceforth she felt sure of my love, and so she abused it.

She came to see me to-day. She could not find words enough to praise her husband. Deeply affected by Matilda's departure, he had succumbed to his wife's pressure, and made her a promise to save appearances by accompanying her to the station, for, she argued, if both he and I were to see her off, her departure would not have the appearance of flight. Moreover, she told me that the Baron, no longer angry with me, had consented to receive me at his house, and, in order to put a stop to the rumours, show himself during the next few days about the town in my company.

I appreciated the generosity of this big, ingenuous child, with the honest heart, and, out of consideration for him, I demurred.

" We're not going to disgrace him like that. Never ! "

" Remember that it is a question of my child's honour."

" Doesn't his honour count for something ? "

But she laughed at the idea of considering other people's honour. Looked upon me as eccentric.

" But that beats everything ! You're making me a byword, you're degrading us all ! It's folly ! It's unworthy ! " I exclaimed.

She cried ; and, after she had sobbed for an hour and overwhelmed me with reproaches, I succumbed to the irresistible weapon of her tears, and consented to do her bidding. But I cursed the despot, I cursed the falling crystal drops which increased tenfold the power of her glances.

She was stronger than both her husband and myself. She was leading us by the nose into disgrace ! Why did she want this reconciliation? Was she afraid of a war to the knife between me and the Baron? Did she dread possible disclosures? . . .

. . . What a punishment she had inflicted on me by compelling me to revisit this dreary house! But, cruel egoist that she was, she had no sympathy with another's terrors. I have had to promise her, on my oath, to deny the whole story of the illicit relationship which existed between the Baron and her cousin, so as to stop all slander. I went to this last meeting with slow steps and a sinking heart.

The little garden smiled at me with its blossoming cherry trees, its sweet-scented daffodils. The shrubbery, where her marvellous beauty had bewitched me, was bursting into leaf; the turned-up flower-beds looked like black shrouds spread out on the lawn; I pictured the forsaken little girl wandering about there alone, looked after by a servant, and learning her lessons; I pictured her growing up, awakening to the facts of life, and being told one day that her mother had deserted her.

I mounted the stairs of the fatal house, which was built against a sand quarry, and called up the memories of my childhood. Friendship, family, love, all had been jeopardised, and, in spite of our efforts to comply with the law of the land, crime had stained its threshold.

Who was to blame?

The Baroness opened the folding doors and secretly kissed me between the wings. I could not suppress a momentary feeling of loathing, and indignantly pushed her aside. It reminded me of the servants' flirtations at the back door, and filled me with disgust. Behind the door! Slut! without pride, without dignity!

She pretended that I was reluctant to enter the drawing-room, and asked me in a loud voice to come in, at the very moment when, embarrassed by the humiliating situation in which I found myself, I hesitated, and was on the point of retracing my footsteps. A flash from her eyes, and my hesitation was gone; paralysed by her self-command, I gave in.

Everything in the drawing-room pointed to the breaking up of the household. Underlinen, dresses, petticoats were scattered all over the furniture. The writing-table was littered with a pile of stockings, a short time ago the delight of my eyes, to-day an abomination. She came and went, counted and folded up, brazenly, shamelessly.

"Had I corrupted her in so short a time?" I asked myself, gazing at this exhibition of a respectable woman's underclothing.

She examined one piece after another, and put on one side everything which needed repairing; she noticed that on one garment the tapes were missing; she laid it aside with perfect unconcern.

I seemed to be present at an execution; I felt sick with misery, while she listened absent-mindedly to my futile conversation about unimportant details. I was waiting for the Baron, who had locked himself into the dining-room and was writing letters.

At last the door opened; I started apprehensively, but it was only the little girl who came in, puzzled to know the reason of all this upset. She ran up to me, accompanied by her mother's spaniel, and held up her forehead to be kissed. I blushed. I felt angry, and turned to the Baroness.

"You might at least have spared me this!

But she did not understand what I meant.

"Mamma is going away, darling, but she'll soon be back and bring you lots of toys."

The little dog begged for a caress—he, too!

A little later the Baron appeared.

He walked up to me, broken, crushed, and pressed my

hand, unable to utter a word. I honoured his evident grief by a respectful silence, and he withdrew again.

The dusk was beginning to gather in the corners of the room. The maid lighted the lamps without seeming to notice my presence. Supper was announced. I wanted to go. But the Baron added his pressing invitation to that of the Baroness, and in so touching and sincere a manner that I accepted and stayed.

And we sat down to supper, the three of us, as in the old days. It was a solemn moment. We talked of all that had happened, and with moist eyes asked one another the question: "Who is to blame?" Nobody, destiny, a series of incidents, paltry in themselves, a number of forces. We shook hands, clinked our glasses together and spoke of our undying friendship exactly as in the days gone by. The Baroness alone kept up her spirits. She made the programme for the following day: the meeting at the railway station, the walks through the town, and we agreed to everything.

At last I rose to go. The Baron accompanied us into the drawing-room. There he laid the hand of the Baroness into mine and said, with a choking voice—

"Be her friend. My part is played out. Take care of her, guard her from the wickedness of the world, cultivate her talent: you are better able to do it than I, a poor soldier. God protect you!"

He left us; the door closed behind him, and we were alone.

Was he sincere at that moment? I thought so at the time, and I should like to think so still. He was of a sentimental nature, and, in his way, fond of us; doubtless, the thought of seeing the mother of his child in the hands of an enemy would have been painful to him.

It is possible that later on, under adverse influence, he boasted of having fooled us. But such a thing would really have been foreign to his character—and is it not a well-known fact that no one likes to admit having been duped?

It was six o'clock at night. I was pacing the large hall of the Central Station. The train for Copenhagen would leave at six-fifteen, and neither the Baron nor the Baroness had appeared.

I felt like the spectator of the last act of a terrible tragedy, I was longing wildly for the end. Another quarter of an hour and there would be peace. My nerves, disordered by these successive crises, required rest, and the coming night would restore some of the nerve force which I had used up and squandered for the love of a woman.

She arrived at the last moment, in a cab, drawn by a mare which the driver was leading by the bridle.

Always careless and always too late!

She rushed towards me like a lunatic.

"The traitor! He has broken his word! He's not coming!" she exclaimed so loudly that she attracted the attention of the passers-by.

It was certainly unfortunate, but I could not help respecting him for it.

"He's quite right. He has common-sense on his side," I said, seized with a spirit of contradiction.

"Be quick! Take a ticket for Copenhagen, or I shall stay here!" she ordered.

"No! If I went with you it would look like an elopement. All Stockholm would talk about it to-morrow."

"I don't care. . . . Make haste!"

"No! I won't!"

But I could not help pitying her at the moment, and the situation was becoming unbearable. A quarrel, a lover's quarrel was inevitable.

She knew it instinctively, and, seizing my hands, she

implored me with her eyes; the ice melted; the sorceress won; I wavered . . . I succumbed. . . .

"To Katrineholm then!"

"Very well, if you'd rather."

She was having her luggage registered.

Everything was lost, including honour, and I had before me the prospect of a painful journey.

The train moved out of the station. We were alone in a first-class compartment. The Baron's non-appearance had depressed us. It was an unforeseen danger and a bad omen. An uneasy silence reigned in the carriage; one of us had to break it. She was the one to speak.

"Axel, you don't love me any more!"

"Perhaps not," I replied, worn out by a month of chaos.

"And I have sacrificed everything to you!"

"Sacrificed everything? . . . To your love, perhaps, but not to me. And have I not sacrificed my life to you? You are angry with Gustav and you're venting your anger on me . . . be reasonable."

Tears, tears! What a wedding tour! I steeled my nerves, put on my armour. I became indifferent, impenetrable.

"Restrain your emotions! From to-day you must use your common-sense. Weep, weep until the source of your tears is dry, but then lift up your head. You are a foolish woman, and I have honoured you as a queen, as a ruler! I have done your bidding because I thought myself the weaker of the two! Unfortunately! Don't make me despise you. Don't ever try to blame me alone for what has happened. I admired Gustav's shrewdness last night. He has realised that the great events in life have always more than one cause. Who is to blame? You? I? He? She? The threatening ruin, your passion for the stage, your internal trouble, the inheritance from your thrice-married grandfather? Your mother's hatred of bearing children which is the cause of your vacillating disposition? The idleness of your husband, whose profession left him too much leisure? My instincts? The instincts of the man who has risen from the lower classes? My accidental meeting with your Finnish friend who brought us together? An endless number of motives, a few of which only are known to us. Don't debase yourself before the mob who will unanimously condemn you to-morrow; don't believe, like those poor in spirit, that you can solve such an intricate problem by taking neither the crime nor the criminal seriously!. . . And, moreover, have I seduced you? Be candid with yourself, with me, while we're here alone, without witnesses."

But she would not be candid.

She could not, for candour is not a woman's characteristic.

She knew herself to be an accomplice in crime; she was tortured by remorse. She had but one thought, to ease her conscience by throwing the whole blame on me.

I left her to herself, and wrapped myself in a callous silence.

Night fell. I opened the window and leaned against the door, gazing at the quickly-passing black Scotch firs, behind which the pale moon was rising. Then a lake passed, surrounded by birch trees; a brook bordered by alders; cornfields, meadows, and then Scotch firs again, a long stretch of them. A mad desire to throw myself out of the carriage seized me; a desire to escape from this prison where I was watched by an enemy, kept spell-bound by a witch. But the anxiety for her future oppressed me like a nightmare; I felt responsible for her, who was a stranger to me, for her unborn children, for the support of her mother, her aunt, her whole family, for centuries to come.

I should make it my business to procure for her successes on the stage; I should bear all her sorrows, her disappointments, her failures, so that one day she could throw me in the dust like a squeezed-out lemon—me, my whole life, my brain, the marrow of my spine, my life-blood; all in exchange for the love which I gave her, and which she accepted and called " sacrificing herself to me." Delusions of love! hypnotism of passion!

She sat without moving until ten o'clock, sulking. One more hour and we should have to say good-bye.

All at once, with a word of apology, she put her two feet on the cushioned seat, pretending to be worn out with fatigue. Her languid glances, her tears had left me unmoved; I had kept my head, my strength of purpose in spite of her fallacious logic. Now everything collapsed. I beheld her adorable boots, a tiny piece of her stocking.

Down on your knees, Samson! Put your head in her lap, press your cheeks against her knees, ask her to forgive you for the cruel words with which you have lashed her— and which she didn't even understand! Slave! Coward! You lie in the dust before a stocking, you, who thought yourself strong enough to conquer a world! And she, she only loves you when you debase yourself; she buys you cheaply at the price of a few moments of gratified passion, for she has nothing to lose.

The engine whistled; the train glided into the station; I had to leave her. She kissed me with motherly affection, made the sign of the cross on my forehead—although she was a Protestant—commended me to the Lord, begged me to take care of myself, and not to give way to fretting.

The train steamed out into the night, choking me with its bituminous smoke.

I breathed—at last—the cool evening air, and enjoyed my freedom. Alas! but for a moment. No sooner had

I arrived at the village inn than I broke down. I loved her, yes, I loved her, just as I had seen her at the moment of parting ; for that moment recalled to me the first sweet days of our friendship, when she was the lovely, womanly tender mother, who spoiled and caressed me as if I had been a little child.

And yet I loved her ardently, desired to make this stormy woman my wife.

I asked for writing material, and wrote her a letter in which I told her that I would pray to God for her happiness.

Her last embrace had led me back to God, and, under the influence of her parting kiss, still fresh on my lips, I denied the new faith, which teaches the progress of humanity.

The first stage in the downfall of a man had been reached ; the others were sure to follow—to utter degradation, to the verge of insanity.

PART II

I

ON the day after our departure the whole town knew that Baroness X had eloped with one of the librarians of the Royal Library.

This was only what was to be expected, to be dreaded! After all my efforts to save her good name, we had forgotten everything in a moment of weakness.

She had spoiled all our plans, and all that remained for me to do was to take the responsibility on my own shoulders and grapple to the best of my ability with the consequences which threatened to ruin her theatrical career; there was only one theatre where she could possibly appear, and loose morals were not likely to increase her chances of an engagement at the Royal Theatre.

On the morning after my return I made an excuse to call on the chief librarian, who was slightly unwell and unable to go out. The sole object of my visit was the establishment of an alibi. After leaving him I strolled through the main streets and thoroughfares and arrived at my office at the usual hour. I spent the evening at the Press Club, and deliberately set the rumour afloat that there was but one reason for the divorce, and that was the Baroness's determination to enter the theatrical profession. I maintained that husband and wife were on the best of terms, and that their separation was but the inevitable result of class prejudice.

If I had only known what harm I was doing myself by spreading these rumours and proclaiming her innocence! . . . But no, I should not have acted otherwise.

The papers scrambled eagerly for the smart society scandal, but the public scoffed at this irresistible love of art, a more or less doubtful phenomenon always, but more especially when the stage is concerned. The women in particular were sceptical, and the forsaken child remained an ugly fact which nothing could explain away.

In the meantime I received a letter—a perfect howl of anguish—from Copenhagen. Tortured by remorse, by a yearning for her deserted child, she asked me to come to her at once, complaining bitterly of her relatives who, she asserted, were making her life one long drawn-out agony. She charged them with having suppressed, in collusion with her husband, an important document, which was essential for the final decision in the case.

I refused to leave town, but wrote a few angry lines to the Baron. His reply was so insolent that it led to a complete rupture between us.

One or two telegrams passed, and peace was re-established. The document was found, and the proceedings went on.

I spent my evenings in writing long letters to her, giving her minute instructions how to comport herself in the circumstances. These letters were intended to cheer and encourage her. I advised her to work, to study her art, to visit the theatres. In my anxiety to supplement her income, I urged her to write on anything which she found interesting, and undertook to get her articles accepted by a first-class paper.

No answer. I had every reason to believe that her independent spirit resented my well-meant interference.

A week passed; a week full of care, unrest and hard work. Then, early one morning, before I was up, I received a letter from Copenhagen.

The tone of her letter was calm and serene; she seemed unable to hide a certain pride on account of the quarrel between the Baron and myself. (She was in a fair position to form an opinion, since she had received the respective letters from both of us.) She found the "duel" not without style, and admired my pluck. "It is a pity," she concluded her letter, "that two men like you and the Baron should not be friends." Further on she gave me a detailed account of what she was doing to while away the time. She was evidently enjoying herself; she had made her way into second-rate artistic circles, a fact which I did not like. She described an evening spent at some assembly-rooms in the company of a number of young men, who paid her a great deal of attention; she had made the conquest of a musician, a youth who had sacrificed his family to his art. "What a strange similarity between our two cases!" she remarked. Then followed a detailed biography of the interesting martyr and the request not to be jealous.

"What did she mean?" I wondered, taken aback by the half-sarcastic, half-familiar tone of her letter, which appeared to be written between two entertainments.

Was it possible that this coldly voluptuous madonna belonged to the class of born wantons, that she was a coquette, a cocotte?

I sat down at once and indited a furious scolding; I painted her picture as she then appeared to me. I called her Madame Bovary; I entreated her to break the spell which was leading her to a precipice.

In reply, "as a proof of her absolute faith in me," she sent me the letters which the young enthusiast had written to her. Love letters!

The same old use of the term friendship, the inexplicable sympathy of the souls, and the whole list of the trite and to us both so familiar words : brother and sister, little mother, playmates, and so on, cloaks and covers under which lovers are wont to hide, to abandon themselves ultimately to their passions.

What was I to think? Was she mentally deranged?

L 2

Was she an unconscious criminal who remembered nothing of the terrible experience of the last two months, when the hearts of three people were on fire for her? And I who had been made to play the part of a Cinderella, a scape-goat, a man of straw, I was toiling to remove all obstacles from her way to the irregular life of the theatre.

A fresh blow! To see the woman whom I adored wallow in the gutter.

My soul was filled with unspeakable compassion, I had a foreboding of the fate which awaited her, perverse woman that she was, and vowed to lift her up, to strengthen and support her, to do everything in my power to shield her from a fatal catastrophe.

Jealous! That vulgar word invented by a woman in order to mislead the man she has deceived or means to deceive. The hoodwinked husband shows his anger, and the word jealous is flung in his face. Jealous husband— husband betrayed! And there are women who look upon jealousy as synonymous with impotence, so that the betrayed husband can only shut his eyes, powerless in the face of such accusations.

She returned after a fortnight, pretty, fresh, in high spirits, and full of bright memories, for she had thoroughly enjoyed herself. She was wearing a new dress with touches of brilliant colouring, which struck me as vulgar. I was puzzled. The woman who used to dress so simply, so quietly, with such exquisite taste, was adopting a colour scheme which was positively garish.

Our meeting was colder than either of us had expected; there was a constrained silence at first, followed by a sudden outburst.

The flatteries of her new friends had turned her head; she gave herself airs, teased me, made fun of me. She spread her gorgeous dress over my old sofa, to hide its shabbiness. Her old power over me reasserted itself, and for a moment I forgot all resentment in a passionate kiss;

nevertheless, a slight feeling of anger remained at the bottom of my heart, and presently found vent in a torrent of reproaches. Subdued by my impetuosity, which contrasted so strangely with her own indolent nature, she took refuge in tears.

"How can you be so absurd as to imagine that I was flirting with that young man?" she sobbed. "I promise you never to write to him again, although I'm sure he'll think it rude of me."

Rude! One of her favourite catchwords! A man pays her attention, in other words makes advances to her, and she listens politely, for fear of being rude. What a woman!

But fate was against me. I was lying at her feet, her beautiful little feet, encased in tiny shoes. She was wearing black silk stockings, which added to my confusion; her leg was a little fuller than it had been; the black legs in a cloud of petticoats were the legs of a she-devil.

Her constant fear of motherhood irritated me; I lied to her; I told her that she had nothing to fear from me; that I knew how to cheat nature. I repeated my assurances until I finished by believing in them myself, and in the end succeeded in setting her mind at ease by promising to be responsible for all consequences.

She was living with her mother and aunt in the second story of a house in one of the main thoroughfares. As she threatened to visit me in my own room if they prevented me from seeing her, I was allowed to call. But the thought of the supervision of these two old women, whom I knew to be watching us through the keyhole all the time, was almost beyond bearing.

The divorced husband and wife were beginning to realise how much they had lost. The Baroness, once a respected married woman, mistress of an aristocratic establishment, had returned to the conditions of her childhood. She was under the control of her mother, almost a prisoner in one room, kept by two old women, who were themselves in needy circumstances. The mother never lost an opportunity of reminding her of her careful bringing up and how she had been fitted to take an honourable social position, and the daughter remembered the happy days following her release from the parental yoke. Bitter words were spoken on both sides, tears and insults were all too frequent, and I had to pay for them when I called in the evening . . . to visit a prisoner under the eyes of a warder and witness.

When the strain of these painful meetings became unbearable, we ventured to meet two or three times in the park. But we only jumped from the frying-pan into the fire, for now we were exposed to the contemptuous stare of the crowd. We hated the spring sunshine which illuminated our misery. We missed the darkness, we longed for the winter, which made it easier for us to hide our shame. Alas! the summer was coming with its long nights, which know no darkness.

Our former friends dropped us, one after the other. Even my sister, intimidated by the now universal gossip, grew suspicious and estranged when the ex-baroness, at a little supper party, tried to keep up her spirits by taking too much wine, became intoxicated, proposed a toast, smoked cigarettes, and generally behaved in a way which excited the disgust of the women and the contempt of the men.

"That woman's a common prostitute! " said a respectable married man and father of a family to my brother-in-law, and the latter took the first chance to repeat the remark to me.

When on the following Sunday evening we arrived at my sister's house, where we had been invited to supper, the servant informed us, to our consternation, that her master and mistress were out.

We spent the evening in my room, a prey to anger

and despair, seeking comfort in the thought of suicide.
I pulled down the blinds to shut out the daylight, and we
sat together in misery, waiting for night and darkness,
before we ventured out again into the street.   But the
summer sun did not set until late, and at eight o'clock
we both felt hungry.   Neither of us had any money, and
there was nothing to eat or drink in the cupboard.   These
moments were some of the most wretched moments of
my life, and gave me a foretaste of misery to come.
Reproaches, cold kisses, floods of tears, remorse, disgust.

I tried to persuade her to go home and have supper
with her mother, but she was afraid of the daylight;
moreover, her heart sank at the thought of the necessary
explanation.   She had eaten nothing since two o'clock,
and the melancholy prospect of going to bed supperless
aroused the wild beast hunger in her.

She had grown up in a wealthy home, and had been
used to every kind of luxury; she had no idea what poverty
meant, and consequently she was completely unstrung.
I, who had been familiar with hunger from childhood,
suffered torture to see her in such a desperate position.
I ransacked my cupboard, but could find nothing; I
searched the drawers of my writing-table, and there,
amongst all sorts of keep-sakes, faded flowers, old love-
letters, discoloured ribbons, I found two sweets which I
had kept in remembrance of a funeral.   I offered them to
her just as they were, wrapped in black paper and tinfoil.
A distressing banquet indeed, these sweets in their
mourning dress !

Depressed, humiliated, apprehensive, I raged and
thundered furiously against all respectable women whose
doors were closed to us, who would have none of us.

"Why this hostility and contempt?   Had we committed a crime?   Surely not; it was but a question of a
straightforward divorce; we were complying with all the
rules and requirements of the law."

"We have been behaving too correctly," she said, trying to comfort herself. "The world is but a pack of knaves. It winks at open, shameless adultery, but condemns divorce. A high standard of morality indeed!"

We were agreed on the subject. But the facts remained. The crime continued to hang over our heads, which drooped under its weight.

I felt like a boy who has robbed a bird's nest. The mother had flown away, the little ones lay prostrate, chirping plaintively, bereft of the protecting warmth of the mother's wings.

And the father? He was left desolate in the ruined home. I pictured him of a Sunday evening, an evening like this, when the family assembles round the fireplace, alone in the drawing-room, with the silenced piano; alone in the dining-room, eating his solitary dinner; alone always. . . .

"Oh, no, nothing of the kind!" she interrupted my musings; ". you are quite mistaken! You would be much more likely to find him lounging on the comfortable sofa at Matilde's brother-in-law's; he has had a good dinner with plenty of wine, and is gently squeezing the hand of my poor, dear, libelled little cousin, laughing at the outrageous stories told of his wife's ill-conduct—his wife, who refused to countenance his infidelity. And both of them, surrounded and upheld by the sympathy and applause of this hypocritical world, are eager to throw the first stone at us."

Her words set me thinking, and after a while I expressed the opinion that the Baron had led us by the nose; that he had schemed to rid himself of a troublesome wife, so as to be able to marry again, and had managed to secure her dowry, in spite of the law.

She became indignant at once.

"You have no right to say anything against him! It was all my fault!"

" Why have I no right to say anything against him ?
Is his person sacred ? "

One might almost have thought so, for whenever I
attacked him she took his part.

Was it the freemasonry of caste which prompted her to
stand up for him ?   Or were there secrets in her life which
made her fear his enmity ?   I could not solve the riddle,
nor discover the reason of her loyalty to him, which no
disloyalty on his part could shake.

The sun set at last, and we parted.   I slept the sleep
of the famished ; I dreamed that I was making desperate
efforts to wing my way heavenwards, with a millstone
round my neck.

Misfortune dogged our footsteps.   We approached
one of the theatrical managers with the request to give
us a date for her first appearance.   He replied that he
could not, in his official position, have anything to do with
a runaway wife.

We left no stone unturned, but all our efforts were
doomed to failure.   A year hence her resources would be
exhausted, and she would be thrown on the street.   It
was my business, the business of the poor Bohemian, to
save her from that fate.

To avoid every possibility of a misunderstanding, she
called on an old friend of hers, a former tragedienne,
whom up to quite recently she had constantly met in
society, and who had cringed like a dog before the
" golden-haired Baroness," her " little fairy."

The great actress, a notoriously unfaithful wife, grown
grey in vice at the side of her husband, received the
honest sinner with insults and closed her door to her.

We had tried everything !

There remained nothing but revenge.

" Very well," I said to her, " why not try writing ?
Write a play, get it produced at this very theatre ?   Why

descend when there is a possibility of rising? Put your foot on that old woman! With one stride rise far above her head! Show off this lying, hypocritical, vicious society, which opens its houses to prostitutes, but closes them to a divorced wife. It's good stuff for a play."

But she was one of those soft natures, very susceptible, very easily impressed, but unable to strike back.

"No, no revenge!"

And cowardly and revengeful at the same time, she left vengeance to God; it came to the same thing in the end, but it put the responsibility on a man of straw.

But I persevered, and at last fortune favoured me. I had an order from a publisher to edit an illustrated book for children.

"Write the text," I suggested; "you will be paid a hundred francs for it."

I supplied her with reference books; I made her believe that she had done the work unaided, and she pocketed the hundred francs. But I paid a heavy penalty. The publisher stipulated that my name, which had come before the public as that of a playwright, should appear on the title-page. It was literary prostitution, and my enemies, who had predicted my incapacity of distinguishing myself in literature, triumphed.

After that I persuaded her to write an article for one of the morning papers. She acquitted herself fairly well. The article was accepted, but the paper made no payment.

I wore myself out in trying to raise a sovereign, and, succeeding after endless efforts, I handed it over to her with the white lie that it represented her remuneration from the paper.

Poor Marie! She was delighted to give her small earnings to her old mother, who supplemented her income by letting furnished apartments.

The old ladies began to look upon me as their saviour; copies of translations, unanimously rejected by theatrical managers in bygone days, appeared from drawers, where they had long lain forgotten. I was credited with the wondrous capacity to effect their acceptance, and burdened with futile commissions which interfered with my work and caused me no end of trouble. I had to fall back on my small savings because I wasted my time and used up my nervous energy; I could only afford one meal a day, and reverted to my old habit of going to bed without supper.

Encouraged by her few little successes, Marie undertook to write a play in five acts. I seemed to have sown into her soul all the sterile seed of my poetic inspirations. In this virgin soil it germinated and grew, while I remained unproductive, like a flower which shakes out its seed and withers. My soul was lacerated, sick to death. The influence of that little female brain, so different from the brain of a man, disturbed and disordered the mechanism of my thoughts. I was at a loss to understand why I thought so highly of her literary gifts, why I kept on urging her to write, for with the exception of her letters to me, which were mostly personal and frequently quite commonplace, I had no proof that she could write at all. She had become my living poem; she had taken the place of my vanished talent. Her personality was grafted on mine and was dominating it. I existed only through her; I, the mother-root, led an underground life, nourishing this tree which was growing sunwards and promising wonderful blossoms. I delighted in its marvellous beauty, never dreaming that the day would come when the offshoot would separate from the exhausted trunk, to bloom and dazzle independently, proud of the borrowed splendour.

The first act of her play was finished. I read it. Under the spell of my hallucination I found it perfect; I loudly expressed my sincere admiration and heartily congratulated the author. She was herself astonished at her talent, and I prophesied for her a brilliant future. But all of a sudden our plans were changed. Marie's mother remembered a friend, an artist, a very wealthy woman with a fine estate, and, what was of greater importance still, closely in touch with one of our leading actors whose wife was the rival and sworn enemy of the great tragedienne, Marie's former friend.

The artist, a spinster, vouched for the high moral standard of this couple, and they expressed themselves ready to undertake the guidance and supervision of Marie's studies until her first appearance in public. Marie was invited to stay for a fortnight with her mother's friend to discuss the matter. There she was to meet the great actor and his wife who, to fill her cup of happiness, had used their influence with the manager of the theatre on her behalf with very satisfactory results. His former reported refusal was thereby entirely contradicted, and turned out to have been a fabrication of her mother's, invented for the sole purpose of keeping her daughter off the stage.

Marie's future appeared to be safe. I could breathe freely, sleep undisturbed, work.

She stayed away for a fortnight. To judge from her scanty letters she was anything but dull. Her new friends, to whom she had given proofs of her talent, had told her that she would do well on the stage.

On her return she engaged rooms in a farmhouse and arranged with the farmer's wife to board her. She was free of her warders now, and we could spend unchaperoned week-ends together. Life was smiling at us, a little sadly, it is true, for a certain melancholy, the effect of her divorce, always remained. But in the country the burden of convention weighs less heavily than in town, and the summer sun soon dispelled the gloom which hung over our lives.

II

HER appearance under the patronage of the two famous actors was announced in the autumn and put a stop to all gossip. I did not like the part chosen for her. It was a small character-part in an old-fashioned play. But her teacher and patron counted on the sympathy of the audience and the effect of a good scene, in which she refused an aristocratic suitor who saw in her a rare ornament for his drawing-room, and declared that in her eyes the noble heart of the poor young man was infinitely more precious than all the wealth and title of the nobleman.

As I was dismissed from my post as her teacher, I was able to devote all my time and attention to my scientific studies, and the writing of a paper destined for some academy or other. This was necessary in order to prove myself a man of letters and efficient librarian. With ardent zeal I gave myself up to ethnographical research in connection with the farthest East. It acted like opium on my brain, which was exhausted by the struggles, cares and pains I had undergone. Inspired by the ambition to show myself worthy of my beloved, whose future appeared in the rosiest hues, I achieved wonders of industry; I shut myself up in the vaults of the Royal Castle from morning till night; I suffered from the damp and icy atmosphere without a complaint; I defied poverty and need.

Marie's appearance in public was postponed by the death of her little daughter, who died of brain fever; another month of tears, reproaches and remorse followed.

"It is a judgment on you," declared the child's grand-

157

mother, glad to thrust the poisoned dagger into the heart of the daughter-in-law whom she hated because she had brought dishonour on her name.

Marie was broken-hearted, and spent day and night at the bedside of the dying child, under the roof of her former husband, chaperoned by her late mother-in-law. The father was overcome with grief at the death of his only child, and, bowed down with sorrow, he longed to meet again the friend of former days, the witness of the past. One evening, a few days after the little girl's funeral, my landlady informed me that the Baron had called and had left a message to the effect that he hoped to see me at his house.

Considering the unusual circumstances which had led up to the breach, I wanted anything but a reconciliation. I sent him a polite refusal.

A quarter of an hour had hardly elapsed when Marie herself appeared, dressed in deep mourning, her eyes full of tears, and begged me to comply with the request of the inconsolable Baron.

I found this mission in abominable taste. I rated her soundly, and pointed out to her how ambiguous and unjustifiable in the eyes of the world such a situation would be. She upbraided me with my prejudices, implored me, appealed to my generous disposition, and ended by overruling all my objections; I agreed to the indelicate proposal.

I had sworn never again to enter the house in which the drama had been enacted. But the widower had removed. He had taken rooms not far from us; I was glad to be spared a renewed visit to the old place, and accompanied the divorced wife on her visit to her late husband.

The mourning, the evident grief, the grave and gloomy appearance of the house all combined to rob our meeting of any trace of strangeness or embarrassment.

The habit of seeing these two people together was a bar to any feeling of jealousy on my part, and the tactful and cordial bearing of the Baron helped to reassure me completely.

We dined together, we drank and played cards just as in the old days.

On the following day we met in my room; on a third evening at Marie's, who was now living in the house of an old lady. We fell into our former habits, and Marie was happy to see us together. It comforted her, and since we had ourselves under perfect control nobody was offended or aggrieved. The Baron looked upon us as being secretly engaged, his love for Marie seemed to be dead. Sometimes he even talked of his unhappy love-affair, for Matilda was carefully watched by her father and out of his reach. . . . Marie teased and comforted him alternately, and he made no secret, now, of his true feelings.

At parting their intimacy was more marked, but instead of rousing my jealousy it merely excited my disgust.

One day Marie told me that she had been to see the Baron, and stayed to have dinner with him; she justified her visit by saying that she had to talk to him on urgent business in connection with her daughter's estate which the Baron inherited.

I objected to this want of taste; in fact, I told her that her conduct was downright indecent. She burst out laughing, teasingly reminded me of my former railings against prejudice, and in the end I joined in her laughter. It was ridiculous, it was unusual, but it was good form to laugh at everything, and a splendid thing to see virtue rewarded.

After that she visited the Baron whenever she pleased, and I believe he helped her to study her part.

Up to now we had had no quarrels, for any jealousy I

might have felt disappeared as soon as I got used to the state of things, and I never quite lost the old illusion that they were husband and wife. But one evening Marie came to see me alone. On helping her to remove her cloak I noticed that her dress was somewhat deranged. It roused my suspicions. She sat down on the sofa opposite the looking-glass, talking volubly all the time. Her conversation struck me as forced, she cast furtive glances at her reflection and stealthily tried to smooth her hair.

A horrible thought flashed into my mind. Unable to control my agitation, I exclaimed—

" Where have you been ? "

" With Gustav."

" What did you do there ? "

She started, but quickly suppressing her emotion, she replied—

" I was studying my part."

" It's a lie ! "

She made an angry exclamation ; she accused me of being absurdly jealous, deluged me with explanations. I wavered, and as we were invited out that evening I had to postpone all further investigation.

Thinking of this incident to-day, I would swear a solemn oath that she committed bigamy in those days, to say the least of it. But at that time I was completely deceived by her trickery. What had happened? . . . Probably this—

She had dined alone with the Baron ; they had had coffee and liqueurs ; she was seized with that after-dinner lassitude ; the Baron advised her to lie down on the sofa and rest awhile, a proposal which did not displease her . . . and the rest followed as a matter of course. Solitude, complete confidence, old memories, increased temptation, and the lonely man succumbed. Why deny themselves, as long as no one knew? She was her own mistress, since she had never taken money from her lover, and to break a promise—what is that to a woman! Perhaps she already regretted his loss; perhaps she had come to the conclusion that he understood her needs better than I; perhaps, now that her curiosity was satisfied, she yearned again for the stronger man; for in the struggle for the love of a woman the sensitive and delicate lover, may he be never so ardent, is always beaten by the athlete.

It was more than probable that she gave herself to him, more especially as she was free from responsibility and her woman's heart pitied the lonely man. Had I been in the place of the offended husband should I have acted otherwise? I hardly think so.

But since the beloved lips never tired of using the sublime words "honour," "decency," "morality," I refused to harbour any suspicions.

For these reasons a woman will always get the better of her lover, if he be a man of honour. He flatters himself that he is the only one, because he wants to be the only one, and the wish is father to the thought.

To-day Marie's loyalty seems to me in the highest degree improbable, incredible, impossible.

It was also a significant fact that the Baron, when we were alone together, always manifested a lively interest in other women; and one evening, after dining with him at a restaurant, he went so far as to ask me for certain addresses. Doubtless this was done in order to deceive me.

Another thing which struck me was his attitude towards Marie; he treated her with a somewhat contemptuous courtesy; she behaved like a cocotte, and her passion for me seemed to be more and more on the wane.

M

III

At last Marie appeared before the footlights. She was a success for many and complex reasons. Firstly, everybody was curious to see a baroness on the stage; secondly, the middle-classes were sympathetic because they delighted in the blow dealt to aristocratic prestige by this divorce; the bachelors, the sexless, the enemies of matrimonial slavery, lavished flowers on her; not to forget the friends and relations of the great actor, who were interested in her because he had been her teacher and was bringing her out.

After the performance the Baron asked both of us, and the old lady with whom Marie was living, to supper.

Everybody was charmed with the result and intoxicated with the success. I was displeased with Marie's appearance because she had not removed her make-up, and her hair was still dressed as she had worn it on the stage. She was no longer the virginal mother with whom I had fallen in love, but an actress with insolent gestures, bad manners, boastful, overbearing, behaving with a kind of offensive foppishness.

In her imagination she had scaled the highest summits of art, and she dismissed all my remarks, my suggestions, with a shrug of her shoulders or a condescending, "My dear, you know nothing about it."

The Baron wore a look of dejection, like an unhappy lover. But for my presence he would have kissed her. Under the influence of an incredible quantity of Madeira he opened his heart to us, and regretted that art, the divine, should claim so many cruel sacrifices.

162

The press—which had been well-managed—confirmed her success, and an engagement seemed likely to follow.

Two photographers fought for the honour of being permitted to photograph the débutante. A successful little magazine sold the portrait of the new star, together with her biography.

What struck me most in looking at these new portraits was the fact that not one of them resembled the old one in my possession. Was it possible that her character, the expression of her face, could have changed in so short a time, in a year? Or was she a different woman when she reflected the love, the tenderness, the compassion which my eyes radiated as soon as I looked at her? The expression of her face on these portraits was vulgar, hard and insolent, every feature expressed a cruel coquetry, a challenge. One pose in particular disgusted me. She was represented leaning over the back of a low chair in such a manner that the beholder could see her bosom, which was only partly hidden by a fan resting against the upper part of her dress. Her eyes seemed riveted on the eyes of an invisible person, not myself, for my love, coupled with respect and tenderness, never caressed her with the shameless sensuality which roused in her the passion of a wanton. The photograph reminded me of those obscene pictures which are furtively offered to the passers-by at the doors of low coffee-houses under cover of the night.

When she offered me this portrait I refused to accept it.

" What! " she exclaimed in a piteous voice, which for a moment revealed her carefully concealed want of true refinement, " you refuse my photograph? Then you don't love me any more! "

When a woman says to her lover, " You don't love me any more," she has already ceased to love him.

I knew from this moment that her love was growing

M 2

cold. She realised that her feeble soul had drawn from me the courage, the boldness necessary to arrive at her goal, and she wanted to be rid of the troublesome creditor. She had been stealing my thoughts while she seemed to scorn them with her contemptuous, "You know nothing about it, my dear!"

This uncultured woman, whose only accomplishment was her fluent French, whose education had been neglected, who had been brought up in the country, who knew nothing of literature or the stage, to whom I had given the first lessons in the correct pronunciation of Swedish, to whom I had explained the secrets of metrics and prosody, treated me as if I were an idiot.

I advised her to select for her second appearance in public, which was to take place shortly, the principal part in the best melodrama on the repertoire. She refused. But a few days later she informed me casually that the idea had occurred to her to choose this particular part. I analysed it for her, sketched the costumes, drew her attention to all the points to be made, showed her how to make her entrances and exits, and pointed out to her the features which should be specially emphasized.

A secret struggle went on between the Baron and myself. He, who stage-managed the performances of the Royal Guards, instructed the play-acting soldiers, fondly imagined himself to be better acquainted with theatrical affairs than I was. Marie valued his so-called hints more highly; accepted him as her authority, scorned my suggestions. Oh! the vileness of his conception of æsthetics! He extolled the commonplace, the vulgar, the banal, because, as he said, it was true nature.

I admitted his arguments as far as modern comedy was concerned, for here the characters are depicted among the thousand details of everyday life. But his theory became impossible when applied, for instance, to English melodrama; great passions cannot be expressed in the same way as the whims and witticisms of a drawing-room conversation.

But this distinction was too subtle for a mediocre brain, which could only generalise and assume that because a certain thing happened in one case, it must infallibly become the rule and happen in all others.

On the day before her appearance Marie showed me her dresses. In spite of my opposition and entreaties she had chosen a dull grey material, most unbecoming to her because it gave her complexion an ashen hue. Her only reply had been a curt repulse and the truly feminine argument—

" But Mrs. X., the great tragedienne, created the part in a grey dress !"

" True, but Mrs. X. is not fair like you! And what suits a dark woman doesn't always suit a fair one."

She had not been able to see my point and had only been angry with me.

I had prophesied a fiasco, and her second appearance really was a dead failure.

The tears, the reproaches, the insults even which followed !

As misfortune would have it, a week later the great actress appeared in the same part, in a special performance, and received cart-loads of flowers.

Of course Marie was furious with me and made me responsible for her failure, simply because I had prophesied it ; the grief and disappointment brought her still nearer to the Baron; it drew them together with the sympathy which always unites inferior characters.

I, the man of letters, the playwright, the dramatic critic, at home in all the literatures, through my work and position at the library in correspondence with the finest intellects of the world, I was cast aside like a worn-out garment, treated like an idiot, considered of no more importance than a footman or a dog.

But although her second appearance had been a failure, she was engaged with a pay of 2,400 crowns [1] per annum. She had acquitted herself fairly well, but she had no great career before her. She would never rise above the level of a " useful actress " ; she would be cast for small parts, society women, mere dressed-up dolls, and spend her days at the dressmaker's. Three, four, sometimes five different dresses on one and the same evening would swallow up her insufficient pay.

What bitter disappointments, what heart-rending scenes, as she watched her parts grow smaller and smaller, until they consisted of a few sentences only. Her room had the appearance of a dressmaker's workshop, littered with dress materials, patterns and millinery. The mother, the real *grande dame* who had left her drawing-rooms, renounced dress and fashion, to devote her life to a lofty ideal of art, had become a bungling seamstress who worked at her sewing machine till midnight, so that she might play before an indifferent bourgeoisie for a few minutes the part of a society woman.

The waste of time behind the scenes during rehearsal, when she stood in the wings for hours waiting for her cue which should bring her before the footlights to say two or three words, developed in her a taste for gossip, for idle talk and risky stories; it killed all honest striving to rise above her condition; the soul was shorn of its wings and was flung to earth, into the gutter.

The disintegrating process went on. She continued to deteriorate, and after her dresses had been remodelled again and again for want of means to buy new ones, she was deprived of even her small parts and degraded to the rôle of a walker on. Poverty was staring her in the face, and her mother, a modern Cassandra, made life a burden

---

[1] A Swedish crown is equivalent to 1s. 4d.

to her; the public, well acquainted with her sensational divorce, and the premature death of her little girl, cried out against the unfaithful wife, the unnatural mother. It was but a question of time and the manager of the theatre would not be able to protect her against the antipathy of the audience; the great actor, her teacher, disowned her and admitted his mistake in believing in her talent.

So much ado, so much unhappiness, to humour a woman who did not know her own mind.

And still matters grew worse, for Marie's mother suddenly died of heart disease, of a broken heart, as it was called, broken with sorrow, caused by her unnatural daughter. Again my honour was involved. I was furious with the injustice of the world, and made a desperate effort to vindicate her honour. I proposed the foundation of a weekly paper, for the discussion of the drama, music, literature and art, and she, thankful now for every effort to help her, gratefully accepted my proposal. In this paper she was to make her début as a critic and writer of feuilletons, and so gradually become acquainted with publishers. She sunk two hundred crowns in the enterprise. I undertook the editorial work and proof-reading. Since I was well aware of my complete incapacity as a business manager, I left her to attend to the sale and advertisements, the proceeds of which she was to share with the manager of her theatre, who was also the proprietor of a news stall.

The first number was set and looked very well indeed. It contained a leader written by one of our rising artists; an original article from a correspondent in Rome; another one from Paris; a critique on a musical performance by a distinguished writer and contributor to one of the first Stockholm papers; a literary review written by myself; a feuilleton and reports on first nights by Marie.

It would have been impossible to improve the arrangements made; the great thing was to publish the first number at the time advertised. Everything was ready, but at the last moment we lacked the necessary funds and credit.

Alas! I had put my fate into the hands of a woman! On the day of the publication she remained calmly in bed and slept till broad daylight.

Convinced that everything was well, I went to town, but everywhere on my way I was greeted with sarcastic smiles.

"Well, where is the wonderful paper to be had?" I was asked the question dozens of times by the numerous people interested in its appearance.

"Everywhere!"

"Or nowhere!"

I went into a newspaper shop.

"We haven't received it yet," said the assistant behind the counter.

I rushed to the printing-office. It had not left the press yet.

A complete failure! We had an angry scene. Her inborn carelessness and ignorance of the publishing trade exonerated her to some extent. She had completely relied on her friend, the theatrical manager.

The two hundred crowns were gone. My time, my honour, the eager thought I had devoted to the scheme, all were wasted.

In this general shipwreck one haunting thought remained: our condition was hopeless.

I proposed that we should die together. What was to become of us? She was quite broken down and I had not the strength to lift her up a second time.

"Let us die," I said to her. "Don't let us degenerate into walking corpses and obstruct the path of the living."

She refused.

What a coward you were, my proud Marie! And how cruel it was of you to make me a witness of the spectacle of your downfall, the laughter and sneers of the onlookers!

I spent the evening at my club, and when I went home that night I was intoxicated.

I went to see her early on the following morning. The alcohol seemed to have made me more clear-sighted. For the first time I noticed the change in her. Her room was untidy, her dress slovenly, her beloved little feet were thrust into a pair of old slippers, the stockings hung in wrinkles round her ankles. What squalor!

Her vocabulary had become enriched by some ugly theatrical slang; her gestures were reminiscent of the street, her eyes looked at me with hatred, an expression of bitterness drew down the corners of her mouth.

She remained stooping over her work, without looking at me, as if she were thinking evil thoughts.

Suddenly, without raising her head, she said hoarsely—

"Do you know, Axel, what a woman is justified in expecting from the man with whom she is on intimate terms, such as we are?"

Thunderstruck, unwilling to trust my ears, I faltered—

"No . . . what?"

"What does a woman expect from her lover?"

"Love!"

"And what else?"

"Money!"

The vulgar word saved her from further questioning, and I left her, convinced that I had guessed correctly.

"Prostitute! Prostitute!" I said to myself, stumbling through the streets, the autumnal appearance of which depressed my spirits. We had arrived at the last stage. . . . All that remained to do was to make payment for pleasures received, to admit the trade without shame.

If she had been poor, at least, suffering from want!

But she had just come into her mother's money, the entire furniture of a house, and a number of shares, some of doubtful value, but nevertheless representing two or three thousand crowns; moreover, she was still receiving her pay regularly from the theatre.

I could not understand her attitude . . . until suddenly I remembered her landlady and intimate friend.

She was an abominable, elderly woman, with the suspicious manners of a procuress; nobody knew how she lived; she was always in debt, yet always extravagantly and strikingly dressed; somehow she managed to ingratiate herself with people, and she always ended by asking them for a small loan, eternally bewailing her miserable existence. A shady character, who hated me because I saw through her.

Now I suddenly remembered an incident which had happened two or three months ago, but which had not interested me at the time. The woman had extracted a promise from a friend of Marie's to lend her a thousand crowns. The promise had remained a promise. Eventually Marie, giving way to pressure and anxious to save the reputation of her friend, who was badly compromised, guaranteed to find the money, and actually raised the sum. But instead of gratitude she reaped nothing but reproaches from her friend, and when it came to explanations, the old woman insisted on her perfect innocence and laid the full blame on Marie's shoulders. I had at the time expressed my dislike and distrust of her, and urged Marie to have nothing to do with an individual whose manipulations came very close to blackmail.

But she had exonerated her false friend at the time. . . . Later on she told a different story altogether, talked of a misunderstanding; in the end the whole incident became "an invention of my evil imagination."

Possibly this woman had suggested to Marie the vile idea of "presenting me with the bill." It must have

been so, for the suggestion had not been made easily and
was most unlike her. I tried to make myself believe it,
hope it.

If she had merely asked me for the money which she
had invested in the paper, the money which had been
lost through her fault—that would have been female
mathematics. Or, if she had insisted on an immediate
marriage! But she had no wish to be married, I was
sure of that. It was a question of paying for the love,
the kisses she had given me. It was payment she demanded. . . . Supposing I sent her in my bill : for my
work according to time and quality, for the waste of
brain power, of nerve force, for my heart's blood, my
name, my honour, my sufferings ; the bill for my career,
ruined, perhaps, for ever.

But no, it was her privilege to send in the first bill ;
I took no exception to that.

I spent my evening at a restaurant, wandered through
the streets and pondered the problem of degradation.
Why is it so painful to watch a person sink? It must
be because there is something unnatural in it, for nature
demands personal progress, evolution, and every backward
step means the disintegration of force.

The same argument applies to the life of the community
where everybody strives to reach the material or spiritual
summits. Thence comes the tragic feeling which seizes
us in the contemplation of failure, tragic as autumn,
sickness and death. This woman, who had not yet
reached her thirtieth year, had been young, beautiful,
frank, honest, amiable, strong and well-bred ; in two short
years she had been so degraded, had fallen so low.

For a moment I tried to blame myself ; the thought that
the fault was mine would have been a comfort to me, for
it would have made her shame seem less. But try as I
would, I did not succeed, for had I not taught her the cult
of the beautiful? the love of high ideals? the longing to do

noble acts? While she adopted the vulgarities of her theatrical friends, I had improved, I had acquired the manners and language of fashionable society, I had learned that self-control which keeps emotion in check and is considered the hall-mark of good breeding. I had become chaste in love, anxious to spare modesty, not to offend against beauty and seemliness, for thus only can we forget the brutality of an act which to my mind is much more spiritual than physical.

I was rough sometimes, it is true, but never vulgar. I killed, but never wounded. I called a spade a spade, but never hinted and insinuated; my ideas were my own, prompted by the situations in which I happened to find myself; I never tried to dazzle with the witticisms of musical comedies or comic papers.

I loved cleanliness, purity, beauty in my daily surroundings; I preferred to refuse an invitation to accepting it and appearing badly dressed. I never received her in dressing-gown and slippers; I may not always have been able to offer a guest more than bread and butter and a glass of beer, but there was always a clean table-cloth.

I had not set her a bad example; it was not my fault that she had deteriorated. Her love for me was dead, therefore she did not want to please me any longer. She belonged to the public, it was that fact which had made her the wanton who could calmly present her bill for so many nights of pleasure. . . .

During the next few days I shut myself up in my library. I mourned for my love, my splendid, foolish, divine love. All was over, and the battlefield on which the struggle had raged was silent and still. Two dead and so many wounded to satisfy a woman who was not worth a pair of old shoes! If her passion had at least been roused by the longing for motherhood, if she had been guided by the unrealised instincts which force those unfortunates who are mothers on the streets! But she detested children; in her eyes motherhood was degrading. Unnatural and perverse woman that she was, she debased the maternal instinct to a vulgar pleasure. Her race was doomed to extinction because she was a degenerate, in the process of dissolution; but she concealed this dissolution under high-sounding phrases, proclaimed that it was our duty to live for higher ends, for the good of humanity at large.

I loathed her now, I tried to forget her. I paced the room, up and down, up and down, before the rows of book-shelves, unable to rid myself of the accursed nightmare which haunted me. I had no desire for her, or for her company, for she inspired me with disgust; and yet a deep compassion, an almost paternal tenderness made me feel responsible for her future. I knew that if I left her to her own devices, she would go under, and end either as the mistress of her late husband, or the mistress of all the world.

I was powerless to lift her up, powerless to struggle out of the morass into which we had fallen. I resigned myself to remain tied to her, even if I had to witness and share in her downward course. She was dragging me down with her—life had become a burden to me, I had lost all enthusiasm for my work. The instinct of self-preservation, hope, were dead. I wanted nothing, desired nothing. I had developed into a complete misanthrope; I frequently turned away from the door of my restaurant and, for-going dinner, returned home, threw myself on my sofa and buried myself under my rugs. There I lay, like a wild beast that has received its death wound, rigid, with an empty brain, unable to think or sleep, waiting for the end.

One day, however, I was sitting in a back room of my restaurant, a private room where lovers meet and shabby coats hide themselves, both afraid of the daylight. All at once a well-known voice woke me from my reverie : a man wished me a good afternoon.

He was an unsuccessful architect, a lost member of our late Bohemia, which was now scattered to all the winds.

" You are still among the living, then ? " he said, sitting down opposite me.

" I am . . . but what about you ? "

" I'm so-so . . . off to Paris to-morrow . . . some fool left me ten thousand crowns."

" Lucky dog ! "

" Unfortunately I have to devour it all by myself . . ."

" The misfortune is not so great, I know a set of teeth ready to help you."

" Really ?   Would you care to come ? . . ."

" Only too glad to ! "

" Is it a bargain then ? "

" It's a bargain."

" To-morrow night, by the six o'clock train, to Paris. . . ."

" And afterwards ? . . ."

" A bullet through the head ! "

" The devil !   Where did you get this idea from ? "

" From your face !   Suicide is plainly written on it ! "

" Haruspex !   Well, pack up and come along ! "

When I saw Marie that night I told her the good news. She listened with every appearance of pleasure, wished me a pleasant time, and repeated again and again that it would do me a world of good, would refresh me mentally.   In short, she seemed well pleased, and overwhelmed me with affection, which touched me deeply.

We spent the evening together, talking of the days which had gone by.   We made no plans, for we had lost faith in the future.   Then we parted. . . . For ever ? . . . The question was not mooted ; we silently agreed to leave it to chance to reunite us or not.

IV

THE journey really rejuvenated me. It stirred up the memories of my early youth and I felt a mad joy surging in my heart; I wanted to forget the last two years of misery, and not for one single moment did I feel inclined to speak of Marie. The whole tragedy of the divorce was like a repulsive heap of offal, from which I was eager to fly without turning round. I could not help smiling in my sleeve at times, like a fugitive who is firmly resolved not to be taken again; I felt like a debtor who has escaped from his creditors and is hiding in a distant country.

For two weeks I revelled in the Paris theatres, museums and libraries. I received no letters from Marie, and was beginning to hope that she had got over our separation and that everything was well in the best of all possible worlds.

But after a certain time I grew tired of wandering about, and sated with so many new and strong impressions; things began to lose their interest. I stayed in my room and read the papers, oppressed by vague apprehensions, by an inexplicable uneasiness.

The vision of the white woman, the Fata Morgana of the virginal mother began to haunt me and disturbed my peace. The picture of the insolent actress was wiped out of my memory; I remembered only the Baroness, young, beautiful; her fragile body transfigured and clothed with the beauty of the Land of Promise, dreamed of by the *ascètes.*

I was indulging in those painful and yet delicious dreams
175

when I received a letter from Marie, in which she informed me in heartbreaking words that she was about to become a mother, and implored me to save her from dishonour.

Without a moment's hesitation I packed my portmanteau. I left Paris by the first train for Stockholm. I was going to make her my wife.

I had no doubt about the paternity of the expected baby. I looked upon the result of our irregular relations as a blessing, as the end of our sufferings; but also as a fact which burdened us with a heavy responsibility, which might spell ruin; at the same time, however, it was the starting point into the unknown; something quite new. Moreover, I always had a very high conception of married life; I considered it the only possible form under which two persons of opposite sex could live together. Life together held no terror for me. My love received a fresh stimulus from the fact that Marie was about to become a mother; she arose purified, ennobled, from the mire of our illicit relationship.

On my arrival at Stockholm she received me very ungraciously and accused me of having deceived her. We had a painful scene—but need she have been so surprised after all that had happened during the last twelve months?

She hated matrimony. Her objectionable friend had impressed upon her that a married woman is a slave who works for her husband gratuitously. I detest slaves, and therefore proposed a modern ménage, in keeping with our views.

I suggested that we should take three rooms, one for her, one for myself and a common room. We should neither do our own housekeeping, nor have any servants in the house. Dinner should be sent in from a neighbouring restaurant, breakfast and supper be prepared in the kitchen by a daily servant. In this way expenses were easily calculated and the causes for unpleasantness reduced to a minimum.

To avoid every suspicion of living on my wife's dowry, I suggested that it should be settled on her. In the North a man considers himself dishonoured by the acceptance of his wife's dowry, which in civilised countries forms a sort of contribution from the wife, and creates in her the illusion that her husband is not keeping her entirely. To avoid a bad start it is the custom in Germany and Denmark for the wife to furnish the house; this creates the impression on the husband that he is living in his wife's house, and in the latter that she is in her own home, maintaining her husband.

Marie had recently inherited her mother's furniture, articles without any intrinsic value, their only claim to distinction being a certain sentimental merit of old association and an air of antiquity. She proposed that she should furnish the rooms, arguing that it would be absurd to buy furniture for three rooms when she had enough for six. I willingly agreed to her proposal.

There only remained one more point, the main one, the expected baby. We were agreed on the necessity of keeping its birth a secret, and we decided to place it with a reliable nurse until such time as we could adopt it.

The wedding was fixed for the 31st of December. During the remaining two months I strained every nerve to make adequate provision for the future. For this purpose, and knowing that Marie would soon be compelled to renounce her work at the theatre, I renewed my literary efforts. I worked with such ease that at the end of the first month I was able to offer for publication a volume of short stories, which was accepted without difficulty.

Fortune favoured me; I was appointed assistant-librarian with a salary of twelve hundred crowns, and

N

when the collections were transferred from the old building to the new one I received a bonus of six hundred crowns. This was good fortune indeed, and taken together with other favourable omens I began to think that a relentless fate had tired of persecuting me.

The first and foremost magazine in Finland offered me a post on the staff as reviewer at fifty crowns for each article. The official Swedish Journal, published by the Academy, gave me the much-coveted order to write the reviews on art for thirty-five crowns the column. Besides all this I was entrusted with the revision of the classics which were being published at that time.

All this good fortune came to me in those two months, the most fateful months of my whole life.

My short stories appeared almost immediately and were a great success. I was hailed as a master of this particular style; it was said that the book was epoch-making in the literature of Sweden, because it was the first to introduce modern realism.

It was unspeakable happiness to me to lay at the feet of my poor, adored Marie a name which, apart from the titles of a royal secretary and assistant-librarian, was beginning to be known, with every prospect of a brilliant future.

Some day I should be able to give her a fresh start, to re-open her theatrical career, which for the moment had been interrupted by, perhaps, undeserved misfortune.

Fortune was smiling at us with a tear in the eye. . . .

The banns were published. I packed my belongings and said good-bye to my attic, the witness of many joys and sorrows. I marched into that prison which all fear, but which, perhaps, we had less cause to dread than others, since we had foreseen all dangers, removed all stumbling blocks. . . . And yet . . .

PART III

I

WHAT inexpressible happiness it is to be married! To be always near the beloved one, safe from the prying eyes of the fatuous world. It is as if one had regained the home of one's childhood with its sheltering love, a safe port after the storm, a nest which awaits the little ones.

Surrounded by nothing but objects which belonged to her, mementoes and relics of her parents' house, I felt as if I were a shoot grafted on her trunk; the oil paintings of her ancestors deluded me into thinking that I had been adopted by her family, because her ancestors will also be the ancestors of my children. I received everything from her hand; she made me wear her father's watch and chain; my dinner was served on her mother's china; she poured on me a continuous stream of trifling presents, relics of old times, which had belonged to famous warriors celebrated by the poets of her country, a fact which impressed me not a little. She was the benefactress, the generous giver of all these gifts, and I entirely forgot that it was *I* who had reclaimed *her*, lifted her out of the mire, made her the wife of a man with brilliant prospects; forgot that she had been an unknown actress, a divorced wife condemned by her sisters, a woman whom very probably I had saved from the worst.

What a happy life we led! We realised the dream of freedom in marriage. No double-bed, no common bedroom, no common dressing-room; nothing unseemly degraded the sanctity of our union. Marriage as we understood and realised it was a splendid institution. The tender good-nights, repeated again and again; the joy of wishing each other good-morning, of asking how we had slept, were they not due to the fact that we occupied separate rooms? How delightful were the stolen visits to each other, the courtesy and tenderness which we never forgot! How different compared with the brazen boldness, the more or less graciously endured brutalities which are as a rule inseparable from matrimony.

I got through an amazing amount of work, staying at home by the side of my beloved wife who was sewing tiny garments for the expected baby. What a lot of time I had wasted in rendezvous and idleness in the days gone by!

After a month of the closest companionship Marie was laid up with a premature confinement. We had a tiny daughter, hardly able to draw breath. Without a moment's delay the baby was taken charge of by a nurse whom we knew to be a decent woman, and two days later it passed away as it had come, without pain, from sheer want of vitality, just after it had received private baptism.

The mother received the news with regret, but it was regret not unmingled with relief. A burden of infinite cares and worries had fallen off her shoulders, for well she knew that social prejudice would not have permitted her to keep the prematurely-born infant under our own roof.

After this incident we firmly made up our minds to one thing: No more children! We dreamed of a life together, a life of perfect comradeship, of a man and a woman, loving and supplementing each other, but living their own lives, restlessly straining every nerve to realise their individual ambitions.

Now that every obstacle had been removed, every threatening danger overcome, we began to breathe freely and reconsider our position. I was ostracised by my relations, no meddlesome member of my family threatened the peace of our home, and since the only relative of my wife's who lived on the spot was her aunt, we were spared the frequent calls and visits which so often give rise to serious troubles and trials in a young *ménage*.

II

Six weeks later I made the discovery that two intruders had insinuated themselves into my wife's confidence.

One of them was a dog, a King Charles, a blear-eyed little monster, which greeted me with deafening yelping and barking every time I entered the house, just as if I had been a stranger. I always disliked dogs, those protectors of cowards who lack the courage to fight an assailant themselves; but I particularly disliked this dog, because it was a relic of her first marriage, a constant reminder of her late husband.

The first time I protested, and ordered it to lie down, my wife reproached me gently, and made excuses for the little beast, which she called her late daughter's legacy, pretending to be horror-struck at this suddenly revealed strain of cruelty in my disposition.

One day I found traces of the little monster on the drawing-room carpet. I punished it, and she called me a coward who ill-treated dumb creatures.

"But what else could I do, my dear? It's no use arguing with animals; they don't understand our language."

She began to cry, and sobbingly confessed that she could not help being afraid of a cruel man. . . .

And the monster continued to dirty the drawing-room carpet.

I decided to take the trouble to train the dog, and did my utmost to convince her that a little perseverance does wonders with an intelligent animal.

She lost her temper, and for the first time drew

my attention to the fact that the carpet belonged to her.

"Take it away, then; I never undertook to live in a pig-sty."

The carpet remained where it was, but the dog was watched more carefully; my remonstrances had some effect.

Nevertheless fresh catastrophes occurred.

In order to keep down our expenditure and save the trouble and expense of a kitchen fire, we decided to have a cold supper in the evening. Entering the kitchen accidentally on one occasion, I was amazed to find a roaring fire and the maid engaged in frying veal cutlets.

"Who are these cutlets for?"

"For the dog, sir."

My wife joined us.

"My dear girl——"

"Excuse me, I paid for them!"

"But I have to be content with a cold supper! I fare worse than your dog. . . . And I, too, pay."

She paid!

Henceforth the dog was looked upon as a martyr. Marie and a friend, a brand-new friend, adopted the habit of worshipping the beast, which they had decorated with a blue ribbon, behind locked doors. And the dear friend heaved a sigh at the thought of so much human malice incarnate in my detestable person.

An irrepressible hatred for this interloper who was everywhere in my way, took possession of me. My wife, with a down pillow and some blankets, made a bed for it which obstructed my way whenever I wanted to say good-morning or good-night to her. And on every Saturday, the day I looked forward to through a week of toil, counting on a pleasant evening with her alone when, undisturbed, we could talk of the past and make plans for the future, she spent three hours with her friend in the kitchen; the maid made up a blazing fire; the whole place was turned upside down—and why? Because Saturday was the monster's tub-day.

"Don't you think you are treating me heartlessly, cruelly?"

"How dare you call her heartless?" exclaimed the friend. "A gentler soul never breathed. Why, she doesn't even shrink from sacrificing her own and her husband's happiness to a poor forsaken animal!"

Some little time after I sat down to a dinner which was below criticism.

For some time past the food which was sent in daily from a neighbouring restaurant had been steadily deteriorating, but my beloved wife, with her irresistible sweetness, had made me believe that I had grown more fastidious. And I had not doubted her word, for I always took her at her own valuation and looked upon her as the soul of truth and candour.

The fatal dinner was served. There was nothing on the dish but bones and sinews.

"What is this you are putting before me?" I asked the maid.

"I am sorry, sir," she replied, "but I had orders to reserve the best pieces for the dog."

Beware of the woman who has been found out! Her wrath will fall on your head with fourfold strength.

She sat as if struck by lightning, unmasked, shown up as a liar, a cheat even, for she had always insisted that she was paying for the dog's food out of her own pocket. Her pallor and silence made me feel sorry for her. I blushed for her, and hating to see her humiliated, I behaved like a generous conqueror, and tried to console her. I playfully patted her cheek and told her not to mind.

But generosity was not one of her virtues. She burst into a torrent of angry words : My origin was very evident ; I had no education, no manners, since I rebuked her before a servant, a stupid girl who had misunderstood her instructions. There was no doubt that I, and I only, was to blame. Hysterics followed, she grew more and more violent, jumped up from her chair, threw herself on the sofa, raved like a maniac, sobbed and screamed that she was dying.

I was sceptical, and remained untouched.

Such a fuss, and all about a dog !

But she continued to scream ; it was a frightful scene ; a terrible cough shook her frame, which since her confinement had grown even more fragile ; I was deceived after all, and sent for the doctor.

He came, examined her heart, felt her pulse, and surlily turned to go ; I stopped him on the threshold.

" Well ? "

" H'm ! nothing at all," he answered, putting on his overcoat.

" Nothing ? . . . But. . . ."

" Nothing whatever. . . . You ought to know women. . . . Good day ! "

If I had only known then what I know now, if I had known the secret, the remedy for hysteria which I have discovered since ! But the only thing which occurred to me at the time was to kiss her eyes and ask her pardon. And that was what I did. She pressed me to her heart, called me her sensible child who should take care of her because she was very delicate, very weak, and would die one day if her little boy had not the sense to avoid scenes.

To make her quite happy I took her dog upon my knees and stroked its back ; and for the next half hour I was rewarded with looks full of the tenderest affection and gratitude.

From that day the dog was allowed to do exactly as it liked, and it dirtied the place without shame or restraint. Sometimes it seemed to me that it did it out of revenge. But I controlled my temper.

I waited for a favourable opportunity, for the happy chance which would deliver me from the torture of a life spent in an unclean home. . . .

And the moment arrived. On returning to dinner one day, I found my wife in tears. She was in great distress. Dinner was not ready. The maid was looking for the lost dog.

Hardly able to conceal my joy, I made every effort to comfort my inconsolable wife. But she could not understand my sympathy with her grief, for she realised my inward satisfaction in finding the enemy gone.

" You are delighted, I know you are," she exclaimed. " You find amusement in the misfortunes of your friends. That shows how full of malice you are, and that you don't love me any more."

" My love for you is as great as ever it was, believe me, but I detest your dog."

" If you love me, you must love my dog too ! "

" If I didn't love you, I should have struck you before now ! "

The effect of my words was startling. To strike a woman ! Carried away by her resentment, she reproached me with having turned out her dog, poisoned it.

We went to every police-station, we paid a visit to the knacker, and in the end the disturber of our peace and happiness was recovered. My wife and her friend, regarding me as a poisoner, or at any rate a potential poisoner, celebrated its recovery with great rejoicings.

Henceforth the monster was kept a prisoner in my wife's bedroom ; that charming retreat of love, furnished with exquisite taste, was turned into a dog's kennel.

Our small flat became uninhabitable, our home-life full

of jars. I ventured to make a remark to the effect, but my wife replied that her room was her own.

Then I started on a merciless crusade. I left her severely alone; and by and by she found my reserve unbearable.

"Why do you never come to say good-morning to me now?"

"Because I can't get near you."

She sulked. I sulked too. For another fortnight I lived in celibacy. Then, tired out, she found herself compelled to make friends. She took the first step, but she hated me for it.

She decided to have the troublesome interloper destroyed. But instead of having it done forthwith, she invited her friend to assist her in the enactment of a farewell farce, entitled "The Last Moments of the Condemned." She went to the length of begging me on her knees to embrace the wretched little brute as a proof that I harboured no ill-will, arguing that dogs might possibly have an immortal soul and that we might meet again in another world. The result was that I gave the dog its life and freedom, an action which found its reward in her gratitude.

At times I fancied that I was living in a lunatic asylum, but one does not stand upon trifles when one is in love.

This scene, "The Last Moments of the Condemned," was renewed every six months during the next three years.

You, reader, who read this plain tale of a man, a woman and a dog, will not deny me your compassion, for my sufferings lasted three times three hundred and sixty-five days of twenty-four hours each. You will perhaps admire me, for I remained alive. If it be true, however, that I am insane, as my wife maintains, blame no one but myself, for I ought to have had the courage to get rid of the dog once and for all.

III

Marie's friend was an old maid of about forty years, mysterious, full of ideals with which I had lost all sympathy long ago.

She was my wife's consoler. In her arms she wept over my dislike of her dog. She was a ready listener to Marie's abuse of matrimony, the slavery of women.

She was rather reserved and careful not to interfere; anyhow I noticed nothing, for I was completely pre-occupied with my work. But I had an idea that she was in the habit of borrowing small sums from my wife. I said nothing until one day I saw her carrying off some of the table silver with the intention of pawning it for her own benefit.

I said a word or two about it to Marie, and gave her to understand that even under the dotal system this sort of comradeship was very unwise. She never dreamed of helping me, her husband and best friend, in this way, although I was in difficulties and worried by debts.

"Since you listen to such proposals from strangers," I said to her, "why not lend me your shares? I could raise money on them."

She objected, arguing that the shares had fallen so low as to be practically valueless and consequently unsale-able. Moreover it was against her principles to transact business with her husband.

"But you don't object to a stranger, who can give you no security whatever, who lives on a pension of seventy-five crowns per annum! Don't you think it wrong to refuse to help your husband who is trying to make a career, and provision for you when you have spent your own money, not to mention the fact that your interests are identical with his? "

She yielded, and the loan of three thousand five hundred francs, or thereabouts, in doubtful shares, was granted.

From this day onward she looked upon herself as my patroness, and told everybody who cared to listen that she had safeguarded my career by sacrificing her dowry. The fact of my being a well-known writer before I had ever set eyes on her was quite lost sight of. But it was bliss to me to look up to her, to be indebted to her for everything : my life, my future, my happiness.

In our marriage contract I had insisted on settling all her property on herself, partly because her financial affairs were chaos. The Baron owed her money ; but instead of paying her in cash, he had guaranteed a loan which she had raised. In spite of all my precautions I was requested by the bank on the morning after our wedding to guarantee the sum. My objections were so much waste of breath ; the bank did not look upon my wife as responsible, since by her second marriage she had again legally become a minor. To my great indignation I was compelled to sign the guarantee, to put my signature by the side of that of the Baron.

In my perfect simplicity I had no idea of what I was doing. It merely seemed to me that what every man of the world would have done in my place, was the right thing to do.

One evening, while I was closeted in my room with a friend, the Baron called. It was his first call since our wedding. My predecessor's visit seemed to me in bad taste, to say the least of it ; but since he did not mind meeting me, I pretended to be pleased to see him. When I accompanied my friend to the door, however, I did not think it necessary to introduce him.   Later on, my wife reproached me for the omission, and called me unmannerly. I accused both her and the Baron of tactlessness.

A violent quarrel ensued, in which she called me a boor.   One word led to another, and certain pictures were mentioned which had once belonged to the Baron, but were now decorating my walls.   I begged her to send them back to him.

"You cannot return presents without hurting the giver," she exclaimed.   "He doesn't dream of returning the presents you gave him, but keeps them as a proof of his friendship and trust."

The pretty word "trust" disarmed me.   But my eye fell on a piece of furniture which awakened unpleasant memories.

"Where does this writing-table come from?"

"It was my mother's."

She was speaking the truth, although she omitted to add that it had passed through her first husband's house.

What a strange lack of delicacy, what bad form, how utterly regardless of my honour!   Was it done intentionally so as to depreciate me in the eyes of my fellow-men? Had I fallen into a trap set by an unscrupulous woman? I wondered. . . .

Yet I surrendered unconditionally without struggling against her subtle logic, convinced that her aristocratic bringing-up ought to serve me as a guide in all doubtful cases where my education did not suffice.   She had a ready answer to everything.   The Baron had never bought a single piece of furniture.   Everything belonged to her— and since the Baron did not scruple to keep my wife's furniture, I need not scruple to accept all articles which belonged to my own wife.

The last phrase : "Since the Baron did not scruple to keep my wife's furniture," caused me lively satisfaction.

Because the pictures which hung in my drawing-room were proofs of a noble trust and evidenced the ideal character of our relationship, they remained where they were; I even carried simplicity to the length of telling all inquisitive callers who cared to know who the giver of those landscapes was.

I never dreamed in those days that it was I, the man belonging to the middle-classes, who possessed tact and delicacy, instincts which are as frequently found amongst the lower strata of society as they are wanting in men and women of the upper ones, where coarse minds are only too often cleverly concealed under a thin layer of veneer. Would that I had known what manner of woman she was in whose hands I had laid my fate!

But I did not know it.

IV

As soon as Marie had got over her confinement, which compelled her to live quietly for a time, she was seized with a craving for excitement. Under the pretext of studying her art, she visited the theatres and went to public entertainments while I stayed at home and worked. Protected by the title of a married woman, she was received in circles which had been closed to the divorced wife. She was anxious that I should accompany her, for she considered the fact of her husband's absence prejudicial to her best interests. But I resisted, and while claiming for myself personal freedom, according to our verbal agreement, I allowed her absolute liberty, and let her go where she pleased.

"But no one ever sets eyes on the husband," she objected.

"People will understand him," I replied.

The husband! The very way in which she pronounced the word conveyed opprobrium; and she fell into the habit of treating me with a certain amount of superciliousness.

During the solitary hours which I spent at home I worked at my ethnographical treatise, which was to be the ladder on which I hoped to climb to promotion at the library. I was in correspondence with all the learned authorities in Paris, Berlin, Petersburg, Irkutsk and Peking, and, seated at my writing-table, I held in my hand the threads of a perfect net of inter-relations which stretched all over the world. Marie did not approve of this work. She would have preferred to see me engaged

192

in writing comedies, and was angry with me. I begged her to await results, and not condemn my work prematurely as waste of time. But she would have none of these Chinese researches which brought in no money. A new Xanthippe, she severely tried my Socratic patience by reiterating that I was frittering away her dowry—her dowry!

My life was a strange mingling of sweetness and bitterness, and one of my greatest worries was Marie's theatrical career. In March it was rumoured that the company of the Royal Theatre would be reduced at the end of May, the period when contracts were renewed. This gave rise to fresh floods of tears during the next three months, in addition to the usual every-day grievances. The house was overrun by all the failures from the Royal Theatre. My soul, broadened and uplifted by the knowledge I had acquired, and the growth and development of my talent, rebelled against the presence of these unfit ones, these incapables who possessed no culture, who were detestable on account of their vanity, their ceaseless flow of banalities, uttered in the slang of the theatre, which they called new truths.

I became so sick of the torture of their tittle-tattle that I begged to be in future excused from my wife's parties. I urged her to cut her connection with those mental lepers, those disqualified ones, whose presence must of necessity depress us and rob us of our courage.

" Aristocrat! " she sneered.

" Aristocrat, if you like, but aristocrat in the true sense of the word," I replied; "for I yearn for the summits of genius, not for the mole-hills of the titled aristocracy. Nevertheless, I suffer all the sorrows of the disinherited."

When I ask myself to-day how I could have lived for years the slave of a woman who treated me disgracefully, who shamelessly robbed me in company of her friends

o

and her dog, I come to the conclusion that it was thanks
to my moderation, to my ascetic philosophy of life, which
taught me not to be exacting, especially in love. I loved
her so much that I irritated her, and more than once she
plainly showed me that my passionate temperament bored
her. But everything was forgotten and forgiven at those
rare moments when she caressed me, when she took my
throbbing head into her lap, when her fingers played with
my hair. This was happiness unspeakable, and like a fool
I stammered out the confession that life without her
would be impossible, that my existence hung on a thread
which she held in her hand. In this way I fostered a
conviction in her that she was a higher being, and the
consequence was that she treated me with flattery and
blandishments as if I were a spoilt child. She knew that
I was in her power, and did not scruple to abuse it.

When the summer came she went into the country and
took her maid with her. She moreover persuaded her
friend to accompany her, for she was afraid of feeling
lonely during the week when my work kept me at the
library. It was in vain that I objected, that I reminded
her that her friend was not in a position to pay, and that
our means were limited; Marie looked upon me as a
"spirit of evil," and reproached me with speaking ill of
everybody. I gave in eventually, in order to avoid
unpleasantness. I gave in—alas! I always gave in.

After a whole week's loneliness I welcomed Saturday
as a red-letter day. With a jubilant heart I caught an
early train and then set out joyfully for half-an-hour's
walk under the scorching sun, carrying bottles and pro-
visions for the week. My blood danced through my
veins, my pulses throbbed at the thought of seeing Marie
in a few moments; she would come to meet me with open
arms, her hair flying in the breeze, her face rosy with
the sweet country air. In addition I was hungry and

looking forward to a gay little dinner, for I had eaten nothing since my early breakfast. At last the cottage among the fir-trees, close to the lake, came in sight. At the same time I caught a glimpse of Marie and her friend, in light summer dresses, stealing away to the bathing vans. I shouted to them with all the power of my lungs. They could not help hearing me, for they were well within earshot. But they only hastened their footsteps, as if they were running away from me, and disappeared into a bathing van. What did it mean?

The maid appeared as soon as she heard my footsteps in the house; she looked uneasy, afraid.

" Where are the ladies? "

" They have gone to bathe, sir."

" When will dinner be ready? "

" Not before four o'clock, sir. The ladies have only just got up, and I have been busy helping the young lady to dress."

" Did you hear me call? "

" Yes, sir."

. . . So they had really run away from me, driven from my presence by an uneasy conscience, and, hungry and tired as I was, I had to wait for a couple of hours for my dinner.

What a reception after a week full of hard work and longing! The thought that she had run away from me like a school-girl caught breaking the rules stabbed me like a dagger.

When she returned to the house I was fast asleep on the sofa, and in a very bad temper. She kissed me as if nothing had happened, trying to prevent the storm from breaking. But self-control is not always possible. A hungry stomach has no ears, and a distressed heart is not soothed by deceitful kisses.

" Are you angry? "

O 2

"My nerves are on edge, don't irritate me."

"I'm not your cook!"

"I never said you were, but don't prevent the cook we have from doing her work!"

"You forget that Amy, as our paying guest, is entitled to the services of our maid."

"Didn't you hear me calling?"

"No!"

She was telling me lies. . . . I felt as if my heart would break.

Dinner—my eagerly-looked-for dinner—was a long torture. The afternoon was dismal; Marie wept and inveighed against matrimony, holy matrimony, the only true happiness in the world, crying on the shoulder of her friend, covering her villainous little dog with kisses.

Cruel, false, deceitful—and sentimental!

And so it went on during the whole summer in infinite variety. I spent my Sundays with two imbeciles and a dog. They were trying to make me believe that all our unhappiness was due to my irritable nerves and persuade me to consult a doctor.

I had intended to take my wife for a sail on Sunday morning, but she did not get up before dinner time; after dinner it was too late.

And yet this tender-hearted woman, who tortured me with pin-pricks, cried bitterly one morning because the gardener was killing a rabbit for dinner, and confessed to me in the evening that she had been praying that the poor little beast's sufferings might be short.

Not long ago I saw somewhere a statement made by a psychopathist to the effect that an exaggerated love for animals combined with indifference towards the sufferings of one's fellow-creatures is a symptom of insanity.

Marie could pray for a rabbit and at the same time torment her husband with smiling lips.

On our last Sunday in the country she took me aside, talked in flattering terms of my generosity, appealed to my kind heart and begged me to cancel Miss Amy's debt to us, pleading her very small means.

I consented without discussing the matter, without telling her that I had anticipated the suggestion, foreseen the trick, the inevitable trick. But she, armed to the teeth with arguments, even when she was unopposed, continued—

"If not, I could, if necessary, pay her share for her!"

No doubt she could have done so. But could she have paid for the annoyance and trouble caused by her friend? . . .

Ah, well—husband and wife must not fall out over trifles.

V

In the commencement of the new year a general crisis shook the credit of the old country, and the Bank which had issued the shares lent to me by Marie failed. I received notice that the loan would be called in. I was forced to pay cash for the sum I had been compelled to guarantee. It was a heavy blow, but after endless difficulties I came to terms with the creditors, who agreed to a year's respite. It was a terrible year, the worst period of my life.

As soon as things were a little more settled I began to make every effort to extricate myself.

In addition to my work at the library I started a novel on modern morals and customs; filled newspapers and periodicals with essays, and completed my scientific treatise. Marie, at the expiration of her contract with the theatre, was re-engaged for another year, but her pay was reduced to fourteen hundred crowns. . . . Now I was better off than she, for she had lost her capital in the general smash.

She was in a vile temper, and made me suffer for it. To re-establish the equilibrium, and thinking of nothing but her independence, she attempted to raise a loan, but these attempts proved abortive and only led to unpleasantness. Acting thoughtlessly, despite her good intentions, she did me harm with her efforts to save herself and render my task more easy. I appreciated her good intentions, but I could not help remonstrating.

Always capricious and wayward, she showed unmistakable signs of malice and fresh events disclosed a state of mind which filled me with apprehension.

A fancy-dress ball, for instance, was given at the theatre, and I had her promise not to attend the ball in male attire. She had bound herself by a solemn oath, for I had been very emphatic on the subject. On the morning after the ball I was told that she had not only broken her promise, but that she had gone to supper later on with some of her male friends.

I was angry because she had lied to me, and the thought of the subsequent supper made me feel uneasy.

"Well," she replied, when I expostulated with her, "am I not free to please myself?"

"No, you are a married woman! You bear my name, and we are responsible to each other. Whenever you compromise yourself, you compromise me, and, in fact, you do me a greater injury than you do yourself."

"That means that I am not free?"

"Nobody can be absolutely free in a community where every individual is inextricably mixed up with the fate of others. Supposing I had invited some women friends to supper, what would you have said?"

She insisted that she was free to do as she liked; that she was at liberty, if she felt so inclined, to ruin my reputation; that her freedom was, in fact, absolute. She was a savage; freedom, as she interpreted it, was the rule of an autocrat who trampled the honour and happiness of her fellow creatures into the dust.

This scene, which began with a quarrel, led to floods of tears and ended with hysterics, was followed by another which made me feel even more uneasy, more especially as I was not sufficiently initiated into the secrets of sexual life to deal with its anomalies, which terrified me, like all anomalies which are difficult of explanation.

One evening, when the maid was busy making up Marie's bed for the night, I heard a half-suppressed scream and smothered laughter, as if some one were being tickled. I felt a sudden fear; an inexplicable terror and a wave of passionate anger swept over me; I opened the door quickly and caught Marie, with her hands on the girl's shoulders, in the act of pressing her lips upon her white throat.

"What are you doing?" I exclaimed furiously, "are you mad?"

"I am only teasing her," answered Marie cynically. "What has that to do with you?"

"It has everything to do with me! Come here!"

And under four eyes I explained to her the nature of her offence.

But she accused me of a vicious imagination, told me that I was perverted and saw vice everywhere.

It is a fatal thing to catch a woman red-handed. She deluged me with abuse.

In the course of the discussion I reminded her of the love she had confessed to have felt for her cousin, pretty Matilda. With an expression of angelic innocence she replied that she herself had been amazed at the strength of her feelings, as she had never thought it possible for one woman to be so deeply in love with another.

This naïve confession reassured me. I remembered that one evening, at my brother-in-law's, Marie had quite openly spoken of her passionate love for her cousin, without blushing, without being conscious that there was anything at all unusual in her conduct.

But I was angry. I recommended her to beware of fancies which, though harmless to begin with, degenerated only too often into vice and led to disastrous results.

She made some inane reply, treated me like a fool—she loved treating me as if I were the most ignorant of ignoramuses—and finished off by saying that I had been telling her a pack of lies.

What was the use of explaining to her that offences of

that sort were legal offences? What was the use of trying
to convince her that medical books termed caresses calculated to arouse amorous feelings in others " vicious "?

I, I was the debauchee, steeped in vice. Nothing could
persuade her to stop her innocent gambols.

She belonged to that class of unconscious criminals
who should be confined in a house of correction and not
allowed to be at large.

Towards the end of the spring she introduced a new
friend, one of her colleagues, a woman of about thirty,
a fellow sufferer, threatened, like Marie herself, with the
lapse of her contract, and therefore, in my opinion,
worthy of compassion. I was sorry to see this woman,
once a celebrated beauty, reduced to such straits. No
one knew why her contract was not to be renewed, unless
it was because of the engagement of the daughter of a
famous actress; one triumph always demands hecatombs
of victims.

Nevertheless, I did not like her; she was self-assertive
and always gave me the impression of a woman on the
look-out for prey. She flattered me, tried to fascinate
me, in order, no doubt, to take advantage of me.

Jealous scenes took place occasionally between the old
friend and the new one, one abused the other, but I
refused to take sides. . . .

Before the summer was over Marie was expecting
another baby. Her confinement would take place in
February. It came upon us like a bolt from the blue.
It was now necessary to strain every effort to make port
before the fatal day dawned.

My novel appeared in November. It was an enormous
success. Money was plentiful, we were saved!

I had reached the goal. I breathed freely. I had made
my way; I was appreciated at last and hailed with
acclamations as a master. The years of trouble and black

care were over; we were looking forward to the birth of this child with great joy. We christened it in anticipation and bought Christmas presents for it. My wife was happy and proud of her condition, and our intimate friends fell into the habit of asking how "the little chap" was, just as if he had already arrived.

Famous now and content with my success, I determined to rehabilitate Marie and save her ruined career. To achieve this I planned a play in four acts, and offered it to the Royal Theatre. It contained a sympathetic part in which she had every chance of reconquering the public.

On the very day of her confinement I heard that the play was accepted and that she had been cast for the principal part.

Everything was well in the best of all worlds; the broken tie between me and my family was firmly reknitted by the birth of the baby. The good time, the spring-time of my life had arrived. There was bread in the house, and even wine. The mother, the beloved, the adored, was taking new pleasure in life, and had regained all her former beauty. The indifference and neglect with which she had treated her first baby were transformed into the tenderest care for the newborn infant.

VI

SUMMER had come again. I was in a position to ask for a few months' leave, which I purported spending with my family in the solitude of one of the green islands on the shores of the Stockholm Archipelago.

I was beginning to reap the harvest of my scientific researches. My treatise was read by the Académie des Inscriptions et Belles Lettres in the Institut de France. I was elected a member of several foreign scientific societies, and the Imperial Russian Geographical Society conferred its medal upon me.

At the age of thirty I had won an excellent position in the literary and scientific world and a brilliant future lay before me. It was pure happiness to lay my trophies at Marie's feet. . . . But she was angry with me because I had "disturbed the equilibrium." I had to make myself small to spare her the humiliation of having to look up to her husband. Like the good-natured giant in the fable I allowed her to pull my beard, and as a consequence she presumed on my good-nature. She took a pleasure in belittling me before the servants and before her friends who were on visiting terms with us, especially her women friends. She gave herself airs ; raised by me on a pedestal, she posed as my superior, and the more insignificant I pretended to be, the more she trampled on me. I deliberately fostered in her the delusion that I had to thank her for my frame, which she did not understand and which she apparently thought little of. I took a positive delight in making myself out to be inferior to her. I contented myself with being no more than the husband of a charming woman, and eventually she came to believe that she, and not I, possessed genius. This applied even to the details of everyday life. Being an excellent swimmer myself, for instance, I taught her to swim. In order to encourage her, I simulated nervousness, and the pleasure she took in ridiculing my efforts and talking of her own grand achievements was a constant source of amusement to me.

The days passed; into the worship of my wife as mother a new thought stole and began to haunt me persistently : I was married to a woman of thirty—a critical age, the beginning of a period full of dangers and pitfalls—I could see indications every now and then which made me feel nervous, indications, perhaps not fraught with disaster for the moment, but which carried in them the germ of discord.

After her confinement physical antagonism came to be added to incompatibility of temper; sexual intercourse between us became odious. When her passion was aroused, she behaved like a cynical coquette. Sometimes she took a malicious delight in making me jealous; at other times she let herself go to an alarming extent, possibly, I thought, under pressure of licentious and perverse desires.

One morning we went out in a sailing boat, accompanied by a young fisherman. I took charge of tiller and mainsail, while the lad was attending to the foresail. My wife was sitting near him. The wind dropped and silence reigned in the boat. All at once I noticed that the young fisherman, from under his cap, was casting lewd glances in the direction of my wife's feet. . . . Her feet? . . . Perhaps there was more to be seen; I could not tell from where I sat. I watched her. Her passionate eyes devoured the young man's frame. In order to remind her of my presence I made a sudden gesture, like a dreamer rousing himself from a dream. She pulled herself together with an effort, and, her eyes resting on the huge tops of his boots, she clumsily extricated herself from an awkward position by remarking—

"I wonder whether boots of this sort are expensive?"

What was I to think of such a stupid remark?

To divert her mind from the voluptuous current of her thoughts, I made the lad change places with me under some pretext or other.

I tried to forget this irritating scene; tried to persuade myself that I had been mistaken, although similar scenes were stored up in my memory, recollections of her burning eyes scrutinising the lines of my body underneath my clothes.

A week later my suspicions were re-awakened by an incident which once and for all destroyed all my hopes of ever seeing this perverse woman realise my ideal of motherhood.

One of my friends spent a week-end with us. He made himself very agreeable to her. She rewarded his courtesy by flirting with him outrageously. It grew late; we said good-night to each other and separated. I thought that she had gone to bed.

Half-an-hour later I heard voices on the balcony. I stepped out quickly, and found wife and friend sitting together, drinking liqueurs. I treated the matter as a joke, but on the following morning I reproached her with making me a public laughing-stock.

She laughed, called me a man of prejudices, cursed with a fantastic and vicious imagination . . . in fact, deluged me with her whole repertory of futile arguments.

I lost my temper; she had hysterics and played her part so well that I apologised for doing her an injustice.

Doing her an injustice—when I considered her conduct absolutely culpable!

Her final words silenced me completely.

"Do you think," she said contemptuously, "I could bear to go through divorce proceedings a second time?"

And brooding over my troubles I slept with the calm of the duped husband.

What is a coquette? . . . A woman who makes advances. Coquetry is nothing but making advances.

And what is jealousy? . . . The fear of losing one's most precious possession. . . . The jealous husband? A ridiculous individual because of his absurd objection to lose his most precious possession.

VII

SUCCESS followed success. All our debts were paid. It rained money. But although a great proportion of my income went towards household expenses, our financial position was chaos. Marie, who kept the accounts and had the cash, was always clamouring for more money, and her constant demands were the cause of violent scenes.

Her contract with the theatre was not renewed. It goes without saying that I had to bear the consequences. It was all my fault! . . . If only she had never married me! . . . The part which I had written for her was forgotten; she had indeed completely ruined it, for she had bungled it, and played it without the slightest conception of its subtleties.

About this time much interest was aroused in what has been called the "woman question." The famous Norwegian male blue-stocking had written a play on the subject, and all feeble minds were obsessed by a perfect mania of finding oppressed women everywhere. I fought against those foolish notions, and consequently was dubbed "mysogynist," an epithet which has clung to me all my life.

A few home-truths on the occasion of our next quarrel threw Marie into a violent fit of hysterics. It was just after the greatest discovery of the nineteenth century in the treatment of neurotic diseases had been made. The remedy was as simple as all great truths.

When the screams of the patient were at their loudest, I seized a water-bottle and thundered the magic words—

"Get up, or I shall pour this water over you!"

She stopped screaming at once—and shot at me a look of sincere admiration, mingled with deadly hatred.

For a moment I was taken aback, but my reawakened manhood would not be denied. . . .

Again I lifted the water-bottle—

"Stop your screaming, or I shall pour this water over you!"

She rose to her feet, called me a blackguard, a wretch, an impostor—signs that my remedy had been effective.

Husbands, duped or otherwise, believe me, for I am your sincere friend : this is the secret of the great cure for hysterics; remember it, maybe the time will come when you need it.

From that day my death was irrevocably settled. My love began to detest me. I knew too much of female cunning; there was no room for me in this world. The sex had determined my physical and mental destruction, and my own wife, as the avenging fury, had accepted the awful and difficult mission of torturing me to death.

She began her task by introducing her friend into the house as a tenant, persuading her to rent a furnished room contiguous to our flat; she did that in spite of my most violent opposition. She went to the length of suggesting that she should take her meals with us, a proposition which I fought tooth and nail. But notwithstanding my protest and all my precautions, I was constantly brought into contact with the intruder. I could almost fancy that I was a bigamist. The evenings which I should have spent in my wife's company I spent by myself, for she remained invisible, closeted with her friend. They enjoyed themselves in her room at my expense, smoking my cigarettes and drinking my wine. I hated the woman, and since I could not hide my feelings—at any rate not sufficiently—I many a time brought on my head Marie's

wrath for having been found wanting in courtesy towards
the "poor child."

Not satisfied with having estranged Marie from husband
and child—the baby was boarded out with a neighbour,
a termagant of forty-five years of age—the fair friend
demoralised the cook ; the consumption of beer rose to the
almost incredible quantity of five hundred bottles a
month ; my cook sat in the kitchen intoxicated, fast
asleep ; the food was wasted.

The fair friend was a *mangeuse d'hommes*, and I was
her prey.

One day Marie showed me a cloak which she said she
wanted to buy. I disapproved of colour and cut, and
advised her to choose another. The friend, who happened
to be present, kept it for herself, and I forgot all about
it. Two weeks later I received a bill for a cloak bought
by my wife.. I inquired into the matter and found that
Marie had lent herself to a trick well known by the
theatrical demi-monde.

As usual, she was furious with me when I asked her
to break off her connection with the adventuress. . . .

And things grew worse and worse.

A few days later Marie, trying to work on my feelings,
posing as the submissive wife, asked me, quite humbly,
whether I had any objection to her chaperoning the "poor
child " on a visit to an old friend of her late father's,
whom she intended to ask for a loan. The request struck
me as so strange that it set me thinking, especially when
I took into account her friend's bad reputation. I
implored Marie, for our child's sake, to open her eyes,
to rouse herself from the trance in which she seemed to
live, and which would surely end with her complete ruin—
her only reply was a repetition of her old phrase : " Your
base imagination. . . ."

And still matters declined.

P

Her friend gave a luncheon for the secret purpose of beguiling on this occasion a well-known actor into making her a proposal of marriage. A fresh revelation awaited me, a revelation which effectually roused me from my lethargy.

Champagne had been drunk, and the ladies had taken more than was good for them. Marie was reclining in an arm-chair, and before her knelt her friend, kissing her on the lips. The famous actor, interested in the strange spectacle, called to one of his friends, and pointing at the couple as if he were bringing proof of an accusation, exclaimed—

"Look here! D'you see?"

Doubtless he was alluding to certain rumours, and there was a hidden meaning in the laughing words.

As soon as we arrived home, I implored Marie to shake off this fatal infatuation and be more careful of her reputation. She made no secret of the pleasure she found in kissing pretty women; her friend was not the only one of her colleagues whom she treated in this way; at the theatre, in the dressing-rooms she bestowed the same favour on others.

She had no intention of denying herself this pleasure, this innocent pleasure, which in my perverted imagination only was vicious.

It was impossible to make her see her conduct in a different light; there was but one remedy. . . .

She was again going to be a mother; this time she was furious, but her condition kept her at home for a time.

VIII

AFTER her confinement she changed her tactics. Whether she was influenced by fear of the consequences of her perverted passions, or whether her female instincts had been reawakened, I cannot say. She paid a great deal of attention to young men; but she did it too openly to make me really jealous.

Without an engagement, with nothing to occupy her time, full of whims, despotic, she was bent on war with me to the knife.

One day she tried to prove to me that it was cheaper to keep three servants than two. As I thought it waste of time to argue with a lunatic, I simply turned her out of my room.

She swore vengeance. She engaged a third maid, who was absolutely superfluous in the house. Consequently no work was done at all. Everything was turned upside down, the three girls quarrelled all day long, drank beer and entertained their lovers at my expense.

To complete the picture of my matrimonial happiness, one of my children fell ill. This brought two more servants into the house and the visits of two doctors. At the end of the month I had to face a deficit of five hundred crowns. I redoubled my energies to meet the expenses, but the strain on my nerves was beginning to tell.

She was for ever taunting me with having squandered her more than doubtful dowry, and forced me to make an allowance to her aunt in Copenhagen. This woman accused me of having wasted her "fortune." and her incredibly silly arguments irritated me beyond endurance. She affirmed that Marie's mother, on her deathbed, had distinctly expressed the wish that she should share my wife's inheritance. I failed to see what that had to do with me, for the "fortune" which she was to inherit existed in imagination only; but the fact remained that the burden of the aunt, who was lazy and incapable, was added to my other burdens. I gave way in the matter; I even agreed to guarantee a sum of money, raised by an older friend, adventuress number one, for my beloved wife had hit on the idea of selling me her favour. I admitted everything for the privilege of kissing her; I admitted having wasted her dowry, squandered her aunt's "fortune," ruined her theatrical career by marrying her, even having undermined her health.

Holy matrimony was degraded to legal prostitution.

She carefully treasured up all my admissions, and worked them into a legend which the papers greedily snapped up later on, and which was assiduously spread by all those of her friends whom I had turned out, one after the other.

My ruin had become an obsession with her. At the end of the year I found that I had given her twelve thousand crowns for household expenses, and I was compelled to ask my publishers for a sum in advance.

Whenever I reproached her with her extravagance, she invariably replied—

"Well, why have children and make your wife miserable? When I consider that I gave up a splendid position to marry you. . . ."

But I had an answer to that taunt—

"As Baroness, my dear, your husband gave you three thousand crowns and debts. I give you three times as much, more than three times as much."

She said nothing, but she turned her back upon me,

and in the evening I admitted all her charges; I agreed that three thousand is three times as much as ten thousand! that I was a blackguard, a miser, a "bel ami," who had risen at the expense of his adored wife, adored more especially in her nightgown.

She poured all her venom into the first chapter of a novel, the subject of which was the exploitation of an oppressed wife by a criminal husband. Through my writings, on the other hand, always glided the white wraith of a lovely golden-haired woman, a madonna, a young mother. I was for ever chanting her praises, creating a glorious myth round the figure of the wondrous woman who by God's grace had been sent to brighten the thorny path of a poet. . . .

And the critics never tired of lauding the "good genius" of a pessimistic novelist, of pouring on her full measures of entirely undeserved praise. . . .

The more I suffered under the persecutions of my shrew, the more eagerly I strove to weave a crown of light for her sacred head. The more I was depressed by the reality, the more I became inspired by my hallucinations of her loveliness . . . alas for the magic of love!

IX

MIDSUMMER IN WINTER

Winter night, the streets forsaken,
   Ice-king holds the world in thrall;
Sudden gusts of wind awaken
Eerie sounds, the walls are shaken
   By the wild, rebellious call.

Gay as gods we have been dining,
   All alone, just you and I.
Light the candles, let their shining
Drive out darkness and repining,
   Perfect joy is nigh.

Draw the blinds, the shutters tighten!
   Safely screened from prying eyes,
Take the cup and pledge me! brighten
Winter-gloom with song, and lighten
   Darkness with sweet harmonies.

Sing of woods, or sing the wonder
   Of the sea, serene and bland;
Or the sea, that lashed asunder
Breaks in crashing peals of thunder
   On the foam-flecked sand.

Like a great enchanted river,
   Full of witchcraft is your voice;
See my pelargoniums quiver
Like a leafy wood a-shiver
   In the breeze when daylight dies.

On my screen, her ensign flying,
   Leaps a brig with white sails set;
Snugly on the hearthrug lying
Silky fur with sable vying,
   Sleeps your Persian cat.

In the mirror's clear perspective
   I can see our little home;
Wrapped in dreams, my introspective
Humour conjures up affective
   Scenes of past joys, joys to come.

214

On the desk where I was writing
  Falls the candle's mellow glow ;
Falls on virgin sheets, exciting
Rose-warm blushes, softly lighting
  Their unblemished snow.

In your chamber's sweet seclusion,
  Hung with green, a vernal nook,
I can glimpse a wild confusion—
Tangled skeins in rank profusion
  Cover work and household book.

In the glass our eyes are meeting ;
  Flashing blue, like tempered steel
Are your glances, but a fleeting
Smile from tender lips in greeting,
  Tells me that your heart is leal.

Radiant brow, my soul entrancing,
  Puts the candle-light to shame ;
From your jewels flashing, dancing
Sparks are flying and enhancing
  Long-lashed eyes' alluring flame.

Hush ! the bell disturbs the slumber
  Of the house—the postman's ring !
Let him be ! His dreary lumber
Shall not darken and encumber
  Love's eternal spring.

Letter-box holds proofs and letters
  Safely under lock and key ;
Sing and play ! Till morn unfetters
These officious care-begetters
  Love our guerdon be.

Sing, beloved, my soul's desire !
  World holds naught but you and me ;
Sing with lips no love can tire,
Sing of passion's quenchless fire,
  Fill the night with ecstasy !

X

THERE were times when I had no doubt that my wife hated me and wished to get rid of me in order to marry again.

Sometimes strange reflections in the expression of her face made me suspect her of having a lover, and her coldness towards me strengthened my suspicion; all of a sudden my smouldering jealousy burst into fierce flames, our marriage was shaken to its very foundations, and hell opened wide at our feet.

My wife declared that she was ill, suffering from some vague disease of the spine or the back, she was uncertain which.

I sent for the family doctor, an old college friend of mine. He diagnosed rheumatic knots on the muscles of the back, and prescribed a course of massage. I had no objection to make, for there seemed to be no doubt of the reality of the disease. As I had no idea of the intimate nature of the treatment, I remained completely absorbed in my literary work, and paid no attention whatever to the progress of the cure. My wife did not appear to be dangerously ill, for she came and went as usual, visited the theatres, never refused an invitation, and was always the last to leave a party.

One evening, at a small gathering of friends, some one suddenly began to bewail the dearth of lady doctors. The speaker maintained that it must be very unpleasant for a woman to undress before a stranger, and, turning to Marie, he said—

" Am I not right ?   Isn't it very unpleasant ? "

"Oh! a doctor doesn't count."

The nature of the treatment was revealed to me by a sudden flash. I noticed an expression of sensuality on Marie's face, an expression which had puzzled me for some time, and a terrible suspicion gripped my heart. She undressed before a notorious voluptuary! And I had been completely ignorant of it.

When we were alone, I asked her for an explanation.

She described the treatment, apparently quite unconcerned.

"But don't you mind?"

"Why should I mind?"

"You always appeared to me almost prudish in your modesty."

Two days later the doctor called to see one of the children. Seated in my room, I overheard a more than strange conversation between him and my wife. They were laughing and whispering.

Presently they entered my room, the smile still on their lips. Plunged in sinister speculations, my mind kept wandering from the subject of our conversation; by and by it drifted to women patients.

"You thoroughly understand women's complaints, don't you, old boy?" I said.

Marie looked at me. She was furious. There was so much hatred blazing in her eyes that I felt a cold thrill running down my back.

When the doctor had left, she turned on me furiously.

"Prostitute!" I flung the word into her face. It escaped my lips against my will, giving expression to an intuitive flash which I had not had time to analyse. The insult came home to me and oppressed me. My eyes fell on the children, and with a contrite heart I apologised.

But she remained angry, so angry that nothing would soften her.

To make amends for the great injustice which I had done her, and to some extent, also, influenced by her hatred, I conceived the idea of arranging for her a pleasure trip to Finland in the shape of a theatrical tour, extending over several weeks.

I started negotiations with theatrical managers, succeeded in coming to terms, and raised the money.

She went to Finland, where she won patriotic victories and a number of laurel wreaths.

I was left alone with the children. I fell ill. Believing myself to be on the point of death, I sent her a telegram, asking her to return home. As she had fulfilled all her engagements, this did not interfere with business.

On her return I was better; she accused me of having brought her back on false pretences, telegraphed lies, merely to take her away from her relations and her native country. . . .

Soon after her return I noticed a new phase, a phase which filled me with increased uneasiness. Contrary to her former habits, she gave herself to me unreservedly.

What was the reason? I wondered, but I felt no inclination to probe too deeply. . . .

On the next morning and the days which followed she talked of nothing but the pleasant time she had spent in Finland. Carried away for the moment by her memories, she told me that she had made the acquaintance of an engineer on the steamer, an enlightened, up-to-date man, who had convinced her that there was no such thing as sin in the abstract, and that circumstances and destiny alone were responsible for all happenings.

"Certainly, my dear," I agreed, "but for all that our actions do not fail to draw their consequences after them. I admit that there is no such thing as sin, because there is no personal God; nevertheless we are responsible to those we wrong. There may be no sin in the abstract, but crime will exist as long as there is a Law. We may smile at the theological conception of it, but vengeance or, rather, retribution, remains a fact, and the aggressor never escapes."

She had grown grave, but pretended not to understand me.

" Only the wicked revenge themselves," she said at last.

" Agreed ; but with so many wicked people in the world, who can be sure that he is dealing with a man brave enough not to retaliate ? "

" Fate guides our actions."

" True ; but Fate also guides the dagger of the avenger."

. . . At the end of the month she had a miscarriage, sufficient proof, I thought, of her infidelity. And from that moment suspicion grew slowly into certainty and filled my heart with bitterness.

She did her utmost to persuade me that I was " mad," that my suspicions were but the figments of an overworked brain. And once again she forgave me. To mark our reconciliation I wrote a play containing a splendid part for her, a part which it was impossible to ruin. On the seventeenth of August I handed her the play together with the deed of gift, which conferred on her all the rights. She could do with it what she liked as long as she herself played the part which I had written for her. It was the result of two months' strenuous work. She accepted it without a word of thanks, a sacrifice due to Her Majesty, the second-rate actress.

XI

Our housekeeping went from bad to worse. I was unable to interfere, for she regarded every opinion expressed by me, every suggestion of a change made by me, as an insult. I had to remain passive, powerless in face of the wanton extravagance of the servants who wasted the food and neglected the children.

There was nothing but misery, discomfort and quarrels.

When she returned from her journey to Finland, the expenses of which I had paid in advance, she had two hundred crowns in her pocket, the financial result of her performances. . . . Since she kept the cash I made a mental note of the sum, and when she asked me for money, long before the date on which it was due, I asked her, surprised by the unexpected demand, what she had done with her money? She replied that she had lent it to her friend, and argued that according to the law she was free to dispose of all moneys earned by her.

" And I? " I replied. . . . Moreover, to withdraw housekeeping money is not disposing. . . .

" It's a different thing in the case of the woman! "

" In the case of the oppressed woman, you mean? In the case of the female slave who permits the man to defray the whole expenses of the household? These are the logical consequences of the humbug called ' the emancipation of woman.' "

Emile Augier's prophesies in the *Fourchambault*, with reference to the dotal system have indeed been fulfilled. The husband has become the slave of the wife. And there are plenty of men who allow themselves to be

deceived to such an extent that they dig their own graves.
Fools!

While the misery of my married life slowly unfolded
itself, as a ribbon winds off a spool, I took advantage of
my literary reputation to tilt at foolish prejudice and
attack antiquated superstitions. I wrote a volume of
satires. I threw a handful of pebbles at the principal
charlatans of the metropolis, not forgetting the sexless
women.

I was at once denounced as a writer of pamphlets.
Marie was strong in her disapproval, and immediately
made friends with the enemy. She was respectability
personified, and complained bitterly of the misery of
being tied to a scandalmonger! She lost sight of the fact
that the satirist was also a famous novelist and had made
a name as a playwright.

She was a saint, a martyr. She deplored the dismal
prospects of her unhappy children. They would have to
bear the consequences of the dishonourable actions of a
father who had squandered their mother's dowry, ruined
her theatrical career, ill-treated her. . . .

One day a paragraph appeared in one of the papers
stating that I was insane; a brochure, written to order
and paid for in cash, spread abroad the martyrdom of
Marie and her friends; not one of the absurdities which
her little brain had hatched was forgotten.

She had won the game.

And as she saw me go down before my enemies, she
assumed the rôle of the tender mother, weeping over the
prodigal son. Amiable to all the world, except to me, she
drew all my friends over to her side, false ones and true
ones alike. Isolated, in the power of a vampire, I abandoned all attempt at defence. Could I raise my hand
against the mother of my children, the woman whom I
loved?

Never!

I succumbed.   She surrounded me with kindness—abroad, at home she had nothing for me but contempt and insults.

I was exhausted by overwork and misery; I suffered much from headaches, nervous irritability, indigestion . . . the doctor diagnosed catarrh of the stomach.

It was a very unexpected result of mental strain.

It was strange that the illness did not break out until after I had decided to go abroad, the only means of escape, so it seemed to me, from the net woven round me by those countless friends who were everlastingly condoling with my wife.   The symptoms of this mysterious malady first showed themselves on the day succeeding a visit to the laboratory of an old friend, from where I had taken a bottle of cyanide; it was to bring me release, and I had locked it in a piece of furniture belonging to my wife.

Paralysed and depressed, I was lying on the sofa, watching my children at play, thinking of the beautiful days that lay behind me, preparing myself for death.

I determined to leave nothing in writing which could throw light on the cause of my death and my sinister suspicions.

I was ready to make my exit, disappear from ken, killed by the woman whom I forgave with my last breath.

Marie was watching me out of the corners of her eyes; wondering, perhaps, how much longer I should linger on this earth, before I left her to enjoy in peace the income which the collected works of the famous writer would yield her, and the sum which doubtless Government would grant her towards the education of the children.

She was a success in my play, so big a success that the critics called her a great tragedienne.   She almost burst with pride. She was allowed to choose her next part; the result was a complete fiasco. Now she could no longer deny the fact that it was I who had made her, that she had to thank me for her laurels, and feeling herself in my debt, the strength of her hatred increased. She besieged the various theatrical managers, but could find no engagement. Eventually I was obliged to reopen negotiations with Finland. I was willing to leave my country, my friends, my publisher, to settle in the midst of her friends who were my enemies. But Finland would have none of her. Her career was over.

During all this time she led the life of a woman free from all duties as mother and wife. My health did not permit me to accompany her to the artistic circles which she frequented, and consequently she went alone. Sometimes she did not come home until early in the morning, very often she was intoxicated and made sufficient noise to wake up the whole house. I could hear her stumbling into the night nursery where she slept.

What is a man to do in a case of this sort? Is he to denounce his own wife? Impossible! Divorce her? No! I looked upon the family as an organism, like the organism of a plant; a whole, of which I was a part. I could not exist independently of it; without the mother, life seemed impossible to me, even if I had had the custody of the children. My heart's blood, transmitted through my wife, flowed through the veins of their small bodies. The whole was like a system of arteries intimately connected and interdependent. If a single one were cut, my life would ebb away with the blood which trickled down and was sucked up by the sand. For this reason the infidelity of the wife is a terrible crime. One cannot help sympathising with the " Kill her ! " of a well-known author, who shows us a father stricken to death because he has come to doubt the legitimacy of his offspring.

Marie, on the other hand, identified herself with the crazy endeavours to increase women's rights and liberties, and fully endorsed the new doctrine that the woman who deceives her husband is not guilty, because she is not his property.

I could not degrade myself to spy on her, I did not want proof which meant death to me. I wanted to deceive myself, live in a world of my own, which I could create at my pleasure.

But I was deeply wounded. I doubted the legitimacy of my children; I was haunted by the suspicion that although they bore my name and were supported by my earnings, they were yet not my children. Nevertheless, I loved them, for they had come into my life as a pledge of my future existence. Deprived of the hope to live again in my children, I floated in mid-air, like a poor phantom, breathing through roots which were not my own.

Marie seemed to lose patience, because I lingered so long. It was true before witnesses she treated me with the tender love of a mother, but when no one was present she tortured me, just as the little acrobat is pinched by his father behind the scenes. She tried to hasten my end by cruelty. She invented a new torture; justifying her conduct with my temporary weakness, she treated me as if I were a cripple. One day, proudly boasting of her physical strength, she threatened to strike me. She rushed at me, but I seized her by the wrists and forced her down on the sofa.

"Admit that I am the stronger, in spite of my illness!"

She did not admit it; she merely looked disconcerted, and, furious at having made a mistake, she left the room, sulking.

In our mutual struggle she had all the advantages of the woman and actress. It was impossible for me, a hardworking man, to hold my own against an idle woman who spent all her time spinning intrigues. In an unequal struggle of this sort the man is certain to be caught in the end in a net which enmeshes him on all sides.

"In love," said Napoleon, that most excellent judge of women, "one only wins by flight." But how could a carefully guarded prisoner escape? and as for a man sentenced to death . . .

My brain recovered after a rest, and I conceived a plan of escape from this stronghold, although it was most carefully guarded by my wife and the friends which she had so successfully duped. I used cunning; I wrote a letter to the doctor in which I expressed a haunting dread of insanity, and suggested a trip abroad as a remedy. The doctor fell in with my suggestion, and I at once informed Marie of his opinion against which there was no appeal.

"By doctor's orders!"

Her very formula when she had successfully dictated to the doctor the treatment she wished him to prescribe for her.

She grew pale when she heard it.

"I don't want to leave my country!"

"Your country? . . . Finland's your country! And as far as I know, there is nothing in Sweden which you could possibly miss; you have no relations here, no friends, no career."

"I refuse to accompany you!"

"Why?"

She hesitated, and after a while continued—

"Because I'm afraid of you! I won't be left alone with you!"

"You are afraid of a lamb that you lead by the nose? You aren't serious!"

"You are a knave, and I won't stay with you unprotected!"

Q

I felt sure that she had a lover. Or else she was afraid of my discovering her indiscretions.

So she was afraid of me, of me who crouched at her feet like a dog, whose leonine mane she had clipped, leaving him but a fringe like a horse's; who waxed his moustache and wore up and down collars, to be better equipped for the struggle with dangerous rivals. Her fear of me increased my dread and stimulated my suspicions.

"This woman has a lover whom she is loath to leave, or else she is afraid of retribution," I said to myself.

After endless discussions she wheedled a promise out of me to stay away no longer than a year.

The will to live returned, and I eagerly finished a volume of poems which was to be published in the winter following my departure.

Summer in my heart, I sang with fresh inspiration. I sang of my beloved wife as she appeared to me on the day of our first meeting, a blue veil fluttering from her straw hat, a blue veil which became the flag which I hoisted when I sailed into the stormy sea. One evening I read this poem to a friend. Marie listened with profound attention. When I had finished she burst into tears, put her arms round me and kissed me.

A perfect actress, she played before my friend the part of the loving wife. And the simpleton regarded me from that day as a jealous fool whom heaven had blessed with the sweetest of wives.

"She loves you, old boy," my friend assured me again and again. And four years later he reminded me of the scene as a convincing proof of her fidelity.

"I swear to you at that moment she was sincere," he reiterated.

Sincere in her remorse, perhaps! Face to face with my love which transformed the wanton into a madonna. It was not very surprising.

XII

SUN-MISTS

HE looked round anxiously to see if everything was there, as if it were possible to see anything at all in that confusion of people and luggage on the upper deck.

He felt guilty of an unknown crime, until the steamer had passed the mill. He was dazzled by the blinding sun, the sea appeared to be boundless, and the hazy blue mountains called him with irresistible force. His eyes fell on the children's perambulator; the one painted white with the blue cover, not the other one; he knew it so well, there were little white milkspots on the blue cover. And over there was the big arm-chair and the drawing-room sofa and the bath with the flower-pots. How dusty the poor things looked, they had spent the whole winter in a cloud of tobacco smoke; the pelargoniums used to stand on the writing-table in the lamplight, in the early spring, when the evenings were still long; the arm-chair stood to the right of the writing-table, and whenever he looked up from his work, whenever the restless pen stopped for a second, he received a friendly nod. But when there was no one sitting in the arm-chair, his tired eyes travelled to the cretonne flowers on the sofa; but there were so many eyes staring into the room, and how the lamp flickered! Ah! it was the sun shining on the upper deck! What was that over there? A pair of eyes familiar last year—how dull they were! Had he been ill? No! They had not met since last year; one never met in town, one was so busy there! One left one's school and went home! The children had had measles. . . . It was cold on deck, he had better go downstairs into the saloon.

There were the eyes again, staring at the sofa and the arm-chair. But they looked happy, longing, yearning for something which must surely happen.

He left his place and stepped forward to let the fresh breeze cool his face. Smoke and the smell of food were rising from the kitchen. There was the cook, taking a rest, trying to grow cool. And the large cabin!

The table-cloth was as white as it had been last year, the silver epergne sparkled as before, the flowers on the sideboard were as new and fresh, the lamps were swinging in their brass brackets; everything was exactly as it had been before, and yet everything was new, thanks to the ever-rejuvenating power of nature, thanks to spring!

And the shore glided past, a long, triumphant march past, now threatening and sinister, now happy and smiling, but always new, endowed with eternal youth.

He was the helpless sport of gloomy dreams; he was pressed in between houses in narrow, dark streets; he was at the bottom of a well; he was trying to creep through a tunnel and was held fast; bricks were being heaped on his breast, when he was awakened by a loud knocking at the window shutters. He jumped up, but the room was pitch dark; he opened the shutters and a sea of light and green greeted his eyes. Oh, Nature! Reality which surpasses all dreams!

Behold, you dreamer, your brain could never invent such a dream, and yet you would talk of cold reality!

The morning sun was shining on an August landscape. He put a piece of bread in his pocket, slung his drinking-cup across his shoulder, took a stick and a basket and went out in search of sport—sport, not bloodshed.

His path lay between oak trees and hazels; autumn flowers grew here, flowers which had waited until after

the passing of the scythe before they appeared, so that
they could enjoy life undisturbed until the frost killed
them. He crossed the stubble field, climbed over the
fence, and the sport began.

On the short, springy turf, woven of reed-grass and
stunted mudwort, the mushrooms lay scattered like new-
laid eggs, waiting for the sun to enable them to fulfil
their destiny before they decayed; but that was impossible
now, since fate had decreed that they should die in their
youth.

He left the battlefield and entered the forest with its
odour of turpentine—health and sick-room—balm for the
wounded breast, as the saying is; he walked below the
branches in a dead calm, while twenty yards above his
head the tempest shrieked. A woodcock flew up; the
branches rattled. If only he had a gun!

Why does a man long for a gun whenever he happens
to come across a harmless creature of the woods? There
are many occasions in life when a gun would be much
more in its place.

Here was a cart track; the wheels of the cart, drawn
by oxen, had cut deeply into the turf; nevertheless, a
red species of the poisonous spit-devils had shot up in the
ruts; maybe they required strake-nails and kicks from
the hoofs of oxen before they could enter into material
existence.

The wood opened out and the path ceased at a place
where many trees had been felled; before him lay what
remained of the giants of the forest, cut down by the axe
because it had been impossible to dig them up with the
roots. He gazed at a huge stump which had been attacked
by a host of fungi of all sizes; they had settled on it as
a swarm of flies settles on carrion, but their crowd was
densest round the decayed parts which they could overcome more easily; they looked starved, pale and bloodless;

they were neither pretty nor poisonous, like the spit-devils; they were merely useful.

Denser and darker grew the wood; the Scotch firs mingled their branches with the moss which covered the ground, embraced the stones and built cool little huts for the yellow merulius which grew embedded in the moss and enjoyed a short life, protected alike from scorching sun and preying insects.

The ground became damp; the bog-myrtle, in times gone by highly valued and eagerly gathered on account of its medicinal qualities, grew undisturbed between tiny hillocks, at the foot of degenerated grey pines which had died of superabundance. A woodpecker hammered high above and stopped every now and then to listen whether the sound betrayed a hollow. The sun's rays were scorching; the ground became stony, the wood opened again; he could hear a low, muffled roar; fresh breezes, laden with the smell of oysters, cooled his face; he caught glimpses of a shining blue expanse through the lower branches of the Scotch firs.

A few more steps up the incline—and before him lay the sea—the sea! The waves leaped up the cliffs and were thrown down again, only to begin their game afresh.

Off with the clothes and down into the deep! What was it that he saw down there for the space of a moment? A different world, where the trees were red like seaweed and the air emerald green like the waves; now he was again on the surface amid the bellowing, fighting breakers; he fought with them until he was tired; he lay on his back and floated; they threw him up sky-high, they dragged him down into dark chasms, as if they meant to throw him into the abyss; he ceased to wish, he ceased to will; he made no resistance; his body had lost all weight; the law of gravity no longer applied to him; he

floated between water and air—in absolute calm, devoid
of all sensation.

He let the waves carry him to the shore, the shallow,
sandy shore, where it formed a lumber-room between the
rocks for the sea's collection of all things it could not
devour; here they lay, sorted, washed and polished;
broken oars, a legion of corks, bark, reed-pipes, staves
and hoops. He sat down and stared at a broken plank.

They had been shut up in the house for a week, for it
was raining. He had established himself in the window-
seat, for one of the panes was all colours with age and
sunlight, and when he looked through it at the grey,
cloud-covered expanse of water, the sun seemed to be shining; the grey reefs, where the seagulls nested, looked red,
the air was flooded with gold, the trees were of a brilliant
emerald green; and if he looked through the window-
pane at a certain angle he could see a rainbow in the
sky, and that kindled in him the hope of fine weather.

Far away, out in the sea, there was a small island, an
island which looked less profaned than the other islands;
the Scotch firs grew more closely together; the cliffs were
greener and the shore was covered with reeds. His soul
yearned for it, for from there he could see the open sea.

And the sun shone again. He set sail and steered for
the little island. The boat danced over the rolling waves,
the channel broadened; far away the green island called
him; it swam nearer steadily, until at last the boat was
moored among the whispering reeds and he landed.

His dream had been realised; he was alone among the
trees and reefs, with the sea before him and the infinite
blue sky above his head. No sound betrayed the dis-
turbing vicinity of a human being, no sail on the horizon,
no cottage on the shore. A solitary oyster-plover flew
away from him, terrified, uttering its impotent: help!

help! A family of creek-ducks, led by the mother, scuddied away, running on the water, frightened by the arrival of dread man; a grey adder uncurled and made good its escape, slipping away between the stones, like a tiny, winding brooklet. The sea-gulls came flying from the reefs to have a look at the intruder, screamed like little children and hurried away again. A crow rose from a large Scotch fir; it fluttered and beat its wings, screamed and threatened and groaned and escaped to outlying reefs; every living thing shunned the dreaded being who had fled from his own kind.

He walked along the sandy shore; he came upon the skeleton of a pine-tree, washed by the sea and bleached by the sun to a deadly pallor; it lay there like a skeleton of a dragon and between its ribs flowered the purple lythrum and the golden lysimachia; little piles of shells lay heaped round the wild aster which lived its life on empty sepulchres; the air was laden with the scent of valerian which grew in profusion on a bed of evil-smelling seaweed.

He left the shore and turned his footsteps towards the wood. How tall and straight the trees were, a little too straight perhaps, but he could see the sea through the trunks, the sea—solitude—nature! The ground was as smooth as if it had been stamped down and flattened by human feet; here was the stump of a tree—the axe had been here; over there a nettle grew, men had been here; there could be no mistake, for the nettle is a parasite which follows in the wake of man and never ventures into the solitude of the woods or the large stretches of meadow-land; the nettle is vermin, supported by man, and can only exist in the vicinity of man; it collects all dust and dirt on its hairy, sticky leaves and burns the finger which touches it,—a magnificent breed, nourished by sin.

He went on. His eyes fell on a sparrow, the denizen of the gutter and backyard—the winged creature which feels at home in the dust, bathes in dirt and should have been a rat since it makes no use of its wings—man's jackal. What was it doing out here where there were no men? What did it live on? On the seed of the nettle?

A few more steps and he found the sole of a shoe; a large foot, a foot deformed by hard work, had trodden heavily on this sole. Between the trunks he came upon a fire-place made of boulders, an altar perhaps, on which Nature's conqueror had sacrificed to Strength. The fire had long been extinct, but the effects of it were still visible. The ground was dug up as if by the hoofs of animals, the trees were stripped of their bark, even the rocks were broken; there was a gigantic well in the mountain, filled with dirty brown water; the bowels of the earth had been laid bare and the broken pieces scattered as if by naughty children, disappointed because they had not found what they sought. But a great piece of mountain was missing. It had been taken away with the feldspar to the china factory, and only when there was no more to be got, man had stayed away.

He fled from the devastation, down to his boat. He noticed the traces of footsteps on the sand. He cursed and turned to fly when he suddenly saw in a flash that he had been cursing himself; and all at once he understood why the seagulls and the adder and all the others had shunned him, and he retraced his footsteps, for he could not escape from himself.

He gazed at the sea through his field-glasses in the direction whence he had come. A white dress and a blue cover shone among the oak-trees. He climbed into the boat, ate his bread, drank a liqueur and muttered, seizing the oars—

"You, whose every desire has been fulfilled, who possess the best of all things Life has to bestow, why are you discontent?"

XIII

At last the house had been cleansed of her friends. The last one, the pretty one, had disappeared in the company of a well-known professor, who had returned from an expedition with four orders and an assured position. Having no home of her own, the fair lady had lived in my house, cost free. She had seized the opportunity, fastened herself on to the poor fellow and seduced him one evening in a cab, where, for some reason or other, she found herself with him; she forced him into marrying her by making a scandalous scene in a third house, to which they had both been invited. As soon as she felt sure of her position she dropped the mask, and at a party, under the influence of too much wine, she called Marie a degenerate. A colleague, who happened to hear the remark, thought it his duty to tell me at once.

Marie, with a few words, proved that the accusation was unjust, and in future my door was closed to the lady, although this meant the loss of my old friend for ever.

I was not sufficiently curious to go more deeply into the meaning of the word "degenerate," but it left its sting in my bleeding flesh. New insults, uttered by the same impure lips, referred to the suspicious life Marie had led during her tour in Finland. My old suspicions arose with fresh vigour, her miscarriage, our conversation on destiny, her complete surrender. . . . All these things strengthened my intention to leave the country.

Marie had discovered the use of a sick poet, and constituted herself sister of mercy, sick-nurse, keeper even, if a keeper was required.

She wove a martyr's crown for her own head, acted with absolute independence behind my back, and, as I discovered later on, went so far as to borrow money from my friends in my name. At the same time valuable pieces of furniture disappeared from our house, and were carted to adventuress No. 1, to be sold by the latter.

All this aroused my attention.

"Had Marie expenses of which I was ignorant?" I often asked myself this question. Was this the cause of those secret sales? The cause of the enormous house-keeping expenditure? And if this was the cause, what was the object of them? I enjoyed the income of a Swedish minister of State, a larger income than that of a Swedish general, and yet I led a miserable life; it was as if my feet were fettered, as if I were dragging a leaden weight with me wherever I went. And yet we lived very simply. Our table was the table of a labourer; the food was cooked so badly that it was at times uneatable. We drank beer or brandy, like a working-man; our cellar was so inferior that our friends upbraided us more than once. I smoked nothing but a pipe. I had hardly any recreation, only very occasionally, about once a month, I spent an evening with friends.

Once only, beside myself with anger, I determined to look into the matter. I asked an experienced lady for advice. She laughed when I asked her whether our house-hold expenses were not rather high, and told me that we must be mad.

I had every reason therefore to believe in extraordinary and secret expenditure. But the object? the object?

Relations? friends? lovers? Nobody cares to enlighten a husband, and so everybody becomes an accessory in crime. . . .

After endless preparations the date of our departure

was fixed. But now a new difficulty arose, a difficulty which I had long foreseen and which was accompanied by a series of unpleasant scenes. The dog was still alive! How much annoyance it had caused me already! especially as so much attention was devoted to him that the children were habitually neglected.

However, the day had dawned when to my inexpressible joy Marie's idol and my evil genius, old, diseased, half-rotten, was to end its days; Marie herself now desired the animal's death, and only the thought of the innocent pleasure which its disappearance would cause me led her to postpone the "dog-question" again and again, and invent fresh annoyances to make me pay for the longed-for relief.

But at last a farewell feast was arranged. She made heart-rending scenes, had a fowl killed, of which I, still a semi-invalid, received the bones, and then—we were in the country at the time—she went to town, taking the dog with her.

After two days' absence she announced her return in a few cold words. What else could a murderer expect? Full of happiness, freed of a burden which I had borne for six years, I went to the landing-stage to meet her, expecting to find her alone. She received me as if I were a poisoner, her eyes were suffused with tears, and when I approached to kiss her, she pushed me aside. Carrying in her arms a large parcel of extraordinary shape, she walked on, slowly, as if she were walking in a funeral procession, with a certain rhythm as if to the strains of a funeral march.

The parcel held the corpse! The funeral ceremony had been reserved for me! She ordered a coffin and sent for two men to dig a grave. Although determined to have nothing to do with the matter, I was compelled to be present at the obsequies of the murdered innocent. It was most touching. Marie collected her thoughts and then prayed to God for the victim and its slayer. Amid the laughter of the onlookers she placed a cross on the grave, the cross of the Saviour who had—at last—delivered me from a monster, innocent itself, but yet terrible as the embodiment and instrument of the malice of a woman who lacked the courage to persecute her husband openly.

After a few days' mourning, during which she refused to have anything to say to me—for she could have nothing to say to a murderer—we left for Paris.

PART IV

I

THE main destination of my journey was Paris, where
I hoped to meet old friends, well acquainted with my
eccentricities; congenial spirits who understood my moods,
knew all about my whims, admired my courage, and were
consequently in a position to gauge accurately the temporary state of my mind. In addition to this some of the
foremost of the Scandinavian poets had just taken up a
permanent abode in Paris; I meant to claim their protection and with their help defy Marie's sinister schemes;
for she intended to have me shut up in a lunatic asylum.

During the whole journey she continued her hostilities
and treated me as a person altogether beneath contempt,
whenever we were without witnesses. She was always lost
in thought, absent-minded, indifferent. In vain I took
her sight-seeing in the towns where we were forced to
spend the nights; she took no interest in anything, saw
nothing, hardly listened to me. My attentions bored her;
she seemed to be fretting for something. But for what?
For the country where she had suffered, in which she had
not left one single friend, but—a lover, perhaps?

During the whole time she behaved like the most
unpractical and ignorant of women; she displayed none of
the qualities of the organiser and manager of which she
had boasted so much. She insisted on staying at the most
expensive hotels, and for the sake of one night she often
had the whole furniture rearranged; a badly served cup

of tea provoked interviews with the hotel proprietor; the
noise which she made in the corridors drew unflattering
comments upon us. We missed the best trains because
she would lie in bed until dinner-time; through her carelessness our luggage went astray; and when we left, her
tips to the servants were of the meanest.

"You are a coward!" she said in reply to one of
my remonstrances.

"And you are ill-bred and slovenly!"

It was a charming pleasure-trip, indeed.

As soon as we had arrived in Paris and settled down
among my friends, who were proof against her spells,
she found that I had got the better of her, and felt like
a wild animal caught in a trap. She was furious because
the leading Norwegian poet received me warmly, and overwhelmed me with kindness. She promptly detested him,
for she sensed in him a friend who might some day raise
his voice in my favour.

One evening, at a dinner given to artists and writers,
he proposed my health, calling me the chief representative
of modern Swedish literature. Marie, poor martyr by
reason of her marriage with the "notorious pamphleteer,"
was present. The applause of the diners depressed her to
a degree which excited my compassion, and when the
speaker tried to make me promise to stay for at least two
years in France, I could no longer resist the wistful
expression of her eyes. To comfort her, to give her
pleasure, I replied that I never took an important decision
without consulting with my wife. My reward was a
grateful look and the sympathy of all the women present.

But my friend remained obdurate. He urged me to
prolong my stay, and with a fine flourish of oratory asked
all those present to support his proposition. All raised
their glasses in response.

My friend's obstinacy always remained inexplicable to me, although I quite well understood at the time that a secret struggle was being fought between my wife and him, the motive of which I could not guess. Maybe he was better informed than I, and had penetrated my secret with the clear-sightedness which frequently accompanies first impressions; moreover, he was himself married to a woman of strange morals.

Marie did not feel at home in Paris, where her husband's genius was generally acknowledged, and after three months' stay she hated the beautiful city. She was indefatigable in warning me of "the false friends who would one day bring me misfortune."

She was again expecting to become a mother, and again life with her was unbearable. But this time I had no reason to doubt the paternity of the expected baby.

Our stay in Paris came to an end; we broke up our tents and slowly made our way to Switzerland.

Isn't It Enough?

It does not matter very much that the wealthy man did not ask Jesus what he should do in order to solve the problem of life, for Jesus would very likely have replied in the same way in which He replied to the question relating to the Kingdom of Heaven: "Go and sell all thou hast and give it to the poor." But it is a pity that the wealthy man did not carry out this suggestion, and above all things that he did not live to see a scorching day in June in the year 1885 in the humble form of a sixty-year-old coster who pushed a heavy barrow down the Avenue de Neuilly, ceaselessly calling out in a voice trembling with hunger and increasing age—

" Cresson de fontaine !
La santé du corps !
Quatre liards la botte !
Quatre liards la botte ! "

He went down on the left side of the avenue, halting
before every door ; but everywhere the porters' wives shook
their heads, for the younger and stronger ones had stolen
a march on the old man, and had already supplied the
necessary requirements for the day. He reached Porte
Mailot and gazed down the avenue which stretched before
him, apparently endlessly, down towards the Seine. He
took off his black cotton cap and with the sleeve of his
blue blouse wiped the perspiration off his forehead. Should
he turn round and walk up on the right side, or should he
go to Paris to try his luck there ? the wonderful luck to
earn the few pence by virtue of which he could keep up
sufficient strength to push his barrow along when to-
morrow had dawned? Should he invest his last shilling
in the payment of the toll and go on to meet the unknown
fate awaiting him ? He took the risk, paid the octroi and
trudged along the Avenue de la Grande Armée.

The sun had risen higher in the sky, and the pavements
were still warm from the previous day ; the gay town
smelled like the close, fetid atmosphere of the bedroom,
which streamed through the open windows and hung
heavily in the still air. The sunbeams heated the dust
which rose in clouds from the carpets beaten against the
doorsteps ; showy advertisements flashed from privies and
news-stalls, and a suffocating smell of ammonia penetrated
through the half-open doors ; cigar ends, tobacco, manure,
orange skins, celery stalks, pieces of paper from forgotten
refuse heaps were carried away by the rushing stream which
gushed from the main and swept everything towards the
gratings of the gutter.

The old man cried his wares, but carts and omnibuses

R

drowned his voice, and no one bought. Tired, forsaken by every one, he sat down on a seat under the plane trees. But the sunbeams found him out, and scorched him in spite of the dusty leaves. How dismal the sun appeared to the worn-out traveller, who longed for an overcast sky and a downpour to relieve the unbearable heat, which robbed his nerves of their strength and shrivelled up his muscles.

Yet the torture of the excessive heat did not make him insensible to the torture of hunger and the dread of the morrow. He rose, seized the shafts of his barrow, and toiled up the steep incline which leads to the Arc de Triomphe, shouting incessantly—

" Quatre liards la botte ! "

At the last street corner a little dressmaker bought two bunches.

He dragged himself through the Champs Elysées, and met the wealthy man, seated in his carriage behind his English coachman, on his way to the Bois de Boulogne, there to brood over the problem of life. The palaces and large restaurants bought nothing ; the fierce rays of the sun dried up the water-cress, and the long green leaves of his cauliflowers hung limp, so that he was obliged to sprinkle them with water at the fountain near the Rond-Point.

It was noon when he passed the Place de la Concorde and arrived at the Quays. Before the restaurants men were sitting and lunching ; some of them had already arrived at the coffee. They looked well-fed, but bored, as if they were fulfilling a melancholy and painful duty by keeping alive. But to the old man they were happy mortals who had staved off death for a few hours, while he felt his soul shrinking like a dried apple.

The barrow rattled past the Pont-Neuf, and every stone

against which the wheels pushed shook the muscles and nerves of his tired arms. He had not broken his fast since the early morning; his voice sounded thin like the voice of a consumptive, so that his cries were more like cries for help now, with little preliminary sighs caused by want of breath.

His feet were burning and his hands trembled; he felt as if the marrow in his spine were melting with the heat, and the thin blood hammered in his temples as he turned towards the city, seeking the shade of the Quai de l'Horloge. He halted for a moment before a wine-shop in the Place de Parvis, half inclined to spend his few pennies on a glass of wine. But he pulled himself together and trudged on, past Nôtre-Dame, towards the Morgue.

He could not drag himself away from this mysterious little house, where so many problems of life have been solved, and he entered. How cool and beautiful it was inside, where the dead lay on marble slabs, the hoar-frost on their hair and beards sparkling as on a beautiful, bright winter day. Some of them looked distressed, because the rush of the water into their lungs, or the stab of the knife into the heart, had given them pain; one of them smiled as if he were glad that all was over; one lay there with an expression of indifference on his face, as if nothing mattered; the problem was solved, at any rate: he had lived until he died. No more clothes required, no more food, no shelter! No sorrow, no cares. All held in their grasp the greatest boon life has to bestow: a calm which neither want, failure of crops, sickness, death, war or famine, American wheat or the hard laws which regulate wages, could disturb. Sleep without dreams, how gentle a sleep! And without an awakening, how splendid!

The old man must have envied the sleepers, for he turned his head on leaving, to feast his eyes once more

R 2

on the sight of those blessed ones, who slept in cool seclusion behind the large glass panes.

He plodded on to the other side of the church and stopped at the principal entrance. He asked the dealer in relics to keep an eye on his barrow, and entered. He stirred the holy water with his right hand and cooled lips and brow. Inside the church it was cool, for the sunbeams were powerless to penetrate the stained-glass windows. The pulpit was occupied by a little abbé, freshly shaved, with traces of powder still visible on his bluish skin; he was speaking, and the old man listened.

"'Consider the lilies in the field,'" said the abbé, "'how they grow; they toil not, neither do they spin, and yet Solomon in all his glory was not arrayed like any one of these! Consider the ravens: for they neither sow nor reap; which neither have store-houses nor barn; and God feedeth them: how much more are ye better than the fowls!'"

"How much more are we better than the fowls!" sighed the old man.

"But rather seek ye the Kingdom of God," concluded the abbé, "and all else will be added to you."

"All else," sighed the old man, "all else! First the Kingdom of God, and then all else."

Leaning against a pillar in the side aisle, the wealthy man, holding a Baedeker in his hand, tried to solve the problem of the essence and origin of life by means of a careful study of the architecture of the past. He did not believe in the Kingdom of God, but he brooded over the purpose of life, and could not understand why a man should go to so much trouble to kill time until he was seventy or at the most eighty years old. Had it not been against all conventions, he would have gone to the old man and said to him who had already passed his allotted time—

"Give me your solution of the problem of life!"

And the old man, unless he had been too exhausted with hunger and thirst, would have answered—

"The problem of life, as I understood it, is the maintenance of one's own life."

"Is that all?" the wealthy man would have answered, astonished.

"All? Isn't it enough? All?"

"We do not understand one another."

"No, we do not understand one another; we have never understood one another."

"Because you are a selfish old man, who has lived but for himself. But humanity. . . ."

"Sir, I too have lived for humanity, for I have brought up and educated four children, a problem which was more difficult perhaps to solve than yours, the solution of which you can buy at any bookseller's. Yes, go, sell all you have and give it to the poor, then you will see whether there is room in life for anything else!"

But the wealthy man preferred to leave the problem unsolved and keep his gold; therefore he continued to study his Baedeker, and did not ask the poor coster for his opinion.

The old man, with faith unshaken, left the church, the abbé's comforting words ringing in his ears: "Take no heed of to-morrow," and crossed to the left shore of the river.

At the corner of the Boulevard St. Michel he was fortunate enough to sell six centimes' worth of his stuff at a reduced price. And on he trudged and turned into the Rue Bonaparte.

It was afternoon, that saddest time of the day when the sun is setting, but darkness has not yet fallen, darkness which brings in its train peace for the weary souls who long to rest and play for a while before they are compelled to face torturing dreams and memories.

He sat down on a stone step and counted his money: eighty centimes; that was twenty centimes less than the franc which he had spent at the gate. How could he pay six francs to the nursery gardener? How could he buy food and drink, how return before nightfall to Suresnes? He saw in imagination the endless Champs Elysées, the long Avenue de la Grande Armée, the terrible Avenue Neuilly. No, it was too far to go back, too far.

He looked about searchingly, and his dim eyes were dazzled by the gleam of the blue and red glass bottles in the chemist's shop on the other side of the street, which sparkled in the rays of the setting sun. They stood on long shelves, filled with bottles and boxes; patent medicines for indigestion; appetite restoratives; powders to calm feverish brains which had brooded too long over the riddle of life; means of protection from over-population or increasing poverty; headache pencils for those who tried to solve social problems; rouge for night-birds, tabloids for nervous ailments and financially independent people. All these things could be bought there.

The old man rose hastily, as if a buyer had beckoned to him, and entered the chemist's shop.

"Six centimes' worth of laudanum, please," he said. "My wife is suffering from convulsions."

And as if to prove his words, he lifted his right hand to show the ring on his third finger. But there was only a white line and a groove in the brown skin.

But the chemist, who, perhaps, had also been waiting for a buyer, took no notice of his gesture; he filled a small bottle with the required liquid, licked a label, bit a cork, took the money, and resumed the study of his pharmacopœia. What business was it of his?

The old man, the bottle in his pocket, staggered out

of the shop, once again seized the shafts, and wandered up the street. He stopped at a bookseller's, and as if to make one more bid for good fortune, he called out for the last time—

"Quatre liards la botte !
Quatre liards la botte !"

Afraid that somebody might beckon to him in reply, he put the bottle to his lips and greedily drank the dark-red liquid, as if to quench a burning thirst. The pupils of his eyes contracted as if he were staring into the sun ; a vivid scarlet flame shot across his cheeks, his knees bent, and he fell on the edge of the gutter. He snored loudly like a man in a sound sleep ; the perspiration stood in large drops on his face, and there was a quivering movement of his legs.

By the time the police had arrived he lay quite still, but the expression of his face plainly betrayed his last conscious thoughts—

"Life was sometimes good, evil every now and then, but the best thing came last. I solved the problem as well as I could, and it was not easy, although the rich man found that it was not enough. But we did not understand one another. It is a pity that men are not meant to understand one another."

II

Arrived in Switzerland, we took rooms in a private hotel, so as to avoid all quarrels on the subject of housekeeping.

Marie made up for lost time, for being alone now, and unbacked by sympathising friends, I was again in her power. From the very beginning she posed as the keeper of a harmless lunatic. She made the acquaintance of the doctor, informed proprietor and proprietress, the waitresses, the servants, the other guests. I was shut off from association with intelligent people of my own kindred who understood me. At meals she revenged herself for the silence to which she had been condemned in Paris. She missed no opportunity of joining in the conversation, and literally inundated us with a never-ending stream of foolish twaddle which, she knew, irritated me horribly. And since the uncultured, commonplace crowd among whom we lived always very politely agreed with her, there was nothing for me to do but to keep silence; they regarded my silence as a proof of my inferiority.

She looked ill and fragile, and appeared to be suffering from a great grief; she treated me with dislike and contempt.

All I loved, she detested : she was disappointed with the Alps because I admired them ; she scorned the beautiful walks ; she avoided being alone with me ; she made a practice of anticipating my wishes so as to thwart them ; she said Yes whenever I said No, and vice versa; there was no doubt that she hated me.

Alone and solitary in a strange country, I was compelled

to seek her society; but since we never talked for fear of quarrelling, I had to be content with merely seeing her at my side, with feeling that I was not quite isolated.

My illness became worse; I was so ill that I could take nothing but beef tea; I lay awake at night, suffering agonies, tortured by an unbearable thirst which I tried to relieve by drinking cold milk.

My brain, keen and refined by study and culture, was thrown into confusion by contact with a coarser brain; every attempt to bring it into harmony with my wife's caused me to have convulsions. I tried to get into touch with strangers. But they treated me with the forbearance which a sane person usually shows to a lunatic.

For three months I hardly opened my lips. At the end of that time I noticed with horror that I had almost lost my voice, and, from sheer want of practice, had no longer any control of the spoken word.

Determined not to be defeated in the struggle, I began a brisk correspondence with my friends in Sweden. But their guarded language, their deep sympathy, their well-meant advice, plainly betrayed the opinion which they had formed of my mental condition.

She triumphed. I was on the verge of insanity, and the first symptoms of persecutional mania showed themselves. Mania? Did I say mania? I *was* being persecuted, there was nothing irrational in the thought.

It was just as if I had become a child again. Extremely feeble, I lay for hours on the sofa, my head on her knees, my arms round her waist, like Michel Angelo's Pieta. · I buried my face in her lap, and she called me her child. "Your child, yes," I stammered. I forgot my sex in the arms of the mother, who was no longer female, but sexless. Now she regarded me with the eyes of the conqueror, now she looked at me kindly, seized with the sudden tenderness which the hangman is said to feel sometimes for his victim.

She was like the female spider which devours her mate immediately after the hymeneal embrace.

While I suffered thus, Marie led a mysterious life. She always remained in bed till the one o'clock dinner. After dinner she went to town, frequently without any definite purpose, and did not return until supper, sometimes even later. When I was asked where she had gone, I replied—

"To town! "

And the inquirer smiled furtively.

I never suspected her. I never thought of playing the spy. After supper she remained in the drawing-room, talking to strangers.

At night she often treated the servants to liqueurs; I heard their whispering voices, but I never stooped so low as to listen at her door. . . .

What was it that held me back? I don't know. Only an instinct, I suppose, which teaches us that those actions are unmanly and dishonourable. Moreover, it had become a sort of religion with me to leave her an absolutely free hand.

Three months passed. Then the fact suddenly struck me that our expenditure was enormous. Now that our expenses were regulated, it was easy to check them.

We paid twelve francs a day at our hotel, that is three hundred and sixty francs a month, and I had given Marie a thousand francs a month. She had therefore spent six hundred francs a month in incidental expenses.

I asked her to account for her extravagance.

"The money has been spent on incidental items! " she exclaimed furiously.

"What! with an ordinary expenditure of three hundred and sixty francs, you spent six hundred francs incidentally? Do you take me for a fool? "

"I don't deny that you have given me a thousand francs, but you have spent the greater part on yourself!"

"Have I? Let's see! Tobacco (very inferior quality), and cigars at one penny each: ten francs; postage: ten francs; what else?"

"Your fencing lessons!"

"I've only had one: three francs!"

"Riding lessons!"

"Two: five francs."

"Books!"

"Books? Ten francs—together thirty francs; let us say one hundred francs; that leaves five hundred francs for incidental expenses. . . . Preposterous!"

"Do you mean to say I'm robbing you? You cad!"

What could I say? Nothing at all! . . .

I was a cad, and on the following day all her friends in Sweden were informed of the progress of my insanity.

And gradually the myth grew and developed. The salient characteristics of my personality became more and more unmistakable as time went on, and instead of the harmless poet, a mythological figure was sketched, blackened, touched up until it closely resembled a criminal.

I made an attempt to escape to Italy, where I felt sure of meeting artists and men after my own heart. The attempt was a failure. We returned to the shores of the Lake of Geneva, there to await Marie's confinement.

When the child was a few days old, Marie, the martyr, the oppressed wife, the slave without rights, implored me to have it baptised. She knew very well that in my controversial writings I had fought Christianity tooth and nail, and was therefore strongly opposed to the ritual of the church.

Although she was not in the least religious herself, and had not set a foot inside a church for the last ten years, or been to communion for goodness knows how long;

although she had only prayed for dogs, fowls and rabbits, the thought of this baptism, which she meant to elaborate into a great festival, completely obsessed her. I had no doubt that the motive which actuated her was the thought of my dislike to ceremonies which I considered insincere, and which are opposed to all my convictions.

But she implored me with tears in her eyes, appealed to my kind and generous nature. In the end I yielded to her importunity, on condition, however, that I was not expected to be present at the ceremony. She kissed my hand, thanked me effusively for what she called a mark of my affection for her, and assured me that her baby's baptism was a matter of conscience to her, a very vital point.

The ceremony took place. After her return from church, she ridiculed the "farce" in the presence of many witnesses, posed as a free-thinker, made fun of the ceremonial, and even boasted that she knew nothing whatever of the church into which her son had just been received.

She had won the game and could afford to laugh at the whole business; the "vital question" transformed itself into a victory over me, a victory which served to strengthen the hands of my adversaries.

Once again I had humiliated myself, laid myself open to attack, in order to humour the fads and fancies of an overbearing woman.

But my measure of calamities was not yet full. A Scandinavian lady appeared on the scene, full of the mania called the "Emancipation of Woman." She and Marie became friends at once, and between them I had no chance.

She brought with her the cowardly book of a sexless writer who, rejected by all parties, became a traitor to his own sex by embracing the cause of all the blue-stockings of the civilised world. After having read *Man and Woman*, by Emile Girardin, I could well understand that this movement was bound to result in great advantages to the hostile camp of the women.

To depose man and put woman in his place by the re-introduction of the matriarchate; to dethrone the true lord of creation who evolved civilisation, spread the benefits of culture, created all great ideals, art, the professions, all that there is great and beautiful in the world, and crown woman who, with few exceptions, has not shared in the great work of civilisation, constituted to me a challenge to my sex. The very thought of having to witness the apotheosis of those intelligences of the iron age, those manlike creatures, those semi-apes, that pack of dangerous animals, roused my manhood. It was strange, but I was cured of my illness, cured through my intense repugance to an enemy who, though intellectually my inferior, was more than a match for me on account of her complete lack of moral feeling.

In a tribal war the less honest, the more crafty, tribe generally remains in possession of the battlefield. The more a man respects woman, the more leisure he leaves her to arm and prepare herself for the fight, the smaller are his prospects of winning the battle. I determined to take the matter seriously. I armed myself for this new duel and wrote a book which I flung, like a gauntlet, at the feet of the emancipated women, those fools who demanded freedom at the price of man's bondage.

In the following spring we changed our hotel. Our new abode was a kind of purgatory where I was continually watched by twenty-five women who, incidentally, furnished me with copy for my book.

In three months' time the volume was ready for publication. It was a collection of stories of matrimonial life with an introduction in which I voiced a great number of disagreeable home-truths.

"Woman," I contended, "is not a slave, for she and her children are supported by her husband's work. She is not oppressed, for nature has ordained that she should live under the protection of the man while she fulfils her mission in life as mother. Woman is not man's intellectual equal; the man, on the other hand, cannot bear children. She is not an essential factor in the great work of civilisation; this is man's domain, for he is better fitted to grapple with spiritual problems than she is. Evolution teaches us that the greater the difference between the sexes, the stronger and more fit will be the resulting offspring. Consequently the aping of the masculine, the equality of the sexes, means retrogression, and is utter folly, the last dream of romantic and idealistic socialism.

"Woman, man's necessary complement, the spiritual creation of man, has no right to the privileges of her husband, for she can only be called ' the other half of humanity ' by virtue of her numbers, proportionally she is merely the sixth part of a sixth. She should not, therefore, invade the labour market as long as it falls to the lot of the man to provide for his wife and family. And the fact should not be lost sight of that every time a woman wrests an appointment from a man, there is one more old maid or prostitute."

The fury of the feminists, and the formidable party which they formed, may easily be imagined when one realises that they demanded the confiscation of my book and brought a lawsuit against me.

But despite their attempt to represent my attack as an offence against religion (the folly of the unsexed actually aspired to raise their cause to the dignity of a religion), they were not clever enough to win their case.

Marie obstinately opposed my intention to go to Sweden

unaccompanied by her ; to take my family with me was out
of the question on account of my limited means. Secretly
she was afraid that I might escape from her strict
guardianship and, worse still, that my appearance in court,
before the public, would give the lie to the rumours con-
cerning my mental condition which she had so sedulously
disseminated.

She pleaded illness, without, however, being able to
make a definite statement as to the nature of her illness,
and kept her bed. Nevertheless I decided to appear
personally in court, and left for Sweden.

The letters which I wrote to her during the following
six weeks, while I was threatened with two years' penal
servitude, were full of love, love rekindled by our separation. My overwrought brain cast a glamour over her
fragile form, wove a resplendent halo round her sweet
face ; restraint and longing clothed her with the white
garments of the guardian angel. Everything that was
base, ugly, evil, disappeared ; the madonna of my first
love-dream reappeared. I went so far as to admit to an
old friend, a journalist, "that the influence of a good
woman had made me more humble and pure-minded."
Probably this confession made the round of the papers
of the United Kingdoms.

Did the unfaithful wife laugh when she read it ?

The public got its money's worth, at any rate.

Marie's replies to my love-letters bore witness to the
keen interest which she took in the financial side of the
question. But her opinion underwent a change in the
same proportion in which the ovations I received in the
theatre, in the street and in court increased, and she called
the judges stupid, and regretted that she was not a
member of the jury.

She met my ardent declarations of love with clever
reserve ; she refused to be drawn into an argument, and

confined herself to the repetition of the words: "To understand one another," "To comprehend each other's nature and ideas." She blamed my failure to understand her for the unhappiness of our marriage. But I could swear that she herself never understood a single word of the language of her learned poet.

Amongst the number of her letters there was one which reawakened my old suspicions. I had mentioned my intention to live permanently abroad, if I was fortunate enough to escape the meshes of the law.

This upset her; she scolded me, threatened me with the loss of her love; she appealed to my pity, went down on her knees before me, as it were, evoked the memory of my mother, and confessed that the thought of never again seeing her country (by which she did not mean Finland) sent cold shudders down her spine and would kill her.

Why cold shudders? I wondered. . . .

To this day I have not found an explanation.

I was acquitted. A banquet was given in my honour, and—oh, irony of fate!—Marie's health was drunk "because she had persuaded me to appear personally before my judges."

It was indeed amusing!

As soon as possible I returned to Geneva, where my family had lived during my absence. To my great surprise Marie, whom I had believed to be ill and in bed, met me at the station; she looked well and happy, but a trifle absent-minded.

I soon recovered my spirits, and the evening and night which followed fully compensated me for all the sufferings I had endured during those six weeks.

On the following day I discovered that we were living in a boarding-house which was mainly patronised by students and light women. While listening to their chatter, it came home to me with a pang that Marie had found pleasure in drinking and playing cards with these shady characters. The familiar tone which prevailed revolted me. Marie posed to the students as the little mother (her old game); she was the bosom friend of the most objectionable of the women; she introduced her to me : a slut, who came down to dinner semi-intoxicated.

And in this hell my children had lived for six weeks! Their mother approved of the place, for she was without prejudices! And her illness—her simulated illness—had not prevented her from taking part in the amusements of this disreputable company.

She lightly dismissed all my remonstrances. I was jealous, a stickler, a snob. . . .

And again it was war between us.

We were now confronted by a new difficulty : the question of the education of the children. The nurse, an uneducated country girl, was made their governess, and, in collusion with the mother, committed the most outrageous follies. Both women were indolent, and liked to stay in bed until broad daylight. Consequently the children were obliged to stay in bed also, during the morning, no matter how wide awake they were; if they insisted on getting up, they were punished. As soon as I became aware of this state of things, I interfered; without much ado I sounded the reveille in the nursery, and was greeted with shouts of delight as a deliverer from bondage. My wife reminded me of our contract : personal freedom —her interpretation of which was the limitation of the liberty of others—but I took no notice of her.

The monomania of weak and inferior brains, that desire to equalise what can never be equal, was the cause of much mischief in my family. My elder daughter, a precocious child, had for years been allowed to play with my illustrated books, and had, besides, enjoyed many of the

s

privileges usually enjoyed by the firstborn. Because I would not extend the same privileges to the younger one, who had no idea of handling an expensive book, I was accused of injustice.

"There ought to be no difference whatever," she said.

"No difference? Not even in the quantity of clothes and shoes?"

There was no direct reply to my remark, but a contemptuous "fool" made up for the omission.

"Every one according to merit and ability! This for the elder, that for the younger one!"

But she refused to understand my meaning, and stubbornly maintained that I was an unjust father, and "hated" my younger daughter.

To tell the truth, I was more attached to the elder one, because she awakened in me memories of the first beautiful days of my life, and because, also, she was sensible in advance of her years; I may also have been influenced by the fact that the younger one was born at a time when I had grave doubts of my wife's fidelity.

The mother's "justice," I may say, evidenced itself in complete indifference to the children. She was always either out or asleep. She was a stranger to them, and they became devoted to me; their preference for me was so marked that it roused her jealousy, and in order to conciliate her, I made a practice of letting her distribute the toys and sweets which I bought for them, hoping that in this way she might win their affection.

The little ones were a very important factor in my life, and in my darkest moments, when I was almost broken by my isolation, contact with them bound me afresh to life and their mother. For the sake of the children the thought of divorcing my wife was unthinkable; an ominous fact, as far as I was concerned, for I was becoming more and more her abject slave.

III

THE result of my attack on the strongholds of the feminists soon made itself felt. The Swiss press attacked me in such a manner that my life in Switzerland became unbearable. The sale of my books was prohibited, and I fled, hunted from town to town, to France.

But my former Paris friends had deserted me. They had become my wife's allies, and, surrounded and hemmed in like a wild beast, I again changed the arena; almost without means I at last made port in a colony of artists in the neighbourhood of Paris.

Alas! I was caught in a net, and I remained enmeshed for ten miserable months!

The society in which I found myself consisted of young Scandinavian artists, recruited from various professions, some of them of strange origin; but, worse still, there was a number of lady-artists, women without prejudices, completely emancipated and so enamoured with hermaphroditic literature that they believed themselves the equals of man. They tried to conceal their sex as far as possible by adopting certain masculine characteristics; they smoked, drank, played billiards . . . and made love to each other. They wallowed in the lowest depths of immorality.

As an alternative to utter isolation, we made friends with two of those monstrous women; one of them was a writer, the other an artist.

The writer called on me first, as is customary when one happens to be a well-known author. My wife was jealous at once: she was anxious to win an ally sufficiently enlightened to appreciate my arguments against the unsexed.

But certain events happened which made my henceforth notorious mania break out in irrepressible fury.

The hotel boasted of an album which contained caricatures of all the well-known Scandinavians, sketched by Scandinavian artists. My portrait was amongst them, adorned with a horn cleverly contrived by the manipulation of a lock of hair.

The artist was one of our most intimate friends. I concluded that my wife's infidelity was an open secret; everybody knew it, everybody except myself. I asked the proprietor of the collection for an explanation.

Marie had taken care to inform him of my mental condition soon after our arrival, and he swore that the decoration of my forehead existed in my imagination only, that there was no trace of it in the sketch, and that I had worked myself into a passion for no reason whatever. I had to be content with this explanation until I was able to obtain more reliable information.

One evening we were sipping our coffee in the hotel garden in the company of an old friend who had just arrived from Sweden. It was still broad daylight, and from where I sat I could watch every expression on Marie's face. The old man gave us all the latest news. Amongst other names he mentioned that of the doctor who had treated my wife by massage. She did not let the name pass without comment, but interrupted him with a defiant—

"Ah! you know the doctor?"

"Oh yes, he is a very popular man. . . . I mean to say he enjoys a certain reputation——"

"As a conceited fool," I interposed.

Marie's cheeks grew pale; a cynical smile drew up the corners of her mouth, so that her white teeth became visible. The conversation dropped amid a general sense of embarrassment.

When I was left alone with my friend, I begged him to tell me frankly what he knew of those rumours which were giving me so much uneasiness. He swore a solemn oath that he knew nothing. I continued urging him, and at last drew from him the following enigmatical words of comfort—

"Moreover, my dear fellow, if you suspect one man, you may be sure that there are several."

That was all. But from this day onward Marie, who had been so fond of telling tales, of mentioning the doctor's name in public, that it sometimes seemed as if she were trying to get accustomed to talk about him without blushing, never again alluded to him.

This discovery impressed me so much that I took the trouble to search my memory for similar evidence. I recollected a play which had appeared at the time of her divorce. It threw light, vague, uncertain light, it is true, but yet sufficient light, on the channel which led up to the source of those rumours.

A play by the famous Norwegian blue-stocking, the promoter of the "equality-mania," had fallen into my hands. I had read it without connecting it in the least with my own case. Now, however, I applied it easily, so easily that the blackest suspicions of my wife's good fame seemed justified.

This was the story of the play—

A photographer (the realism of my writings had won me this designation) had married a girl of doubtful morality. She had been the mistress of a smelter, and funds which she received from her former lover kept her home going. She made herself proficient in her husband's profession ; and while she worked left him to loaf and spend his time in the cafés, drinking with boon companions.

The facts, albeit disguised in this way, must have been plain enough to the publisher; for although the latter knew that Marie was a translator, he did not know that I edited her translations and paid her the proceeds of her work without condition or deduction.

Matters did not improve when the unfortunate photographer discovered that his daughter, whom he idolised, had come into the world prematurely and was not his child at all, that he had been duped by his wife when she had prevailed on him to marry her.

To complete his degradation the deceived husband accepted a large sum from the old lover in lieu of damages.

In this I saw an allusion to Marie's loan which the Baron had guaranteed; it was the same guarantee which I had been compelled to countersign on our wedding-day.

I could not, at first, see any similitude between the illegitimate birth of the child in the play and my own case, for my little daughter was not born until two years after our marriage.

But I reflected. . . . What about the child who died? . . . I was on the right tack! . . . Poor little dead baby! . . . It had been the cause of our marriage which otherwise might never have taken place.

I knew that my conclusion was not altogether sound, nevertheless I had arrived at a conclusion of some sort. Everything fitted in. Marie had visited the Baron after the divorce, he was on friendly terms with us, the walls of my home were decorated with his pictures, there was the loan, and all the rest of it.

I was determined to act, and laid my plans accordingly. I intended to suggest that Marie should draw up an indictment, or rather a defence, which would clear us both, for both of us had been attacked by the feminists' man of straw; he, doubtless, had been bribed into undertaking this profitable job.

When Marie entered my room, I received her in the most friendly manner.

" What is the matter ? " she asked.

" A very serious thing which concerns us both ! " I told her the story of the play, and added that the actor who played the part of the photographer had made up to resemble me.

She reflected, silently, a prey to very evident excitement. Then I suggested the defence.

" If it is true, tell me ; I shall forgive you. If the little one who died was indeed Gustav's baby, well—you were free at the time ; vague promises only bound you to me, and you had never accepted any money from me. As for the hero of the play, he behaved, in my opinion, like a man of heart ; he was incapable of ruining the future prospects of his wife and daughter. The money which he accepted on behalf of the child was nothing but a quite legitimate compensation for an injury done to him."

She listened with great attention ; her small soul nibbled at the bait without, however, swallowing it.

To judge from the calm which smoothed her conscience-stricken features, my assertion that she had a right to dispose of her body because she had never taken money from me pleased her. She agreed that the deceived husband was a man of heart. " A noble heart," she maintained.

The scene ended without my succeeding to draw a confession from her. I showed her the way out of the difficulty ; I appealed to her for advice as to the best means of repairing our honour ; suggested that we should publish our " defence " in the shape of a novel, and so cleanse ourselves before the world and our children from all those infamies. . . .

I talked for an hour. She sat at my writing-table,

playing with my penholder, in a state of intense agitation, without making a sound, only giving vent occasionally to a short exclamation.

I went out for a walk and then played a game of billiards. When I returned, after a couple of hours, I found her still sitting in the same place, motionless, like a statue.

She roused herself when she heard my footsteps.

"You were setting a trap for me!" she exclaimed.

"Not at all! Do you think I want to lose the mother of my children for ever?"

"I consider you capable of anything. You want to be rid of me; you made an attempt some time ago when you introduced a certain friend of yours to me." She mentioned a name which had never before been mentioned in this connection. "You hoped that I should betray you with him, didn't you?"

"Who told you that?"

"Helga!"

"Helga?"

She was Marie's last "friend" before we left Sweden. The revenge of the Lesbian!

"And you believed her?"

"Of course I did. . . . But I deceived you both, him and you!"

"You mean there was a third?"

"I didn't say so!"

"But you just confessed it! Since you deceived both of us, you must have deceived me! That is a logical conclusion."

She fought my arguments desperately, and demanded that I should prove them.

"Prove them! . . ."

Her treachery, surpassing the lowest depths of degradation of which I held a human heart capable, weighed on me like a crushing load. I bowed my head, I fell on my knees, I whined for mercy.

"You believed in the tittle-tattle of that woman! You believed that I wanted to be rid of you! And yet I have never been anything to you but a true friend, a faithful husband; I can't live without you! You complained of my jealousy . . . while I regarded all women who run after me, trying to make love to me, as evil spirits. You believed what that woman said! . . . Tell me, did you really believe it? "

She was moved to compassion, and, all at once, yielding to a prompting to tell the truth, she confessed that she had never really believed it.

"And you deceived me. . . . Confess it, I'll forgive you. . . . Deliver me from the terrible, pitiless thoughts which torment me. . . . Confess it. . . ."

She confessed nothing, and merely confined herself to calling my friend a "scoundrel."

A scoundrel he, my most intimate, my closest friend!

Oh, that I lay before her dead! Life was unbearable. . . .

During dinner she was more than kind to me. When I had gone to bed, she came into my room, and, sitting on the edge of my bed, stroked my hands, kissed my eyes, and at last, shaken to the very foundation of her soul, burst into uncontrollable weeping.

"Don't cry, darling, tell me what's the matter; let me comfort you! . . ."

She stammered unintelligible, disconnected words about my generous heart, my kindness, my forbearance, the great compassion which I extended even to the worst of sinners.

How absurd it all was! I accused her of infidelity, she praised and caressed me.

But the fire had been kindled, and the flames could not be extinguished.

She had deceived me.

I must know the name of my rival!

The following week was one of the darkest of my whole life.

I fought a desperate fight against all those inbred principles which we inherit, or, rather, which we acquire through education. I resolved to open Marie's letters and make sure how I stood with her. And yet, although I allowed her to open all communications which came for me during my absence, I recoiled from tampering with the sacred law of the inviolability of letters, this most subtle obligation imposed on us by silent agreement between the whole community.

But my desire to know the full truth was stronger than my sense of honour, and a day dawned when the sacred law was forgotten. A letter had arrived; I opened it with trembling fingers; my hands shook as if they were unfolding the death-warrant of my honour.

It was a letter from the adventuress, friend No. 1. The subject of it was my insanity, mockingly, contemptuously discussed; it concluded with a prayer that God might soon deliver "her dear Marie" from her martyrdom by extinguishing the last glimmer of my reason.

I copied the worst passages, re-sealed the envelope, and laid the letter aside, ready to hand it to my wife with the evening mail. When the time came I gave it to her, and sat down by her side to watch her while she read it.

When she came to the part where the writer prayed for my death—at the top of the second page—she burst into shrill laughter.

So my beloved wife saw no other way out of her difficulties than my death. It was her only hope of escape from the consequences of her indiscretions. When I was gone, she would cash my life insurance and receive the pension due to the widow of a famous writer; then she would marry again, perhaps, or remain a gay widow all her life . . . my beloved wife. . . .

Moriturus sum! I resolved to hasten the catastrophe by a liberal recourse to absinthe, sole source of happiness now, and in the meantime play billiards to calm my excited brain.

A fresh complication confronted me, worse, if possible, than any of the previous ones. The authoress who had pretended to be in love with me made a conquest of Marie, and Marie became so devoted to her that her attachment gave rise to a great deal of gossip. This roused the jealousy of the authoress's former "inseparable," a fact which was not calculated to contradict the ugly rumours.

One evening Marie asked me whether I was in love with her friend. . . .

"No, on the contrary! A common tippler! You can't be serious!"

"I am mad on her," she replied. "It is strange, isn't it? . . . I am afraid of being alone with her!"

"Why?"

"I don't know! She is so charming . . . delicious. . . ."

"Indeed. . . ."

In the following week we invited some of our Paris friends, artists, without scruples or prejudices, and their wives.

The men came, but alone; the wives sent apologies, so transparent that they amounted to insults.

Dinner degenerated into a perfect orgy. The scandalous conduct of the men revolted me.

They treated Marie's two friends as if they were prostitutes, and when every one was more or less intoxicated I saw one of the officers present repeatedly kissing my wife.

I waved my billiard cue above their heads and demanded an explanation.

"He's a friend of my childhood, a relative! Don't make yourself a laughing-stock, you silly!" replied Marie. "Moreover, it is a Russian custom to kiss in public, and we are Russian subjects."

"Rubbish!" exclaimed one of the convives. "A relative? Humbug!"

I nearly committed a murder then. I had every intention to . . . but the thought of leaving my children without father and mother arrested my arm.

When the company had left I had a scene with Marie.

"Prostitute!"

"Why?"

"Because you submit to being treated like one."

"Are you jealous?"

"Yes, I am jealous; jealous of my honour, the dignity of my family, the reputation of my wife, the future of my children! It is because of your unworthy conduct that we are ostracised by all decent women. To allow a stranger to kiss you in public! Don't you realise that you are mad, that you neither see, nor hear, nor understand what you are doing, that you are absolutely devoid of all sense of duty? I shall have you shut up if you don't mend your ways, and, to begin with, I forbid you to have anything more to do with those two women!"

"It's all your fault! You egged me on!"

"I wanted to see how far you would go!"

"See how far I would go! What proof have you

that the relationship between me and my friends is such
as you suspect?"

"What proof! None! But I have your admissions,
your slippery tales. And didn't one of your friends admit
that in her own country she would fall into the hands
of the law?"

"I thought you denied the existence of vice!"

"I don't care how your friends amuse themselves so
long as their amusements do not interfere with the
welfare of my family. From the moment, however, that
their ' peculiarities,' if you prefer this word, threaten to
injure us, they are, as far as we are concerned, criminal
acts. True, as a philosopher, I don't admit the existence
of vice, but only of physical or moral defects. And, quite
recently, when this unnatural tendency was discussed in
the French parliament, all the French physicians of note
were of opinion that it was not the province of the law
to interfere in these matters, except in cases where the
interests of individual citizens were violated."

I might as well have preached to stone walls. How
could I hope to make this woman, who acknowledged no
other law but her animal instincts, grasp a philosophical
distinction!

To be quite sure of the facts, I wrote to a friend in
Paris and asked him to tell me the plain truth.

In his reply, which was very candid, he told me that my
wife's perverse tendencies were no secret in Scandinavia,
and that the two Danes were well-known Lesbians in Paris.

We were in debt at our hotel, and had no money;
therefore we were unable to move. But the two Danish
ladies got into trouble with the peasants, and were compelled to leave.

We had known them for eight months, and an abrupt
termination of our friendship was impossible; moreover,
they belonged to good families, and were well educated;

they had been comrades in trouble, and I resolved to grant them a retreat with honours. A farewell banquet was therefore arranged in the studio of one of the young artists.

At dessert, when every one was more or less gay with the wine which had been drunk, Marie, overcome by her feelings, rose to sing a song of her own composition. It was an imitation of the well-known song in *Mignon*, and in it she bade farewell to her friend. She sang with fire and genuine feeling, her almond-shaped eyes were full of tears and glowed softly in the reflection of the candle-light; she opened her heart so wide that even I was touched and charmed. There was a candour, an ingenuousness in this woman's love-song to a woman, so pathetic that it kept all unchaste thoughts at bay. And how strange it was! She had neither the appearance nor the manners of the hermaphrodite; she was essentially woman; loving, tender, mysterious, unfathomable woman.

How different from her was the object of her tenderness! She was a pure Russian type, with masculine features, a hooked nose, a massive chin, yellow eyes and bloated cheeks, a flat chest, crooked fingers—a truly hideous woman—a peasant would not have looked at her.

When she had finished her song Marie sat down by the side of this freak; the latter rose, took Marie's head in her two hands and kissed her on the lips. That at least was pure and unadulterated sensuality.

I drank with the Russian until she was quite intoxicated; she stumbled, looked at me with large, bewildered eyes, and, sobbing like an imbecile, clutched the wall to support herself. I had never before seen such ugliness in human shape.

The banquet ended with a row in the street. On the following morning the two Danes left.

Marie passed through a terrible crisis; I was genuinely

sorry for her; her longing for her friend, her suffering, were unmistakable. It was a genuine instance of unhappy love. She went for solitary walks in the woods, sang love-songs, visited the favourite haunts of her friends, exhibited every symptom of a wounded heart. I began to entertain fears for her sanity. She was unhappy, and I could not console her. She avoided my caresses, pushed me aside when I tried to kiss her. My heart was full of hatred for the woman who had robbed me of my wife's love. Perfectly unconscious of herself, Marie made no secret of the identity of the person for whom she was mourning. She talked of nothing but her love and her sorrow. It was incredible!

The two friends carried on a brisk correspondence. Infuriated with her indifference to me, I one day seized one of her friend's letters. It was a genuine love-letter. "My darling, my little puss, my clever, delicate, tender, noble-hearted Marie; that coarse husband of yours is but a stupid brute . . ." and so on. The letter further suggested that she should leave me, and proposed ways and means of escape. . . .

I stood up against my rival, and on the same evening —oh, my God! Marie and I fought in the moonshine. She bit my hands, I dragged her to the river to drown her like a kitten—when suddenly I saw a vision of my children. It brought me to my senses.

I resolved to put an end to myself, but before doing so I determined to write the story of my life.

The first part of the book was finished when the news spread through the village that the Danish ladies had engaged rooms.

I instantly had the trunks packed, and we left for German Switzerland.

IV

Lovely Argovia! Sweet Arcady, where the post-
master tends his flocks, where the colonel drives the only
cab, where the young girls are virgins when they marry,
and the young men shoot at targets and play the drum.
Utopia! land of the golden beer and smoked sausages;
birthplace of the game of ninepins, the House of Habs-
burg, William Tell, rustic merry-makings and naïve
songs straight from the heart, pastors' wives and vicarage
idylls!

Peace returned to our troubled hearts. I recovered,
and Marie, weary of strife, wrapped herself in undisguised
indifference. We played backgammon as a safety-valve,
and our conversations, so fraught with danger, were
replaced by the rolling of dice. I drank good, wholesome beer instead of wine and the nerve-shattering
absinthe.

The influence of our environment soon made itself felt.
I was amazed to find that such serene calm could follow
the storms we had weathered, that the elasticity of the
mind could withstand so many shocks, that we could
forget the past, that I could fancy myself the happiest
husband of the most faithful wife.

Marie, deprived of all society and friends, uncomplain-
ingly devoted herself to her children. After a month
had elapsed the little ones were dressed in frocks which
she had cut out and made with her own hands. She
was never impatient with them, and allowed them to
absorb her completely.

For the first time now I noticed a certain lassitude in
272

her; her love of pleasure was less pronounced, approaching middle-age made itself felt. How grieved she was when she lost her first tooth! Poor girl! She wept, put her arms round me and implored me never to cease loving her. She was now thirty-seven years old. Her hair had grown thinner, her bosom had sunk like the waves of the sea after a storm, the stairs tired her little feet, her lungs no longer worked with the old pressure.

And I, although I had not yet reached my prime, although my strength was increasing and I enjoyed excellent health, I loved her more than ever at the thought that now she would belong entirely to me and her children. Shielded from temptation, surrounded by my tender care, she would grow old in the fulfilment of her duties towards her family. . . .

Her return to a more normal state of mind manifested itself in many pathetic ways. Realising her hazardous position as the wife of a comparatively young man of thirty-eight, she took it into her head to be jealous of me; she was more particular about the details of her dress, and took care of herself during the day, so that she might be fresh and able to please me in the evening.

She need have had no fear, for I am monogamous by temperament, and, far from abusing the situation, I did my utmost to spare her the cruel pangs of jealousy by giving her proof after proof of my renewed love.

In the autumn I made up my mind to make a tour through French Switzerland; I intended to be away for three weeks, and never stay longer than a day at any one place.

Marie, still clinging to the idea of my shattered health, tried to dissuade me.

"I am sure it will kill you," she reiterated.

"We shall see!"

T

The tour was a point of honour with me, an attempt
to win her back completely, to reawaken in her the love
of the virile.

I returned after incredible hardships, strong, brown
and healthy.

There was a look of admiration, a challenge in her eyes
when she met me, which was, however, quickly superseded
by a look of disappointment.

I, on the other hand, after my three weeks' absence
and abstinence, treated her as a man treats a beloved
mistress, a wife from whom he has been parted all too
long. I put my arm round her waist and, like a conqueror, seized my own, after a journey of forty-eight
hours without a break. . . . She did not know what to
think; she was amazed, afraid of betraying her real feelings, frightened at the thought of finding the "tamer"
in her husband.

When my excitement had abated a little, I noticed
that Marie's expression had undergone a change. I
scrutinised her appearance : her missing tooth had been
replaced, a fact which made her look much younger.
Certain details of her dress betrayed a wish to please.
It roused my attention. I soon discovered the reason
in the presence of a young girl of about fourteen, with
whom she was exceedingly friendly. They kissed one
another, went for walks together, bathed together. . . .

There was nothing left for me to do but to take her
away at once.

V

WE took rooms in a German private hotel on the shores of the Lake of Lucerne.

Marie relapsed into her former ways. She paid a great deal of attention to one of the guests, a young officer; played ninepins with him, and took melancholy walks in the garden while I worked.

I noticed at dinner that they exchanged tender glances, although no words were uttered. They seemed to caress one another with the eyes. I resolved to put them to the test at once, and, turning round sharply, looked straight into my wife's face. She tried to throw me off the scent by letting her eyes glide along the young man's temples until thy rested on the wall, on a spot which was adorned by a huge poster advertising a brewery. She made an inane remark to cover her confusion.

"Is that a new brewery?" she stammered.

"Yes . . . but don't imagine that you can hoodwink me," I retorted.

She bent her neck, as if I had pulled in the reins, and remained silent.

Two days later, in the evening, on pretence of being tired, she kissed me good-night and left the room. I too went to bed, and after reading for a little while, fell asleep.

All of a sudden I awoke. Some one was playing the piano in the drawing-room; a voice was singing—it was Marie's voice.

I arose and called the children's nurse.

T 2   275

"Go and tell your mistress to go to bed at once," I said. "Tell her that if she refuses I shall come down myself and shake her in the presence of the whole company."

Marie came up-stairs at once. She seemed ashamed, and with an air of injured innocence she asked me why I had sent her so strange a message; why I would not allow her to stay in the drawing-room, although there were other ladies present?

"I don't mind your staying in the drawing-room," I replied angrily. "But I do object to your sly ways of getting rid of me whenever you want to be there by yourself."

"If you insist, very well, I'll go to bed."

This candour, this sudden submission. . . . What had happened?

Winter had set in in good earnest. There was an abundance of snow; the sky was leaden, and we were cut off from all society. Everybody had left; we were the last guests in the modest hotel. The extreme cold compelled us to take our meals in the large public dining-room of the restaurant.

One morning, while we were at luncheon, a strong, thick-set man, rather nice-looking, evidently belonging to the servant class, entered, sat down at one of the tables, and asked for a glass of wine.

Marie scrutinised the stranger in her free and easy manner, took his measure, as it were, and became lost in a reverie.

The man went away, confused and flattered by her attention.

"A nice-looking man," she remarked, turning to the host.

"He used to be my porter."

"Was he? He really is unusually good-looking for his class! A very nice-looking man indeed!"

And she went into details, praising his virile beauty in terms which puzzled our host.

On the following morning the dashing ex-porter was already in his place when we entered. Dressed in his Sunday best, hair and beard trimmed, he appeared to be fully aware of his conquest. He bowed; my wife acknowledged his bow with a graceful bending of her head; he squared his shoulders and gave himself the airs of a Napoleon.

He returned on the third day, determined to break the ice. He started a polite conversation, reminiscent of the back-door, all the while addressing himself directly to my wife without wasting any time over the usual trick of first conciliating the husband.

It was intolerable!

Marie, in the presence of her husband and children, allowed herself to be drawn into a discussion by a stranger.

Once more I tried to open her eyes, begged her to be more careful of her reputation.

Her only answer was her usual: "You have a nasty mind!"

A second Apollo came to the rescue. He was the village tobacconist, an undersized man, at whose shop Marie was in the habit of making small purchases. More shrewd than the porter, he tried to make friends with me first; he was of a more enterprising nature. At the first meeting he stared impudently at Marie and loudly exclaimed to our host—

"I say, what a distinguished-looking family!"

Marie's heart caught fire, and the village beau returned night after night.

One evening he was intoxicated, and therefore more

insolent than usual. He approached Marie while we were
playing backgammon, and asked her to explain the rules
of the game to him. I answered as civilly as I could
under the circumstances, and the worthy man returned
to his seat, snubbed. Marie, more sensitive than I, was
under the impression that she ought to make amends for
my rudeness; she turned to him with the first question
which came into her mind—

"Do you play billiards?" she said.

"No, madame, or rather, I play badly. . . ."

He rose again, approached a step or two, and offered
me a cigar. I declined.

He turned to Marie. "Won't you smoke, madame?"
Fortunately for her, for the tobacconist and the future of
my family, she too declined, but she refused in a manner
which flattered him.

How dared this man offer a lady a cigarette in a
restaurant in the presence of her husband?

Was I a jealous fool? Or was my wife's conduct
so scandalous that she excited the desire of the first-
comer?

We had a scene in our room, for I regarded her as
a somnambulist whom it was my duty to awaken. She
was walking straight to her doom, without being in the
least aware of it. I gave her an epitome of her sins, old
and new, and minutely criticised her conduct.

Silently, with a pale face and dream-shadowed eyes,
she listened until I had finished. Then she rose and went
down-stairs to bed. But this time—for the first time in
my life—I fell so low as to play the spy. I crept down-
stairs, found her bedroom door, and looked through the
keyhole.

The rich glow of the lamp fell on the children's nurse,
who sat opposite the door, right in the field of my
vision. Marie was pacing the room excitedly, vehemently

denouncing my unfounded suspicions; she conducted her
case as a criminal conducts his defence.

And yet I was innocent, quite innocent, in spite of
all my opportunities to sin. . . .

She produced two glasses of beer, and they drank
together. They sat down, side by side, and Marie looked
at her caressingly. Closer and closer she moved to the
girl, put her head on the shoulders of this new friend,
slipped her arm round her waist and kissed her. . . .

Poor Marie! Poor, unhappy woman, who sought
comfort far from me, who alone could set her mind at
rest and give her peace. All of a sudden she drew herself
up, listened, and pointed towards the door.

"Some one's there!"

I slipped away.

When I returned to my post of observation I noticed
that Marie was half undressed, exposing her shoulders to
the gaze of the girl, who, however, remained quite
unmoved. Then she resumed her defence.

"There can be no doubt that he is mad! I shouldn't
be surprised if he tried to poison me. . . . I suffer unbearable pains in my inside. . . . But no, it's hardly probable . . . perhaps I ought to fly to Finland. . . . What
do you think? . . . Only it would kill him, for he loves
the children. . . ."

What was this, if not the outpourings of an evil conscience? . . . Stung with remorse, she was terror-stricken
and sought refuge on the bosom of a woman! She was
a perverted child; an unfaithful wife, a criminal; but,
above all, she was an unhappy woman.

I lay awake all night, a prey to my tormenting thoughts.
At two o'clock in the morning I heard her moaning in
her sleep. Full of pity, I knocked on the floor to dispel
the visions which terrified her. It was not the first time
that I had done this,

She thanked me on the following morning for having awakened her from her nightmare. I made much of her, and begged her to tell me, her best friend, everything. "Tell you what? . . . I have nothing to tell."

I should have given her absolution for whatever crime she had confessed to me at that moment, for my heart was full of compassion. I loved her with an infinite love, despite of, or perhaps because of, all the misery she had wrought. She was but an unhappy woman. How could I raise my hand against her?

But instead of delivering me once and for all from the terrible doubts which haunted me, she offered me the most strenuous resistance. She had persuaded herself that I was insane; her instinct of self-preservation had built up a legend behind which she could shield herself from the attacks of her anguished conscience.

Sunwards.

Not a single ray of sunlight had gladdened the little village of Gersau on the shore of the Lake of Lucerne for three long weeks, not, in fact, since the beginning of October, when the Foehn began to blow. There had been a dead calm; after sunset I had fallen asleep and slept until I was awakened, in the middle of the night, by the ringing of the church bells and a noise which mingled with the peculiar rushing sound of the tempest as it came sweeping across the Alps, flung itself on the southern shore of the lake, was compressed into the valley and forced into the streets of our village, where it tore at the signs, shook the window shutters, rattled the slates and howled through the branches of trees and shrubs.

The waves of the lake dashed against the dam, foamed over the border and plashed against the sides of the boats. Handfuls of storm-lashed sand were flung at our windows; the leaves, torn from their branches, went dancing and whirling by, the doors of the stoves clattered, the walls shook. I looked out of the window; the church was lighted up, and the bells were ringing to awaken those who still slept. In these parts the Foehn is accounted as full of danger as an earthquake, for it does not only sweep away the houses, but it tears the mountains to pieces and flings them into the valleys. Our house was situated at the base of a mountain which, though only fifteen hundred metres high, carried on its summit a loose litter of rocks, peculiarly adapted to stone-throwing on a large scale. The tempest raged for three hours, then the danger was over; but on the following morning everybody in the village knew that at Schwyz a rock had fallen on a farmhouse and carried away the right wing without injury to those who lived in the left.

After this warm but terrific gale a fog descended on village and lake. The sky was overcast, but no rain fell; yet there was no sunshine. This continued for three weeks, and if the outlook had been grey to begin with, it ended by being black. The beautiful alpine landscape, the unrivalled restorer of flagging spirits, had lost its potency, for it was impossible to see further ahead than a hundred yards up the steep rocks; the heart became heavy as lead and indescribably depressed. The tourists had turned their faces homewards, the hotels were empty, November was upon us, sombre and gloomy. The hours dragged on wearily; one longed for the end of the dreary day and the cheerful light of the lamps; the dismal sky was grey, the lake was grey, the landscape was grey.

No wind, no rain, no thunder. Nature, so varied and diversified, had become monotonous, calm and quiet; so peaceful that an earthquake would have been a relief.

Wherever the light did not fall, greyness reigned;

vision was dimmed, and drowsiness, akin to laziness, enveloped the soul.

One evening, when I complained to the magistrate of the long absence of the sun, he answered with the phlegm which characterises the German-Swiss—

"The sun! You can see the sun all day long on the Hochfluh!"

The Hochfluh was one of the smaller mountain ranges which surrounded the valley in which we lived; it was only two hundred metres lower than the Sulitelma, and consequently a favourite walk of young English tourists. Being a worshipper of the sun, I decided to make a pilgrimage to my deity, and early one November morning I set out on my travels.

The inhabitants of Gersau, living at the base of a mountain which, as I have already mentioned, every now and then transforms itself into a volcano and rains rocks and stones on the valleys, have from time immemorial cultivated the habit of preparing themselves for death by visiting their church three times a day, at morning, noon and evening. I was not surprised, therefore, to meet the church-goers now, at eight o'clock in the morning, carrying their Prayer Books in their hands. Two old women, patiently performing their daily half-mile trudge to morning prayers, were counting their beads on the highroad. One of them started the angelic salutation "Ave Maria!" and her companion joined in the burden "In sæcula sæculorum, Amen." They kept up their monotonous mumbling the whole way, and though this counting of beads may not have done any actual good, it at least prevented any misuse of the tongue; I could not help thinking of the well-known anecdote of the count who made his butler whistle whenever he was busy in the wine cellar.

Soon after I had left the old women and the highroad

behind, and begun the ascent, I came upon some sights which were so striking that they made a lasting impression on me. Close to the first curve of the road grew a walnut tree, to which were nailed a crucifix and a tablet; the inscription on the latter informed the passer-by that farmer Seppi, while busy with the harvest, fell from the tree and was killed. God have mercy on his soul! Pray for him! Amen!

At the next corner there was a queer little shrine built of whitewashed bricks, small like a child's dolls'-house. A peep through the railings disclosed pictures of the Holy Family, painted, perhaps, in the sixteenth century, and a legend to the effect that criminals on their way to execution were allowed a few minutes' respite before the shrine to utter a last prayer. I was, therefore, on the road which led to the gallows, and a few minutes later I arrived at the place of execution, a pleasant open spot on the top of an overhanging cliff which jutted out in the direction of the lake. From this point one had a magnificent view. To bid farewell to life with a last look at such a picture as greets the eye from the summit of Pilatus, Buechserhorn or Buergenstock is quite conceivably a genuine pleasure. Even Voltaire could have felt none of the repugnance which was excited in him by the idea of being hanged in secret, a contingency which filled him with such extreme disgust, that he was quite consistent in accusing Rousseau of a vanity so great that it would permit him to submit cheerfully to being hanged, if he could be sure of his name being nailed to the gallows.

In the distance, near the shore, I could dimly discern a faint outline of a haunted little church, called "Kindli-mord" because a grief-stricken father is said there to have killed his starving child.

I left these four melancholy landmarks behind me in

the grey morning light, and hastened my ascent to those happier heights where the sun was shining.

Very soon beeches took the place of chestnut and walnut trees. I rested for a while in a dairy cottage in the company of fine cattle and a horrible cur, and then entered cloudland. I seemed to be walking in a dense fog, which grew in density and almost completely blotted out the landscape. The effort to see made my eyes ache; trees and shrubs loomed indistinctly through a cloud of smoke; the millions of cobwebs which festooned the branches were richly studded with raindrops; it looked as if the old woman of the wood, if there is such a being, had hung up thousands of lace handkerchiefs to dry.

It was difficult to breathe; the fog hung on my coat, hair, beard and eyebrows, gave out a stale, sickly smell, and rendered the rocks so smooth and slippery that I could hardly keep my footing; it darkened the heart of the wood, where the trunks were quickly swallowed up in a monotonous grey, which limited the range of vision to a few yards.

I had to climb up through this layer of fog, extending about a thousand metres upwards, a cold and damp purgatory, before I could reach the sun; and I struggled on, with sublime faith in the magistrate's word of honour that the fog would cease before the mountain ceased and grey space began.

I had no barometer with me, but I felt that I was ascending, that the fog was growing less dense, and that I was approaching a purer atmosphere.

A feeling of intoxication seized me—a faint glimmer from above dimly illuminated the narrow pass, like the first dawn of day shining through the picture of a landscape painted on a window-blind; the trees stood out more distinctly, the field of vision increased, the tinkling of cowbells—from above—fell on my ear. And now,

right on the summit, there hung a golden cloud; a few
more steps and the stunted beeches and brushwood shone
and glittered, dazzling splashes of gold, copper, bronze
and silver, wherever a stream of broken sunlight fell on
the faded foliage which was still clinging to the branches.
I was standing in an autumn landscape looking out into
a sun-bathed summerland; through my mind flashed the
memory of a sail on the Lake of Mälar; I remembered
how I was sitting in the sunshine, watching the passing
of a black hail-storm no further off than a cable-length
to leeward. And now I, too, stood in the sunlight,
gazing at a northern landscape made up of firs and birch
trees, green fields and red cattle, little brown cottages
with old women on the thresholds, knitting socks for
father, who was toiling far down in the canton of Tessin;
my eyes rested on potato fields and lavender bushes,
dahlias and marigolds.

The sun dried my hair and coat, and warmed my
shivering limbs; I bared my head before the glowing orb,
source and preserver of all there is, completely indifferent
whether I was worshipping unquenchable flames of burning hydrogen, or the not yet scientifically acknowledged
primordial substance, helium. Was it not the All-Father,
who had given birth to the Cosmos, the Almighty, the
Lord of life and death, ice and heat, summer and winter,
dearth and plenty?

My eyes, which had been feasting on summer joy and
green fields, plunged into the gloom of the abyss whence
I had climbed. The mantle of cold and darkness which
had been lying on the surface of the lake was cold and
dark no longer; dazzling clouds, like snowy, sunlit piles
of wool, hid from my gaze the twilight and the polluted
earth; above them rose snow-clad peaks, glistening and
sparkling, fashioned of condensed silver fog, a crystal-
lised solution of air and sunlight, drift-ice on a sea of

newly fallen snow. It was a vision of transcendent beauty, compared to which the cowbell-idyll under the birch trees was commonplace.

The dead silence was suddenly broken by a sound from below, where melancholy men and women toiled and trembled in the grey gloom. It was a splashing sound which approached deliberately; so deliberately that my eyes unconsciously tried to follow its course under the cloud-cover. It sounded like a millstream, a brook swollen with rain, a tidal wave. Then a scream rent the air, loud and wild, as if all the dwellers in the four cantons were calling for help against Uri-Rotstock; it was the shrill whistle of the paddle-boat which, penetrating the layer of clouds, gained in volume in the pure air and was caught up and tossed from rock to rock by the redundant echo of the Hochfluh.

It was noon! Time to begin my descent through the fog down to the greyness, the darkness, the damp, the dirt, and wait for another three weeks, perhaps, for another glimpse of the sun.

VI

AFTER the New Year we left Switzerland and took up
our abode in Germany; we had decided to stay for a
while at the lovely shores of the Lake of Constance.

In Germany, the land of militarism, where the patri-
archate is still in full force, Marie felt completely out
of it. No one would listen to her futile talk about
women's rights. Here young girls had just been forbidden to attend the University lectures; here the dowry
of a woman who marries an officer of the army has to
be deposited with the War Office; here all government
appointments are reserved for the man, the breadwinner
of the family.

Marie struggled and fought as if she had been caught
in a trap. On her first attempt to hoodwink me she
was severely taken to task by the women. For the first
time in my life I found the fair sex entirely on my side;
henceforth she had to play second fiddle. The friendly
intercourse with the officers braced me; their manners
influenced mine; and after ten years of spiritual emascula-
tion my manhood reasserted itself.

I let my hair grow as it liked, and abolished the fringe
on which Marie had insisted; my voice, which had grown
thin from everlastingly speaking in soothing tones to
a woman, regained its former volume. The hollows in
my cheeks filled out, and although I was now beginning
my fortieth year my whole physique gained in strength
and vigour.

I was friendly with all the women in the house, and
soon fell into the habit of taking a very active part in

the conversation, while Marie, poor, unpopular Marie, once again sat in silence.

She began to be afraid of me. One morning, for the first time in the last six years of our marriage, she appeared fully dressed in my bedroom before I was up. I could not understand this sudden move, but we had a stormy scene, during which she admitted that she was jealous of the girl who came into my room every morning to light the fire in my stove.

"And I do detest your new ways!" she exclaimed. "I hate this so-called manliness, and loathe you when you give yourself airs!"

Well, I knew that it had always been the page, the lap-dog, the weakling, "her child" that she loved. The virago never loves virility in her husband, however much she may admire it elsewhere.

I became more and more popular with the women. I sought their society; my whole nature was expanding in the friendly warmth which they emanated, these true women, who inspired the respectful love, the genuine devotion which a man only feels for a womanly woman.

We were discussing our return home. But again my old suspicions tormented me. I shrank from the renewal of old relations with former friends, some of whom might quite conceivably have been my wife's lovers. To put an end to my doubts, I determined to cross-examine her, for my letters to friends in Sweden had been so much waste of paper. I had been unable to elicit a candid statement.

Everybody pitied the "mother." No one cared whether or not the "father" would be ruined by the ridicule which threatened to befall him.

An excellent idea occurred to me. I would make use of the resources of the new science of psychology and thought-reading. I introduced it into our evening amusements, as if it were a game, employing the methods of Bishop and his kind. Marie was suspicious. She charged me with being a spiritualist; laughingly called me a superstitious free-thinker; overwhelmed me with abuse—in fact, used every means in her power to divert my attention from practices the danger of which she apparently anticipated. I pretended to give in, and dropped hypnotism, but I resolved to make my attack some time when she was off her guard.

The opportunity came one evening when we were sitting alone in the dining-room, facing each other. I gradually led the conversation to gymnastics. I succeeded in interesting her so much that she became excited and, compelled either by my will-power or the association of ideas which I had aroused in her mind, she mentioned massage. This suggested the pain caused by the treatment, and remembering her own experience in this connection she exclaimed—

"Oh yes, the treatment is certainly painful—I can feel the pain now when I think of——"

She paused. She bowed her head to hide her pallor; her lips moved as if she were anxious to change the subject; her eyelids flickered. A terrible silence followed which I prolonged as much as possible. This was the train of thought which I had set in motion and guided, full steam on, in the intended direction. In vain she tried to put on the brake. The abyss lay before her; she could not stop the engine. With a superhuman effort she broke from the grip of my eyes and rushed out of the room.

The blow had struck home.

She returned a few minutes later; her face had lost its strained expression. Under pretence of demonstrating to me the beneficial effect of massage, she came behind my

U

chair and stroked my head. Unfortunately the little
scene was acted before a mirror. A furtive glance showed
me her pale, terrified face, her troubled eyes which
scrutinised my features . . . our searching glances met.
Contrary to her habit she came and sat on my knee, put
her arms round me lovingly and murmured that she was
very sleepy.

"What wrong have you committed to-day that you
caress me like this?" I asked.

She hid her face on my shoulder, kissed me and went
out of the room, bidding me good-night.

I am perfectly well aware that this sort of evidence
would not satisfy a jury, but it was sufficient for me,
who knew her so well.

And to my thinking the evidence was strengthened by
the fact that a short time ago my brother-in-law had
forbidden the doctor his house, because the latter had
made advances to my sister.

I was therefore determined not to return to my own
country. At home I should be compelled to associate
daily with men whom I distrusted, and to escape the
ridicule which inevitably falls to the share of the duped
husband, I fled to Vienna.

Alone in my hotel, the vision of the wife I had
worshipped haunted me. Utterly unable to work, I
began a correspondence with her. I wrote her love-letters
twice a day. The unknown town affected me like a
cemetery. I moved through the thronging crowd like a
phantom. But after a while my imagination began to
people this solitude. I invented a romantic story for the
sole reason of introducing Marie into this dreary desert,
and soon life was pulsing everywhere. I pictured her as
a famous singer, and to lend my dream a semblance of
reality and make of the fine city a more convincing back-

ground for her, I made the acquaintance of the director of the Conservatoire. I, who detested the theatre, visited the opera or a concert every night. Everything interested me intensely, because I reported everything to her. No sooner had I arrived at my hotel than I sat down and gave her a minute description of Miss So-and-so's performance, drawing comparisons which were invariably in her own favour.

Her spirit pervaded the picture galleries. I spent an hour before the Venus of Guido Reni in the Belvedere, because she was so like my beloved.

In the end my longing grew so irresistible that I packed my box and returned home as fast as the express could carry me. Surely I was bewitched; there was no means of escape from her.

I had a royal reception.

My love-letters seemed to have rekindled Marie's love. I ran up the little garden to meet her. I covered her face with passionate kisses. I took her little head between my hands.

" Can you really work magic, little witch? "

" What do you mean? Your journey was not an attempt at flight, was it? "

" It was! But you are stronger than I am. . . . I throw down my arms. . . ."

On my writing-table lay a spray of red roses.

" You do love me a little? "

She was covered with confusion like a young girl— she blushed . . . it was all over with me, my honour, my efforts to break the chains which bound me, and which I longed for when I was free.

Six months went by; we lived in a wonderful dream: we chirruped like starlings, we kissed, our love was endless. We played duets and backgammon. The most beautiful days of the last five years were surpassed.

U 2

Spring had returned in the autumn of our lives! And had we not dreaded the approach of the winter?

I was fast again in her toils. She was convinced that the love philtre which she had given me to drink had intoxicated me afresh, and relapsed into her former indifference. She neglected her appearance, and despite all my remonstrances no longer took the trouble to make the best of herself. I foresaw that the result would be coldness on both sides, in spite of ourselves. Even her preference for her own sex reappeared, more dangerous and more pitiable, for this time she made love to young girls.

One evening we had invited the commandant and his fourteen-year-old daughter, our hostess and her daughter, a girl of fifteen, and a third girl of about the same age to a quiet little dinner-party, which was to be followed by a dance.

Towards midnight—to this day I grow hot when I think of it—I saw that Marie, who had been drinking freely, had gathered the young girls round her and, looking at them with lascivious eyes, was kissing them on the lips.

The commandant was watching the scene from a dark corner of the room, hardly able to control himself. In imagination I saw prison, penal servitude, a scandal which we could never live down; I made a rush at the group and broke it up, telling the girls to join in the dancing. . . .

When we were left alone I took Marie to task. We argued and stormed till daylight. Since she had had more wine than was good for her, she lost her head and confessed things which I had never even dreamed of.

Beside myself with anger, I repeated all my indictments, all my suspicions, and added a new charge, in which I did not really believe myself.

" And this mysterious illness, these headaches from which I suffer. . . ."

" What! You blame me for that too ! "

I had not meant what she insinuated; I had merely referred to the symptoms of cyanide poisoning which I had observed in myself.

All of a sudden a reminiscence flashed into my mind; the thought of something which at the time had seemed too improbable that it had left no permanent trace in my memory. . . .

My suspicion was strengthened when I remembered a certain epithet used in an anonymous letter which I had received a short time after Marie's divorce. The letter referred to her as " the prostitute of Soedertelje."

What did it mean? I had made inquiries which had come to nothing. Was I on the point of making a fresh discovery?

When the Baron, Marie's first husband, made her acquaintance at Soedertelje, she was half and half engaged to a young officer, a man with admittedly bad health. Poor Gustav had played the part of a greenhorn. That accounted for the warm gratitude which she felt for him even after the divorce ; she had confessed at the time that he had delivered her from dangers . . . what dangers she had not mentioned.

But " the prostitute of Soedertelje "? I reflected . . . the retired life which the young couple led, without friends, without society; they had been ostracised by the class to which they belonged.

Had Marie's mother, formerly a governess of middle-class origin, who had wheedled Marie's father into a marriage with her; who had fled to Sweden to escape from pressing debts; had she, the widow who so cleverly contrived to conceal her poverty, stooped to sell her daughter when they were living at Soedertelje?

The old woman, a coquette still at the age of sixty, had always inspired me with mingled feelings of compassion and dislike; mean, pleasure-loving, with the manners of an adventuress, a veritable "man-eater," she regarded every man as her legitimate prey. She had made me support her sister; she had deceived her first son-in-law, the Baron, with the story of a dowry swindled out of one of her creditors.

Poor Marie! Her remorse, her unrest, her dark moods were rooted in that shady past. In putting old events by the side of new ones I had the key to the quarrels between mother and daughter, brutal quarrels, frequently verging on violence. I could understand Marie's hitherto incomprehensible words, "I could kick my mother!"

Had her game been to silence the old woman? Probably; for the latter had threatened to ruin our lives by confessing "everything."

There could have been no doubt of Marie's dislike for her mother, to whom the Baron frequently referred as "that old blackguard," an invective which he justified with the half-truth that she had taught her daughter all the tricks of coquetry to enable her to catch a husband.

All these coincidents strengthened my determination to separate from her. It had to be! There was no alternative. And I left for Copenhagen to make inquiries into the past of the woman in whose keeping I had confided my honour.

In meeting my countrymen after several years' absence I found that they had formed very definite opinions of me; the eager exertions of Marie and her friends had borne fruit. She was a holy martyr; I was a madman, whose lunacy consisted in believing himself to be saddled with an unfaithful wife.

Make inquiries? It was like beating my head against

a stone wall. People listened to what I had to say with a furtive smile and stared at me as if I were a rare animal. No information was vouchsafed to me; I was deserted by every one, especially by those who secretly yearned for my ruin, so that they might rise over my fallen body.

I returned to my prison. Marie met me with evident misgivings; I learned more from the expression of her face than I had learned during the whole of my melancholy journey.

For two months I champed upon the bit; then I fled for the fourth time, in the height of summer, this time to Switzerland. But the chain which held me was not an iron chain which I might have been able to break; it was rather an indiarubber cable, elastic and capable of infinite expansion. The stronger the tension, the more irresistibly I was pulled back to the starting point.

Once more I returned, to be rewarded with open contempt; she was sure that another attempt to free myself from her net would kill me, and my death was her only hope.

I fell ill, severely ill, so that I believed myself to be dying; I made up my mind to write the whole story of the past. I could see plainly now that I had been in the power of a vampire. I only wanted to live long enough to cleanse my name from the filth with which she had sullied it. I wanted to live long enough to revenge myself; but first of all I must have proofs of her infidelity.

I hated her now with a hatred more fatal than indifference because it is the antithesis of love. I hated her because I loved her.

It was on a Sunday, while we were dining in the summer-arbour, that the electric fluid which had gathered during the last ten years discharged itself. I cannot remember my actual motive, but I struck her, for the first time in my life. I struck her face repeatedly, and when she tried to defend herself I seized her wrists and forced her on her knees. She gave a terrified scream. The temporary satisfaction which I had felt at my action gave way to dismay, for the children, frightened to death, cried out with fear. It was a horrible moment! It is a crime, a most unnatural crime, to strike a woman, a mother, in the presence of her children. It seemed to me that the sun ought to hide his face. . . . I felt sick to death.

And yet there was peace in my soul, like the calm after a storm, a satisfaction such as is only derived from duty done. I regretted my action, but I felt no remorse. My deed had been as inevitable as cause and effect.

In the evening I saw her walking in the moonlit garden. I joined her; I kissed her. She did not object; she burst into tears. We talked for a few minutes, then she accompanied me to my room and stayed with me until midnight.

How strange is life! In the afternoon I had struck her. At night she held me in her arms and kissed me.

What an extraordinary woman she was, to kiss her executioner with willing lips!

Why had I not known it before? If I had struck her ten years ago I should now have been the happiest of husbands.

Remember this, my brothers, if ever you are deceived by a woman!

But she had no intention of foregoing her revenge. A few days after this incident she came into my room, began telling me a long, rambling story, and after endless digressions gave me to understand that she had once, only once, been violated; it had happened, she said, while on her theatrical tour in Finland.

It was true, then!

She implored me not to think that it had happened more than once; not to suspect her of having had a lover.

That meant several times, several lovers.

"Then it is true that you have deceived me, and in order to deceive the world, too, you have invented the myth of my insanity. To hide your crime more completely you meant to torture me to death. You are a criminal. I have no longer any doubt of it. I shall divorce you!"

She threw herself on her knees, weeping bitterly, and asking me to forgive her.

"I'll forgive you; nevertheless our marriage must be annulled."

On the following day she was very quiet; on the second day she had regained her former self-possession; on the third she behaved in every respect like an innocent woman.

Since she had confessed herself, she was more than innocent; she was a martyr who treated me with insulting condescension.

She did not realise the consequences of a crime such as she had committed, and therefore she did not understand my dilemma. If I continued to live with her, I became a public laughing-stock; on the other hand, to leave her spelled disaster also; my life was ruined.

Ten years of martyrdom to be paid for with a few blows and a day of tears. Was it fair?

For the last time I left my home, secretly, for I had not the heart to say good-bye to the children.

On a beautiful Sunday afternoon I went on board a steamer bound for Constance. I had decided to visit my friends in France, and there to write the story of this woman, the true representative of the age of the unsexed.

At the last moment Marie appeared on the landing-stage, tear-stained, excited, feverish, yet pretty enough to turn the head of any man. But I remained cold, callous, silent, and received her treacherous kiss without returning it.

" Say at least that we are parting friends ! "

" Enemies for the short time which remains for me on earth ! "

We parted.

The steamer started. I watched her walking along the quay, trying to draw me back with the magic of her eyes which had held me under their spell for so many years. She came and went like a forsaken little dog. I waited for the moment when she would jump into the water ; I should jump after her, and we should drown together. But she turned away and disappeared in a little side-street, leaving me with a last impression of her bewitching figure, her little feet, which I had allowed to trample on me for ten years without a murmur. Only in my writings perhaps I had occasionally given vent to my feelings, but even there I had always tried to mislead the reader by concealing her real crimes.

To steel my heart against grief and regret, I went at once into the saloon. I sat down to dinner, but an aching lump in my throat compelled me to rise, and I climbed again on deck.

I watched the green hill gliding past, and thought of the little white cottage with the green shutters which crowned it. My children lived there, but the home was desolate, they were without protection, without means. . . . An icy pang shot through my heart.

I was like the cocoon of the silkworm when the great steam-engine slowly reels off the shining thread. At every stroke of the piston I grew thinner, and as the thread lengthened the cold which chilled me increased.

I was like an embryo prematurely detached from the umbilical cord. What a complete and living organism is the family ! I had thought so at that first divorce, from

which I had recoiled conscience-stricken. But she, the
adulteress, the murderess, had remained unmoved.

At Constance I caught the train for Basle. What a
wretched Sunday afternoon!

I prayed to God, if God there was, to preserve even
my bitterest foes from such agony.

At Basle I was overwhelmed with an irresistible desire
to revisit all those places in Switzerland where we had
stayed together, to gladden my sad heart with memories
of happy hours spent with her and the children.

I stayed for a week in Geneva and some days at Ouchy,
hunted by my misery from hotel to hotel, without peace
or rest, like a lost soul, like the wandering Jew. I spent
my nights in tears, haunted by the little figures of my
beloved children; I visited the places they had visited;
I fed "their" seagulls on the Lake of Geneva, a poor,
restless ghost, a miserable phantom.

Every morning I expected a letter from Marie, but
no letter came. She was too clever to furnish her
opponent with written evidence. I wrote to her several
times a day, love-letters, forgiving her for all her crimes
—but I never posted them.

Doubtless, my judges, if I had been destined to end
my days in a lunatic asylum, my fate would have come
upon me in those hours of keenest agony and bitterest
sorrow.

My power of endurance was exhausted; I wondered
whether Marie's confession had not been a ruse, so as to
get rid of me and begin life all over again with her
unknown lover, or, perhaps, to live with her Danish
friend. I saw my children in the hands of a " stepfather "
or the clutches of a " stepmother "; Marie would be quite
rich with the proceeds of my collected works; she would
perhaps write the story of my life as seen through the eyes
of the unnatural woman who had come between us. The

instinct of self-preservation stirred within me; I conceived a cunning plan. The separation from my family paralysed me mentally; I decided to return to them and stay with them until I had written the story of Marie's crimes. In this way she would become the unconscious tool of my revenge, which I could throw away when I had no further use for it.

With this object in view I sent her a telegram, businesslike, free from all sentimentality; I informed her that my petition for a divorce had been refused; pretended that I required a power of attorney from her, and suggested an interview at Romanshorn, on this side of the Lake of Constance.

I despatched the telegram with a sense of relief. On the following day I took the train and in due time arrived at the appointed place. The week of suffering was a thing of the past; my heart was beating normally, my eyes shone with added lustre; I drew a deep breath at the sight of the hills on the opposite shore, where my children lived. The steamer approached the landing stage; my eyes searched for Marie.

Presently I caught sight of her on the deck, her face woebegone, ten years older. The sight of her, suddenly grown old, wrung my heart. She walked with dragging footsteps, her eyelids were red with weeping, her cheeks hollow and drooping.

At that moment all feeling of hatred and disgust was swamped by pity. I felt a strong temptation to take her into my arms, but I pulled myself together, drew myself up and assumed the devil-may-care expression of a young blood who had come to a tryst. When I looked at her more closely I discovered in her a strange resemblance to her Danish friend; the likeness was really extraordinary; she had the same expression, the same pose, the same gestures, the same way of wearing her hair. Had she played me this last trick? Had she come to me straight from her "friend"?

Warned by these details, I recapitulated the part I meant to play. While I accompanied her to the hotel she was depressed and ill at ease, but she kept her self-possession. She questioned me very intelligently on the projected divorce proceedings, and when she found that I exhibited no trace of grief or emotion, she dropped her woe-begone aspect and began to treat me, as far as she dared, with a certain condescension.

During the interview she reminded me so much of her friend that I was tempted to ask for news of the lady. I was especially struck by a very tragic pose, a favourite one of her friend's, a pose which was accompanied by a certain gesture of the hand which rested on the table . . . ugh!

I rang for wine. She drank greedily and became sentimental.

I took the opportunity to ask after the little ones. She burst into tears; she said that she had suffered greatly during the past week; from morning till night the children had worried her with questions about their father; she did not see how they could get on without me.

All at once she noticed the absence of my wedding-ring; she became agitated.

"Your wedding-ring?" she gasped breathlessly.

"I sold it in Geneva. There's no need to ask what I did with the money."

She grew pale.

"Then we are quits. Shall we make a fresh start?"

"Is that what you call fair play? You committed an act fraught with tragic consequences for the whole family, for through it I am compelled to doubt the legitimacy of my children. You are guilty of having tampered with the lineage of a family. You have dishonoured four people: your three children of doubtful paternity and your husband, whom your infidelity has made a public laughing-stock. What, on the other hand, are the consequences of my act? "

She wept. I remained firm. I said that the divorce proceedings must go on, that I should adopt the children —in the meantime she could remain in my house, if she liked. Would it not be the free life she had always been dreaming of? She had always cursed matrimony.

She reflected for a moment. My proposal did not please her.

"I remember you saying you would like the position of a governess in the house of a widower. Here's the widower for you! "

"Give me time. . . . We shall see. . . . But in the meantime do you intend to live with us? "

"If you ask me to."

"We are waiting for you."

And for the sixth time I returned to my family, but this time firmly resolved to use the remaining weeks to finish my story. . . .

EPILOGUE

SEATED at my writing-table, pen in hand, I fainted; a feverish attack prostrated me. This very inopportune attack frightened me, for I had not been seriously ill for fifteen years. It was not fear of death, oh no. Death held no terrors for me; but I was thirty-nine years old and at the end of a turbulent career, my last word still unsaid, the promises of my youth only partly fulfilled, pregnant with plans for the future. This sudden cutting of the knot was far from pleasing me. For the last four years I had lived with my family in half-voluntary exile; I was at the end of my resources, and had settled down in a small town in Bavaria; I had come into conflict with the law, for one of my books had been confiscated, and I had been banished from my own country. I had but one desire left when I was thrown on my sick-bed—the desire for revenge.

A struggle arose within me; I had not sufficient strength left in me to call for help. The fever shook me as one shakes a feather bed; it seized me by the throat and throttled me; it put its foot on my breast and scorched my brain, so that my eyes started from their sockets. I was alone with Death, who had crept in by stealth and was attacking me.

But I was unwilling to die; I resisted, and an obstinate fight began. The tension of my nerves relaxed, the blood coursed through my veins. My brain twitched like a polypus that has been thrown into vinegar. But before long I realised that I must succumb in this dance of death. I relinquished my hold, fell backwards and submitted to the fatal embrace of the dread monster.

Immediately an indescribable calm came over me, a voluptuous weakness composed my limbs, and perfect peace soothed body and soul, which had lacked all wholesome recreation during so many years of toil.

I fervently desired that it really should be the end. Slowly all will to live ebbed away. I ceased to observe, to feel, to think. I became unconscious, and a delicious sensation of blankness filled the void created by the cessation of the racking pain, the tormenting thoughts, the secret terrors.

When I regained consciousness I found my wife sitting by my bedside and gazing at me with terrified eyes.

" What is the matter with you, dear ? " she said.

"Nothing ; I am ill," I replied.   " And there are times when illness is welcome."

" What do you mean ?   You are jesting ! "

"No, it is the end at last . . . anyhow, I hope it is."

"Heaven forbid that you should leave us in these straits ! " she exclaimed.   " What is to become of us in a strange country, without friends, without means ? "

"There is my life insurance," I said, attempting to console her.   " I know it isn't much, but it is enough to take you home."

She had not thought of this, and she looked a little reassured as she continued—

" But you cannot lie here like this !   I shall send for a doctor."

" No, I won't have a doctor ! "

" Why not ? "

" Because—I won't ! "

The glances which we exchanged spoke volumes.

" I want to die," I said, anxious to put an end to our conversation.   " I am sick of life ; the past is a tangled

skein which I cannot unravel. It is time that my eyes
closed for ever—that the curtain fell! ''

She remained unmoved.

" Your old suspicion . . . is it still alive, then? '' she
asked.

" Yes, still alive. Drive away the spectre, you alone
can do it.''

She assumed her favourite part of little mother, and
gently laid her soft hand on my burning forehead.

" Does that relieve you? ''

" Yes. . . .''

It was a fact. The mere touch of that light hand
which rested so heavily on my life exorcised the
evil spirit, the secret trouble which would not let me
rest.

Another and more violent attack of fever followed.
My wife rose to make me some elder tea.

Left by myself I sat up in bed and looked out through
the window opposite. It was a large window in the shape
of a triptychon, framed by wild vine; I saw a part of
the landscape surrounded by green leaves; in the fore-
ground the beautiful scarlet fruit of a quince tree rocked
gently among the dark green foliage; apple trees, a little
further off, studded the green grass; still further away
the steeple of a small church rose into the radiant air,
behind it a blue spot, the Lake of Constance, was visible,
and far in the background the Tyrol Alps.

We were in the height of summer, and, illuminated
by the slanting rays of the afternoon sun, the whole
scene formed a charming picture.

From below rose the twittering of the starlings which
sat on the vine-props in the vineyards, the chirping of
the young chickens, the strident note of the crickets, the
tinkling cowbells, clear as crystal. The loud laughter of
my children, the directing voice of my wife, who was

x

talking to the gardener's wife about my illness, mingled with these gay sounds of country life.

And as I gazed and listened life seemed good to me, death to be shunned. I had too many duties to perform, too many debts to pay. My conscience tortured me, I felt an overpowering need to confess myself, to ask all men's forgiveness for the wrongs I had committed, to humiliate myself before some one. I felt guilty, stricken with remorse, I did not know for what secret crime; I was burning with the desire to relieve my conscience by a full confession of my fancied culpability.

During this attack of weakness, the result of a sort of innate despondency, my wife returned carrying a cup in her hand; alluding to a slight attack of persecutional mania from which I had once suffered, she tasted the contents before offering it to me.

"You may drink without fear," she said smilingly, "it contains no poison."

I felt ashamed. I did not know what to say. And to make amends for my suspicion I emptied the cup at one draught.

The somniferous elder tea, the fragrance of which recalled in me reminiscences of my own country where the mystic shrub is held sacred by the people, made me feel so sentimental that I there and then gave expression to my remorse.

"Listen to me carefully," I said, "for I believe that my days are numbered. I confess that I have always lived a life of utter selfishness. I have sacrificed your theatrical career to my literary ambition. . . . I will tell you everything now . . . only forgive me. . . ."

She tried to calm me, but I interrupted her and continued—

"In compliance with your wishes we married under the dotal system. In spite of it, however, I have wasted your dowry to cover sums which I had recklessly guaranteed. My greatest grief now is the fact that you cannot touch the proceeds of my works. Send for a notary at once, so that I can settle on you all my nominal or real property. . . . Above everything, promise that you will return to the stage which you gave up to please me.''

She refused to listen any further, treated my confession as a joke, advised me to go to sleep and rest, and assured me that everything would come right, and that I was not on the point of death.

I seized her hand, exhausted. I begged her to stay with me until I had fallen asleep. Grasping her little hand more firmly, I again implored her to forgive me for all the wrong I had done her. A delicious drowsiness stole over me and closed my tired eyelids. Under the radiations of her shining eyes, which expressed infinite tenderness, I felt as if I were melting away as ice melts in the rays of the sun. Her cool lips, touching my forehead, seemed to press a seal on it, and I was plunged into the depths of ineffable bliss.

It was broad daylight when I awoke from my stupor. The rays of the sun fell on a Utopian landscape. To judge from the matutinal sounds which rose from below, it must have been above five o'clock. I had slept soundly during the whole night without dreaming or waking up. On the little table by my bedside stood the cup which had contained the elder-tea; the chair on which my wife had been sitting when I fell asleep was still in its place. I was covered with her cloak; the soft hairs of the fox skins with which it was lined tickled my chin.

My brain felt as refreshed and rested as if I had slept for the first time in ten years. I collected my thoughts, which had been rushing hither and thither in wild disorder, and with this powerful, well-drilled and disciplined

X 2

army I prepared to meet those attacks of morbid remorse which frequently accompany physical weakness.

Looming large, filling my mind completely, were the two ugly blots which, under guise of a confession, I had revealed to my wife on the previous day; the two dark blots which had spoiled my life for so many years.

I resolved to re-examine them at once, to dissect those two "facts" which up to now I had allowed to pass unchallenged, for I had a vague presentiment that they were unsound.

"Let me see," I said to myself, "what have I done that I should look upon myself as a selfish coward, who has sacrificed the artistic career of his wife to his ambition? Let me see what really happened. . . ."

At the time of our betrothal she was playing very small parts. Her position in the artistic world had sunk to a very modest one, once her want of talent, character and originality had made her second appearance in public a fiasco. She lacked all the essentials which go to make a successful actress. On the day before our wedding she was playing the part of a society woman in a very commonplace play; she had only a dozen words to speak.

For how many tears, how much misery was our marriage made responsible! It robbed the actress of all charm, and yet she had been so fascinating as Baroness, divorced from her husband that she might devote her life entirely to art.

It was true, I was to blame for this deterioration, which, after two years' weeping over steadily shrinking parts, resulted in her leaving the stage.

At the very moment when her engagement came to an end I had a success, an undoubted success, as a novelist. I had already conquered the stage with small, unimportant plays. Now I was burning to write a play which would create a sensation; it should be one of those spectacular plays which delight audiences; my purpose, of course, was to help my wife to a re-engagement. It was a repugnant task, for one of my most cherished dreams was the reform of the drama. In writing my new play I sacrificed my literary faith. But I meant to force my wife on a hostile public, throw her at their heads with all the means in my power, move heaven and earth to make her popular. All my efforts were in vain. The public would have none of the divorced wife who had married a second time; the manager hastened to cancel a contract which brought him no advantage.

"Well, was that my fault?" I asked myself, voluptuously stretching my limbs, well satisfied with the result of this first self-examination. Was there a greater blessing than a good conscience?

With a lighter heart I continued my musing—

A miserable year passed, was wept away, despite the happiness it brought us in the birth of a little girl.

And all of a sudden my wife had another attack of stage mania, more violent than the previous one. We besieged the agencies, stormed the managerial offices, advertised ourselves hugely—but everywhere we failed, all doors were closed to us, everybody threw cold water on our schemes.

Disillusioned by the failure of my drama, and on the point of making a name in science, I had sworn never again to write a play round an actress, more especially as this sort of work had no attraction for me. In addition, I was little disposed to break up our home merely to satisfy a passing whim of my wife's, and therefore I resigned myself to bearing my share of the incurable sorrow.

But after a time I found the task beyond my strength. I made use of my connections with a theatre in Finland,

and, thanks to my efforts, my wife was engaged for a number of performances.

I had made a rod for my own back. For a whole month I was widower, bachelor, head of the family, housekeeper. In compensation my wife, on her return, brought home with her two large packing-cases full of wreaths and bouquets.

But she was so happy, so young and so charming, that I took at once the necessary steps to secure a fresh engagement for her. I knew that by doing this I was running the risk of having to leave my country, my friends, my position, my publisher—and for what? For a woman's whim. . . . But let that pass! Either a man is in love or he isn't. . . .

Fortunately for me, my correspondent had no room in his company for an actress without a repertoire.

Was that my fault? At the thought of it I literally rolled over in my bed with pleasure. What a good thing an occasional little self-examination is! It unburdens the heart . . . it rejuvenated me.

But to proceed. Children were born to us at short intervals. One—two—three. But again and again her yearning for the stage returned. One ought to persevere! A new theatre was being opened. Why not offer the manager a new play with a good part for the leading actress, a sensational play, dealing with the " woman question " which loomed so large at the time?

No sooner thought than done. For, as I have already said, either a man is in love, or he isn't.

The play was produced. It contained a splendid part for the leading actress, magnificent dresses (of course), a cradle, much moonshine, a villain ; an abject husband in love with his wife (myself), a wife about to become a mother (a stage novelty), the interior of a convent—and so on.

The actress had an extraordinary success, but from the literary point of view the play was a failure, an awful failure . . . alas!

She was saved. I was lost, ruined. But in spite of everything, in spite of the supper which we gave to the manager at a hundred crowns per head; in spite of a fine of fifty crowns which we had to pay for illegal cheering, late at night before the agent's office—in spite of all our efforts, no engagement was offered to her. It was not my fault. I was blameless in the matter. I was the martyr, the victim. Nevertheless, in the eyes of her sex I henceforth was a ruffian who had ruined his wife's career. For years I had suffered remorse on this account, remorse so bitter that it poisoned my days and robbed my nights of peace.

How often had the reproach been publicly flung into my face! It was always I who was guilty! . . . That things came about in quite a different way, who cared? . . . One career had been ruined, that I admit . . . but which, and by whom?

A horrible thought came into my mind; the idea that posterity might blame me for this ruined career seemed to me no laughing matter, for I was defenceless and without a friend capable of stating the facts undisguised and unmisrepresented.

There remained the spending of her dowry.

I had once been made the subject of a paragraph entitled: " A squanderer of his wife's fortune." I also, on another occasion, had been charged with living on my wife's income, a charge which had made me put six cartridges into my revolver.

Let us examine this charge also, since an investigation has become desirable, and after due examination let us pronounce sentence.

My wife's dowry consisted of ten thousand crowns in doubtful shares; I had raised a mortgage on these shares with a bank of mortgages, amounting to fifty per cent of their face value. Like a bolt from the blue the general smash came. The shares were so much waste-paper, for we had omitted to sell them at the right moment. I was consequently compelled to pay the full amount of my mortgage: fifty per cent of the face value. Later on my wife received twenty-five per cent of her claim, this being the proportion which the creditors received after the bank's failure.

How much did I squander?

Not one penny, in my opinion. The holder of the shares received the actual value of her unsaleable investments which my personal guarantee had increased by twenty-five per cent.

Truly I was as innocent in this connection as in the other.

And the anguish, the despair which had more than once driven me to the verge of suicide! The suspicion, the old distrust, the cruel doubts, began to torture me afresh. The thought that I nearly died as a scoundrel almost drove me mad. Worn out with care, overwhelmed with work, I had never had time to pay much attention to the dark innuendoes, the veiled allusions. And while I, completely absorbed by my daily toil, lived unsuspectingly from day to day, slanderous rumours had been started, which became more and more insistent and definite, although they had no other foundation than the talk of the envious and the idle gossip of the cafés. And I, fool that I was, believed everybody, doubted no one but myself. Ah ! . . .

Was I really never insane, never ill, no degenerate? Was I merely fooled by a trickster whom I worshipped, whose little embroidery scissors had cut off Samson's locks when he laid his weary head on the pillow, worn out by heavy toil, exhausted by care and anxiety on her account and the children's? Trustful, unsuspicious, I' had lost my honour, my manhood, the will to live, my intellect, my five senses, and alas! much more even, in this ten years' sleep in the arms of the sorceress.

Was it possible—the thought filled me with shame—that a crime had been committed in these fogs in which I had lived for years like a phantom? An unconscious little crime, caused by a vague desire for power, by a woman's secret wish to get the better of the man in the duel called matrimony?

Doubtless I had been a fool! Seduced by a married woman; compelled to marry her to save her honour and her theatrical career; married under the dotal system and the condition that each should contribute half of the expenses, I was ruined after ten years, plundered, for I had borne the financial burden on my own shoulders entirely.

At this very moment when my wife denounced me as a spendthrift, incapable of providing the necessities of life; when she represented me as the squanderer of her so-called fortune; at this very moment she owed me forty thousand crowns, her share of the expenses, according to the verbal agreement made on our wedding day.

She was my debtor!

Determined to settle all old accounts once and for ever, I jumped out of bed like a man who has dreamed that he is paralysed, and on awakening flings away the crutches with which he had walked in his dream. I dressed quickly and ran down-stairs to confront my wife.

Through the half-open door my enraptured gaze met a charming spectacle.

She lay, stretched out at full length, on her tumbled bed, her lovely little head buried in the pillow over which the flood of her golden hair waved and curled; her transparent nightgown had slipped off her shoulders, and her virginal bosom gleamed white under the lace insertion; the soft, red-and-white striped coverlet betrayed the swelling curves of her graceful, fragile body, leaving her bare feet uncovered—tiny arched feet with rosy toes and transparent flawless nails—a genuine work of art, perfect, fashioned in flesh after the model of an antique marble statue: and this was my wife.

Light-hearted and smiling, with an expression of chaste motherliness, she watched her three little ones as they were climbing and tumbling about among the flowered down pillows, as if on a heap of newly mown flowers.

The delightful spectacle softened me. But a whispering doubt in my heart warned me: " Beware of the she-panther playing with her cubs! "

Disarmed by the majesty of motherhood, I entered her room with uncertain steps, timid as a schoolboy.

" Ah! You are up already, my dear," she greeted me, surprised, but not as pleased as one might have expected.

I stammered a confused reply, smothered by the children, who had climbed on my back when I stooped to kiss their mother.

Was it possible? Could she really be a criminal? I pondered the question as I went away, subdued by her chaste beauty, the candid smile of those lips which could surely never have been tainted by a lie. No, a thousand times no! . . .

I stole away, convinced of the contrary.

And yet doubt remained, doubt of everything: of my wife's constancy, my children's legitimate birth, my sanity; doubt which persecuted me, relentlessly and unremittingly.

It was time to make an end, to arrest the flood of sterile thoughts. If only I could have absolute certainty! A

crime had been committed in secret, or else I was mad!
I must know the truth!

To be a deceived husband! What did I care, as long
as I knew it! I should be the first to laugh at it. Was
there a single man in the world who could be absolutely
certain that he was his wife's only lover? . . .

When I thought of the friends of my youth, now
married, I could not pick out one who was not, to some
extent, hookwinked. Lucky men whom no doubts
tortured! It was silly to be small-minded. Whether one
is the only one, or whether one has a rival, what does it
matter? The ridicule lies in the fact of not knowing it;
the main thing is to know all about it.

Yet if a man were married for a hundred years he would
still know nothing of the true nature of his wife. However deep his knowledge of humanity, of the whole
cosmos, he would never fathom the woman whose life is
bound up with his own life. For this reason the story
of poor Monsieur Bovary is such pleasant reading for all
happy husbands. . . .

But as far as I was concerned I wanted the truth. I
must have it. For the sake of revenge? What folly!
Revenge on whom? On my favoured rivals? They did
but make use of their prerogative as males! On my
wife? Did I not say one ought not to be small-minded?
And to hurt the mother of my darlings? How could I
do it?

But I wanted to know; I wanted to know everything.
I determined to examine my life, carefully, tactfully,
scientifically; to make use of all the resources of
psychology: suggestion, thought-reading, mental torture
—none should be neglected; I determined to probe the
deepest depths, not even despising the well-worn, old-
fashioned means of burglary, theft, interception of letters,
forged signatures. . . .

I determined to make the most searching investigations. . . . Was that monomania, the paroxysm of rage of a lunatic? It is not for me to say.

I appeal to the reader for a verdict after a careful study of my confession. Perhaps he will find in it elements of the physiology of love, some light on the pathology of the soul, or even a strange fragment of the philosophy of crime.

September 1887—*March* 1888.

Concluding Remarks of the Author

THIS is a terrible book, I fully admit it, and I regret that I ever wrote it.

How did I come to write it?

I had to wash my corpse before it was laid in its coffin.

Four years ago, if I remember rightly, a friend of mine, a writer, a declared enemy of the indiscretions—of others—said to me one day when talking about my first marriage—

"Do you know, it would make excellent copy for the sort of novel which I should like to write."

Certain of my friend's applause, I decided there and then to write it myself.

"Don't be angry with me, dear old fellow, that I, as the original owner, make use of my property."

I also remember, it is twelve years ago now, a remark my future mother-in-law made to me one evening when I was watching her daughter carrying on a flirtation with a group of young men—

"Wouldn't she make a splendid heroine for a novel?"

"With what title?"

"A passionate woman!"

Happy mother, who died in the nick of time, I have carried out your suggestion. The novel has been written. I can die in peace.

MS. 1888.

The other day I met again the hero of this novel. I upbraided him for having induced me to publish the story of his first marriage. He is married again, father of a sweet little girl, and looks ten years younger.

"Dear old boy," he said in reply to my reproaches, "the sympathy which everybody felt for the heroine of the novel, when it was first published, absolves me. You may gauge from this fact the great depth of the love I bore her, for not only did it survive so much brutality, but it communicated itself even to the reader. This, however, has not prevented a French academician from denouncing my constancy as weakness, my steadfast loyalty to my family, including my children, baseness, in view of my wife's brutality, inconstancy and dishonesty. I wonder whether this man would consider an insignificant Caserio superior to an eminent Carnot, simply because the former stabbed the latter?

"Moreover, this book, which you had wanted to write yourself, is only the woof of a fabric the richness of which is known only to those of my countrymen who have followed my literary career as it unfolded itself side by side with the sorrows of my heart, without suffering to be influenced. I could have left the battlefield. I remained steadfastly at my post. I fought against the enemy at home, day and night. Was this not courage?

"The 'poor, defenceless woman' was backed by the four Scandinavian kingdoms, where she counted nothing but allies in her war against a man who was sick, solitary, poor, and threatened with confinement in a lunatic asylum because his intellect rebelled against the deification of woman, this penultimate superstition of the free-thinkers.

"The dear souls who conceal their revengeful thoughts under the term 'divine justice' have condemned my 'Confession' in the name of their Nemesis divina, bringing spurious evidence for their assertion that I had deceived the husband of Marie's first marriage. Let them read the scene where the Baron throws his wife into my arms, when I stood before him with clean hands and confessed to him my guiltless love for the wife he neglected. Let them remember the important fact that I took upon my young shoulders the whole burden of our fault, to save his position in the army and the future of his little girl. Let them then say whether it is just to punish an act of self-sacrifice by an act of brutal revenge.

"One must be young and foolish to act as I have acted, I admit that. But it will not happen again—never again. . . . But . . . enough of it! And then . . . no . . . good-bye!"

He walked away quickly, leaving me under the spell of his perfect honesty.

I never again regretted having published the story of this idealist, who has now disappeared from literature and the world. But I abandoned my former intention to write "The Confession of a Foolish Woman," because, after all, it goes too much against common-sense to allow a criminal to give evidence against her victim.

French Original Edition, 1894.

It was the outspoken account of his first marriage, written in self-defence and as a last testament, for he intended to take his life as soon as the book was finished. For five years the sealed manuscript, which was not meant for publication, was in the safe keeping of a relative. Only in the spring of 1893, under the pressure of circumstances and after public opinion and the press had attacked him in the most unjust manner, did he sell the book to a publisher.

"Separated," 1902.

THE END